For Emma, Stephen, Nicholas and Julian

Famous Kings & Queens of England & Scotland

Endpapers George V and Queen Mary entering St Paul's
Cathedral for the Silver Jubilee Service of Thanksgiving in
1935.
Above The coronation of a medieval king.
Overleaf Henry VIII with Philip of Spain, Princess Mary,
Prince Edward and Princess Elizabeth.
Contents page Queen Victoria and Prince Albert with five of
their nine children.

Famous Kings & Queens of England & Scotland

by Joyce Marlow

with chapters on the Scottish Monarchs contributed by Elspeth McKay

Arco Publishing Company, Inc. New York

Published by Arco Publishing Company Inc.
219 Park Avenue South, New York, N.Y. 10003

Printed in Great Britain

Library of Congress Cataloging in Publication Data

Marlow, Joyce.
    Famous Kings & queens of England & Scotland.

    Includes index.
    1. Great Britain—Kings and rulers—Biography
    I. Title. II. Title: Famous Kings & queens of
England & Scotland.
    DA28.1.M327   941'.00992 [B]   77–7067
    ISBN 0–668–04357–1

Contents

William I

r. 1066-87

'Verily, he was a very great prince.'

William of Normandy is renowned in English history as the Conqueror but to his contemporaries he was known as William the Bastard. His father Robert was the Duke of Normandy but his mother Herleve was the daughter of a Falaise tanner, albeit a prosperous one. Although Herleve bore her ducal lover two children, of whom William was born in either 1027 or 1028, the social gap meant there was no question of marriage. Herleve was later married off to one of Duke Robert's vassals, by which gentleman she had two more sons: Robert who became Count of Mortain and a mighty Anglo–Norman baron, and Odo who became Bishop of Bayeux, an equally mighty prince of the Church.

Bastardy was then common, and being illegitimate was not necessarily a bar to inheriting a natural father's land or title, but when William was born it was becoming more of a handicap. There was a strong reforming movement within the Christian Church which aimed, among other things, to enforce its teachings more strictly, including the sanctity of holy matrimony. When in 1034 Duke Robert decided to go on a pilgrimage to the Holy Land, the good luck necessary in any successful life smiled for the first time on William, for the duke had no legitimate children and therefore decided to recognize his bastard son as his heir. More surprisingly, he managed to persuade the Norman nobility to swear fealty to the boy. While returning from the Holy Land in 1035, Robert died suddenly and the eight- or nine-year-old William found himself Duke of Normandy.

For a while the Norman lords kept their word and recognized the boy as their lawful Duke but with the death of his powerful protector, anarchy reigned. For ten bloody years William's luck held and the warring factions managed to kill each other rather than him, but it was not until 1054, when he was twenty-six or -seven years old, that he finally emerged as the undisputed Duke of Normandy. In the process he had become a man of iron, but he was also a man of God who feared for his immortal soul and he was not without vision and imagination. He appreciated that force was not the sole answer to the problem of ruling men, even if it was a major factor. In the years from 1054 to 1066 William not only consolidated his power in Normandy – and extended it into the bordering country of Maine – he reorganized the structure of Norman society.

As early as 1049, long before he became one of the most powerful rulers in mainland Europe, William had acquired sufficient reputation to negotiate a marriage with Matilda, a daughter of Count Baldwin of Flanders. The alliance was a political coup and despite papal disapproval he went ahead with the marriage, a bold action for a devout Christian ruler. Physically he and Matilda were an ill-assorted pair; she was a little over four feet tall, whereas he was close to six feet, immensely strong and tough, with a harsh guttural voice. Mentally they seem to have been well attuned and the marriage was remarkably successful, particularly if it is remembered that political gain and interest, not love or even compatibility, were the hallmarks of royal alliances. As the Norman empire expanded William was able to leave his wife as regent, a task she performed with great efficiency and loyalty. She bore him at least nine children and he earned a reputation for total fidelity which was even more remarkable than their marital harmony. Fortune again favoured him in his marriage with a wife whom he could *trust*, not a quality of which he had had much experience in the treacherous, turbulent years of his youth.

When thoughts of adding the kingdom of England to the dukedom of Normandy first entered William's mind is a matter of conjecture. It is possible that his determination to marry Matilda was prompted by such an idea, because she was a direct descendant of Alfred the Great, whereas his relationship to the English monarchy was much more tenuous. In fact there was no established right of succession in England at the time, so it was a question of who could lay the best claim to the throne. In the Norman version of events leading up to 1066 – as depicted in the Bayeux tapestry and by the Anglo–Norman chroniclers – Duke William visited King Edward in London in 1051. Edward – known to posterity as the Confessor – had spent much of his childhood in exile at the Norman court and was to an extent Norman-oriented. During the visit he is supposed to have promised that should he die without an heir Duke William would be his rightful successor. Then there is a leap to 1064 and the arrival of Harold Godwinson in Normandy, by which time it had become obvious that King Edward would not produce an heir.

Harold was a member of the family which had established itself as the Earls of Wessex and after some changes of fortune had become the most powerful in England. He had as good (or bad) a claim to the English throne as William, with the extra factor that he was a native of the country. Whether Harold *actually intended* to go to Normandy in 1064 and what his mission was if he did, is now a matter of dispute. The Norman version is that Harold arrived in Normandy, albeit via the domain of Ponthieu, explicitly to reaffirm his allegiance to Duke William as the next rightful King of England, nominated by King Edward. And moreover that he swore allegiance on sacred relics, though where he actually swore his oath varies even in the Norman accounts.

This episode is the crux of the Norman version. Once Edward the Confessor died in January 1066 and Harold Godwinson had himself crowned king, William was morally and legally entitled, even driven, to fight for the inheritance which had been usurped. The version was accepted *at the time* by other European rulers and, most importantly, by the Pope. William was able to land in England with the papal seal of approval for a justified invasion, bearing a holy banner. (His half-brother Odo, who as a Bishop was not supposed to carry arms, arrived wielding a holy sceptre). The Norman account can be accepted as the truth or seen as evidence that in the propaganda war – as it would now be called – Duke William beat King Harold even more decisively than he did in battle.

The last Saxon king of England has since had many apologists. They deride the idea that King Edward would have willed away his crown as early as 1051, or that the Saxon Harold would have gone to Normandy specifically to swear allegiance to a Norman duke; if he did swear, it was under duress and therefore an invalid oath. There is general agreement that as Edward the Confessor lay dying

Opposite top Falaise Castle, the birthplace of William the Bastard.

Below and opposite Two scenes from the famous Bayeux tapestry. In the first Harold swears allegiance to William as the heir to the English throne; the second shows Harold's coronation as King of England in defiance of his oath.

he nominated Harold as his successor and he was thus accepted by the Witanegemot (the assembly of Saxon nobility). But the Normans explained that this nomination was extracted from a dying, unworldly, perhaps slightly senile man and was itself invalid, apart from the fact that Harold had foresworn himself.

Early in 1066 Harold had the crown of England with the consent of his peers, but also with the knowledge that Duke William of Normandy considered it his by right. Harold soon called up the fyrd (a Saxon militia of freemen) in the south of England and they responded. The months went by, the weather was awful and nothing happened; Harold was more or less forced to disband the fyrd because while they were willing to *fight*, they were not disciplined to *wait*. Then in the middle of September another expected invader actually arrived, Harold Hardrada of Norway who was a claimant to the English throne. Hardrada's claim was as good as anybody's: it lay through Edward the Confessor's Anglo–Danish predecessors Kings Canute and Hardacanute and promises allegedly made by them to Hardrada's father.

King Harold marched north and on 25 September inflicted a crushing defeat on Harold of Norway at Stamford Bridge, near York. Again the necessary element of luck was with William,

because as his enemy Harold Godwinson went to kill the other serious claimant Harold Hardrada for him, the weather changed for the better. On 12 September William's forces landed at Pevensey in Sussex, with neither the fyrd nor King Harold's own troops to oppose them. However, there was nothing lucky about the way William overcame his Norman nobles' reluctance to support an invasion of England (they thought he was over-reaching himself), nor in the way he organized his invasion forces. That was a masterly piece of planning and staff-work, assembling men, horses, ships, weapons, supplies and then keeping them disciplined and intact while they waited and waited for favourable weather conditions.

In the meantime, having fought a long, bitter and bloody battle at Stamford Bridge, King Harold marched back to London, had a brief respite, gathered more troops and marched south to meet the Normans. It might have been wiser if Harold had rested longer and reorganized his tired army, particularly as William was being extremely cautious and had done nothing more than establish a bridgehead slightly nearer to Hastings. But Harold presumably believed that attack was the best form of defence and on 14 October an event took place of which virtually everybody in Britain knows the date, the battle of Hastings 1066.

It was, as the Duke of Wellington said later of another battle, a damn close run thing; but as darkness fell King Harold lay dead, though probably not with an arrow in his eye, and the

Saxon forces scattered into the night. By the end of 1066 William had received the formal submission of the nobility and bishops at Berkhamsted, and had been annointed and crowned as King William I of England in Westminster Abbey, the building begun by the man who had allegedly willed him the crown, Edward the Confessor. William had accomplished a truly astonishing feat, the conquest of a rich, well-organized kingdom with the minimum of bloodshed.

Thereafter, there *was* opposition to William and his Norman barons (it was in England that they became known as barons). In 1067 there were risings on the Welsh border and in Kent and by the end of the year William was back in his new kingdom to subdue a more serious uprising in the West Country. During 1070 and 1071 he suppressed rebellions in the Midlands, including that of Hereward the Wake, but Hereward's revolt, though it has attracted historical novelists, was not as threatening as the earlier Northumbrian one. It was in the north that William again showed his ruthlessness, as well as his prowess, as a general. He led his troops across the Pennines in bitter mid-winter on an epic march but he also devastated thousands of square miles. Fifteen years later when the Domesday survey was undertaken, the north of England remained a depopulated wasteland, but the savage tactics had worked and by 1072 England was under William's control. The last rebellions he had to subdue came not from the native inhabitants but from his over-ambitious, rapacious half-brother

Two impressions of King Harold's death at the Battle of Hastings in 1066. In the picture opposite it is William himself who kills him.

Apres seynt Edward rey
na Harald le fiz Gode
wyn. count de kent. a for
ea tort. ix. moys. dunke ue
ent will' bastard. e ly tol
yst la vye e le regne e qquist
la tere. Harald gist al Walthm.

Pis regna Will' bas
tard xxi. an. puis mo
rust e gist a kame en
mundye.

Odo and from like-minded disgruntled Norman barons.

The Domesday survey was decided upon while William was holding court at Gloucester in December 1085. It was a unique idea carried out quickly and thoroughly by royal officers who were despatched into nearly every corner of the land to discover the exact wealth of England, and thereby its customs and much additional information. The Domesday Book, which now resides in the Public Record Office in London, was William's supreme administrative achievement, one which showed his determination, practicality and vision.

1066 and the Norman Conquest are regarded as decisive moments in English history. How much of a revolution did they effect? The country which William conquered had as sophisticated a form of government as any in Europe. In the first place England was a united kingdom, if only loosely so, with the great earls exercising enormous autonomous power. But they all paid homage directly to their king, and homage was a public act of submission and allegiance, while fealty was more of a pact between lord and vassal. The king's writ officially ran throughout England and written charters, though not unknown in other parts of Europe, were an Anglo-Saxon innovation. The method by which the king's justice was enacted was again sophisticated: through a system of shire courts which met twice a year and sub-divisions into 'Hundreds' with their own courts meeting every four weeks. Then there was the geld, a tax based on the number of hides (units of land) owned, and paid by all landowners to the king. The geld was unique, the first form of general taxation in Europe, and there was also an advanced monetary system. The quality of life in Anglo-Saxon England was summed up by a comparatively lowly, albeit free man: 'An equal and like life we share. Lord of himself is each man here; and each is faithful to the other.'

So why did this superior, incipiently democratic civilization collapse so easily before the Normans? Anglo-Saxon enthusiasts claim that might overcame right, as has happened only too frequently in history. William's luck was again with him when Harold Godwinson was killed, thus depriving the Saxons of their leader (the death of a noble, let alone a king, in battle was rare in medieval times). Anglo-Saxon England was not of course idyllic; slavery existed and the king's justice applied only to freemen. The pro-Norman historians have some justice on their side when they claim that Anglo-Saxon England had grown lethargic, and that while there was unity on the surface, society remained basically tribal. (Incidentally, there was much comment at the Norman victory celebrations held in Fécamp at Easter 1067, about the *long-haired* Englishmen who appeared there. This was seen as a sign of Anglo-Saxon degeneracy.)

How much of the existing system did the Normans destroy? and how many of their own customs did they impose? The astute William adopted most of the excellent Anglo-Saxon laws, but the sheriffs at the shire courts now worked directly for him, not through the earls as previously, and the king's writ became an expression of his will. The Witanegemot which had been a consultative assembly turned into the *Curia Regis*, the King's Court, in which William to an extent consulted (with his Norman barons) but also legislated and dictated. The Saxon oath of allegiance was adopted and at Salisbury in 1086 William assembled a great concourse of barons and nobles, Norman and

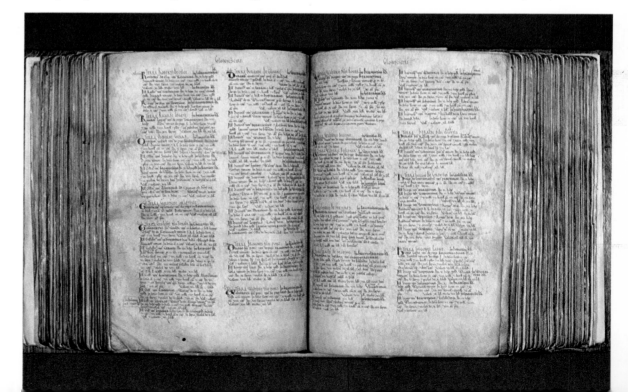

Saxon, and had them pay homage to him as king, as well as swear the Norman fealty to him as duke. It was not so much the laws of England that William changed as the punishments. Murder became an officially punishable crime for the first time – previously the earls had sorted it out between themselves – though this law was enacted mainly because too many Normans were being bumped off by the natives who then displayed an absolute innocence and lack of knowledge of the culprits. But William also banned slavery and the death penalty; instead an offender was to have 'his eyes gouged out and his testicles cut off', which to many people today might sound worse than execution but was in fact a step forward.

The face, character and structure of England were radically altered by the Norman conquest. Its face was changed by the great stone castles which William had built to enforce his rule. The old aristocracy was swept away; in the Domesday survey 20 per cent of the land was owned by the king, 25 per cent by the Church, 50 per cent by the Norman barons and only the remaining 5 per cent by Anglo-Saxons. French became the official language and the thriving Anglo-Saxon culture suffered badly from its imposition. William also purged the Church in England, with the assistance of his old friend and councillor, the scholarly

Lanfranc whom he made Archbishop of Canterbury. If no such thing as 'the feudal system' existed, a new form of feudalism was introduced, a complicated hierarchical structure at whose apex was the king, of land tenure and military service, allegiance and reward with its base the pursuit of war. For to keep everybody happy and rewarded new conquests were required, and Anglo-Saxon England had not been a society organized for war. A vast cleavage occurred between the Norman governors and the Saxon governed which took centuries to bridge, but the Normans brought England firmly into the mainstream of Europe and it was from the slow fusion of Norman and Anglo-Saxon that the English nation started to emerge.

William himself visited England for the last time in 1086, and much of the last year of his life was spent fighting in Normandy, where his eldest son Robert Curthose was among those ranged against him. In a battle for the disputed Vexin territory which lay between the kingdom of France and Normandy, he was thrown from his horse and died six weeks later on 9 September 1086 at Rouen, though he was buried in Caen. Whether one's sympathies are Norman or Anglo-Saxon, without doubt William the Bastard was indeed an extraordinary man.

Opposite The Domesday Book.

Above The Tower of London – one of the many castles built by William to enforce his conquest.

13

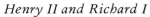
Henry II and Richard I

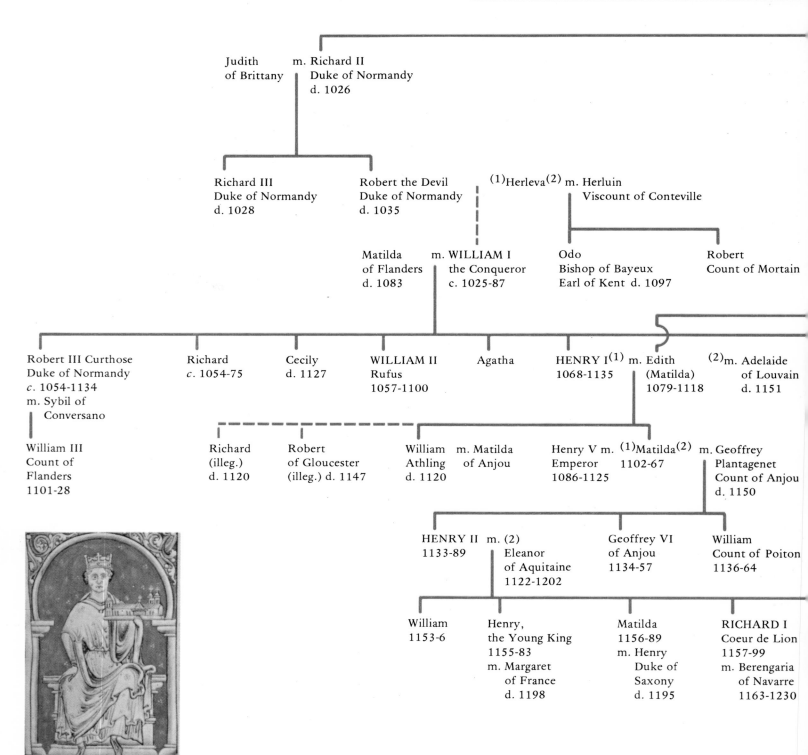

Judith of Brittany   m. Richard II Duke of Normandy d. 1026

Richard III Duke of Normandy d. 1028

Robert the Devil Duke of Normandy d. 1035

(1)Herleva(2) m. Herluin Viscount of Conteville

Matilda of Flanders d. 1083   m. WILLIAM I the Conqueror c. 1025-87

Odo Bishop of Bayeux Earl of Kent d. 1097

Robert Count of Mortain

Robert III Curthose Duke of Normandy c. 1054-1134 m. Sybil of Conversano

Richard c. 1054-75

Cecily d. 1127

WILLIAM II Rufus 1057-1100

Agatha

HENRY I(1) m. Edith (Matilda) 1068-1135   1079-1118

(2)m. Adelaide of Louvain d. 1151

William III Count of Flanders 1101-28

Richard (illeg.) d. 1120

Robert of Gloucester (illeg.) d. 1147

William Athling m. Matilda d. 1120   of Anjou

Henry V m. (1)Matilda(2) m. Geoffrey Emperor 1102-67   Plantagenet 1086-1125   Count of Anjou d. 1150

HENRY II m. (2) 1133-89   Eleanor of Aquitaine 1122-1202

Geoffrey VI of Anjou 1134-57

William Count of Poiton 1136-64

William 1153-6

Henry, the Young King 1155-83 m. Margaret of France d. 1198

Matilda 1156-89 m. Henry Duke of Saxony d. 1195

RICHARD I Coeur de Lion 1157-99 m. Berengaria of Navarre 1163-1230

King John

The Normans and Angevins

Richard I the Fearless m. Gunnor of Denmark
Count of Normandy
d. 996

Elgifu of
Northampton
m. (1)CNUT(2) m. (2)Emma(1) m. (2)ETHELRED II, the Unready(1) m. Elfreda
d. 1035   of Normandy   d. 1016   (Elgifu)

Godwin
Earl of Wessex

Edmund
Ironside
d. 1016

HAROLD I
d. 1040

Swein
King of
Norway
d. 1036

HARTHACNUT
d. 1042

EDWARD the Confessor m. Edith
c. 1005-66   d. 1075

HAROLD II
c. 1022-66

Edward Athling
d. 1057

Malcolm III
King of Scots
d. 1093

m. St Margaret
d. 1093

Edgar
Athling

Adela
d. 1137

m. Stephen Henry
Count of Blois
d. 1102

Edgar
King of Scots
c. 1074-1106

Alexander I
King of Scots
1077-1124

David I
King of Scots
c. 1080-1153

Mary m. Eustace III
Count of
Boulogne

Theobald
Count of Blois

Henry
Bishop of Winchester

STEPHEN
c. 1096-1154

m. Matilda of Boulogne
d. 1151

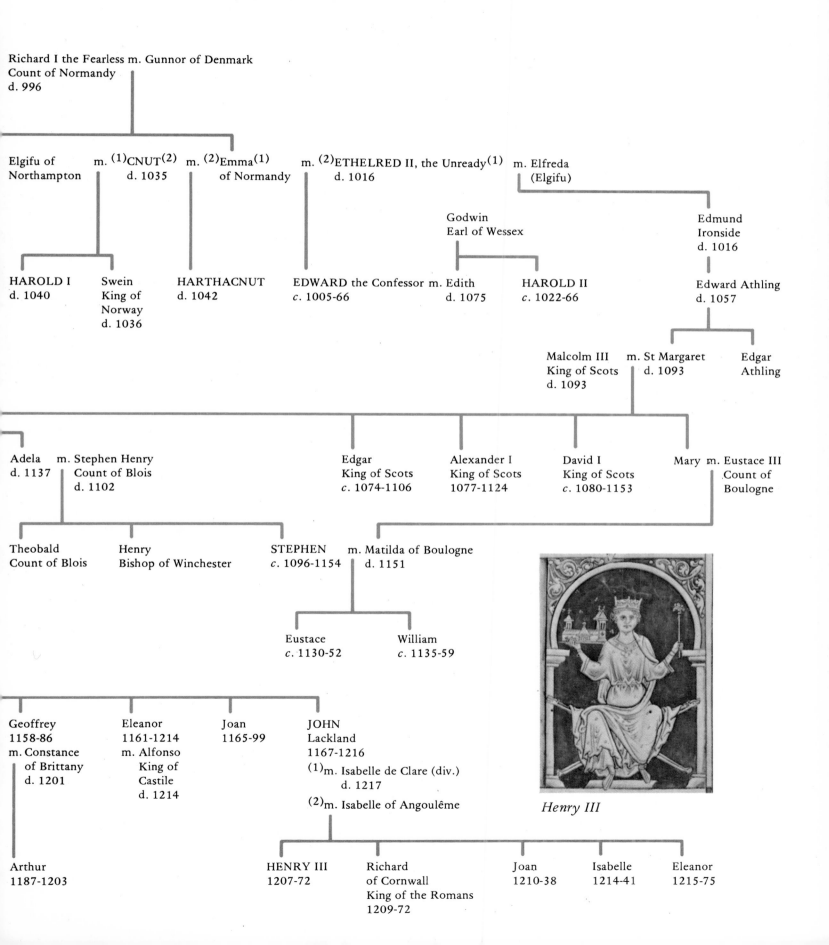

Henry III

Eustace
c. 1130-52

William
c. 1135-59

Geoffrey
1158-86
m. Constance
of Brittany
d. 1201

Eleanor
1161-1214
m. Alfonso
King of
Castile
d. 1214

Joan
1165-99

JOHN
Lackland
1167-1216
(1)m. Isabelle de Clare (div.)
d. 1217
(2)m. Isabelle of Angoulême

Arthur
1187-1203

HENRY III
1207-72

Richard
of Cornwall
King of the Romans
1209-72

Joan
1210-38

Isabelle
1214-41

Eleanor
1215-75

Henry II

r. 1154-89

'From the Devil they came, and to the Devil they shall go.'

Henry's youth was almost as turbulent as his great-grandfather's, William the Conqueror. There was still no defined law of succession to the English throne, though it had become accepted that a close legitimate relative of the monarch should inherit. In theory there was no objection to a woman succeeding to the throne, but in practice it was a man's world. When Henry I had died in 1135 leaving only one legitimate daughter alive, Matilda, and Stephen of Blois seized the throne, many Anglo–Norman barons recognized his claim (Stephen was a grandson of the Conqueror's through his mother). Matilda is one of the many formidable ladies who permeate the annals of medieval history. Her second husband, whom she did not like, was Count Geoffrey of Anjou and eventually a son was born of the reluctant union at Le Mans in March 1133 and christened Henry. When Matilda's father died two years later she fought like a tigress, not so much for her own claim to the English crown, though it was good, but for her infant son's. After nearly two strife-torn decades, during which Stephen and Matilda alternatively held and lost the English throne and young Henry learned the harsh facts of medieval power politics, a treaty was agreed in which Stephen recognized Henry of Anjou as his heir. Fortunately Stephen died soon afterwards, and in December 1154 Henry was crowned in Westminster Abbey.

Henry II was the first of the Plantagenet dynasty (though he and his sons were known as the Angevins). The name derived from Henry's father who was a great hunter and ordered acres of broom (genet in French) to be planted to improve the chase; hence *planta genet*. Apart from his title as King of England, Henry was Duke of Normandy, Duke of Aquitaine, Count of Anjou and Count of Maine, a vast inheritance for a young man of twenty-one, the ruler of lands which stretched from the Scottish border to the Pyrenees. Henry owed his English crown to his mother's lineage and determination; to his father he owed the resubjugation of Normandy and Maine, apart from the direct inheritance of Anjou. But it was to his wife Eleanor that he owed the acquisition of the duchy of Aquitaine, itself an amalgam of Poitou and Gascony.

Eleanor had already been married to King Louis VII of France. It may be noted here, to clarify any confusion, that the actual kingdom of France had shrunk to a small area and what we now know as France was split into dozens of domains such as Normandy, Brittany, Burgundy, Anjou, Blois, Toulouse, Touraine, Aquitaine. But some of these areas were dependencies of the French crown, while others recognized the French king as their overlord. Moreover France was the only *kingdom* in the land and its centre was Paris which had long been an important city. Thus Eleanor's first marriage had been illustrious but after fifteen years, early in 1152, it was annulled for a variety of reasons, not least of which was her failure to produce a male heir. (France adhered to the Salic Law by which only male issue could inherit).

Eleanor was as formidable a lady as Matilda but a more attractive character and her fame, unlike Matilda's, has endured through the centuries. Beautiful, cultured, intelligent, powerful – Eleanor was Duchess of Aquitaine in her own right – once free of King Louis she became the immediate focus for every ambitious ruler in Europe. The one who managed to snap her up was Henry of Anjou and two months after the annulment they were married (he aged nineteen, she about twenty-nine) to the fury of the French who belatedly appreciated the threat presented by a vast, powerful Angevin empire. In 1153, fifteen months after the marriage Eleanor gave birth to a son and to add insult to the French injury she proceeded to bear Henry four more sons. Initially the union was in all directions a success, the marriage of two forceful, passionate, energetic minds and bodies.

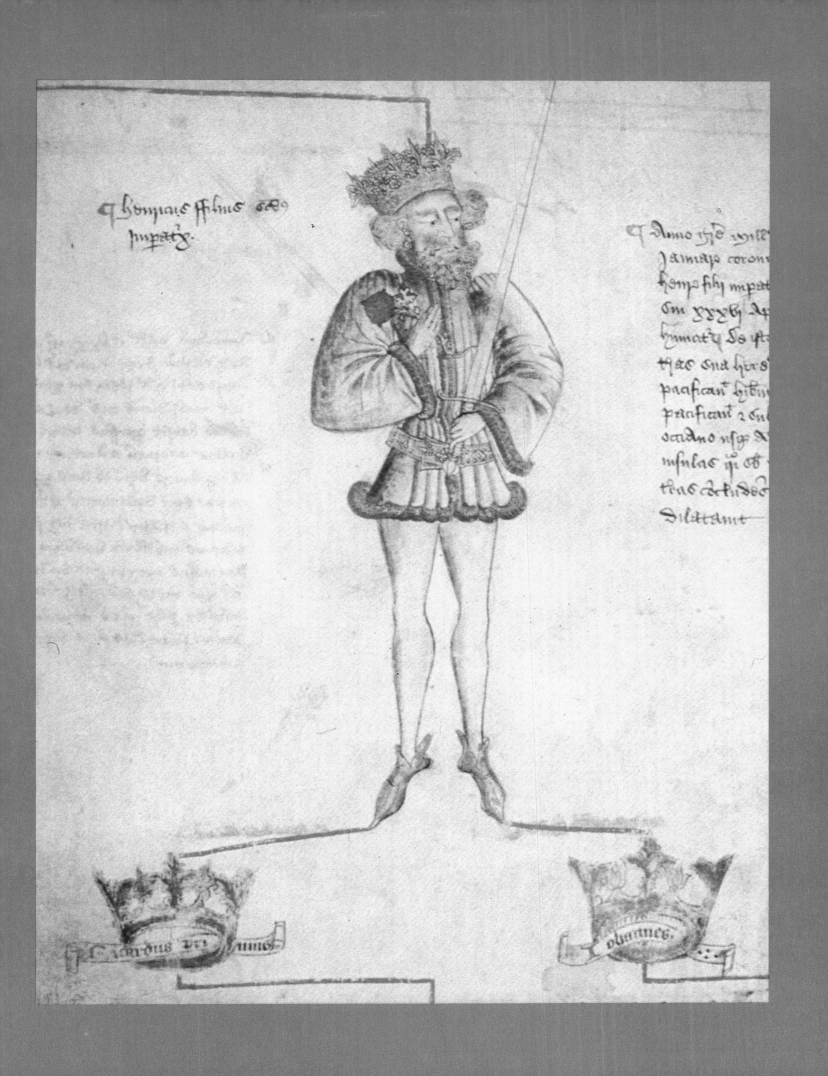

Above Stephen of Blois.

stay throughout the Mass whereas previously she had slipped out before Holy Communion was taken. At the sight of the holy relics Melusine immediately flew through the roof of the church and was seen no more. The trouble with the legend was that among those who believed it were the Angevins themselves. However it was some years before Henry's family began to live up to its image and earned the name of 'the Devil's brood'.

Henry was not born in England but in the early stormy years he had landed several times with his mother and had received some of his education in England while she was temporarily in power. He devoted a considerable amount of his staggering energy towards the many problems of his rich kingdom. The first to which Henry turned his attention was that of the castles which had been built illegally during twenty years of civil warfare. By Norman edict the building of castles was a royal prerogative but many barons had taken advantage of the chaos to strengthen their power. Henry promptly had the illegal castles dismantled, firmly proving *his* power.

The problem with which his name is most closely associated – the long fight with Thomas à Becket – was not peculiar to England but was part of a European struggle between Church and State. The reforming movement within the Church had reached a peak under the great Hildebrand who had become Pope Gregory VII in 1073. His aim had been not only to cleanse the Church of its corruption but to impose papal authority throughout Europe, 'the one seamless garment of Christianity'. It was a breathtaking concept, in effect a united Europe, but the European rulers had no wish to be united under anybody – even God's legate on earth – and thereby stripped of their individual power.

Henry and Becket were both powerful, able, ambitious men who fought on level terms in the battle to decide what should be controlled by the church and what by the king. Initially they had been friends, as Henry was a good judge of talent and generous in promoting it (outside his own family). It was to him that Becket owed his advancement first as Chancellor of England, then as Archbishop of Canterbury. Henry's mistake was thinking he could control his friend once he had invested him with real power, or seen in more ideological terms Henry was the pragmatist who believed in compromise, whereas Becket was the absolutist who considered compromise to be another word for the surrender of principles.

There was friction between Henry and Becket from the moment the latter became Archbishop of Canterbury in 1162 but matters came to a head

Henry's energy was phenomenal, even by the standards of powerful medieval rulers. To govern successfully in unsettled lands amid the jealousies of powerful nobles, frequent journeys were essential, but Henry was constantly on the move. There are accounts of his exhausted retinue packing and unpacking, riding miles over rough country, attending to business at the court, and then being expected to hunt or spend half the night in revelry. Henry may have suffered from the need to prove himself because he was a small man, if powerfully built; he was described as 'short of body' and 'broad breasted'. His small bustling figure was emphasized by the short cloak he habitually wore which earned him the nickname of 'Curtmantle'. (The Anglo-Norman nobility still wore long cloaks.)

What Henry also suffered from was the famed Angevin temper. There were stories of him lying on the ground and in his rage stuffing his mouth with the rushes on the floor – not as a child but when he was adult. But the Angevins were believed to be descended from the devil, for according to legend, Melusine, the daughter of Satan, had married a Count of Anjou and borne him children. Her true identity was finally revealed when she was made to

18

when Henry promulgated the Constitutions of Clarendon in 1164. Three clauses became particularly inflammatory: that the king should have jurisdiction over the Church's lands and patronage; that the clergy would no longer be immune from the laws of the land; and that no clergyman could appeal over the head of the king to the pope. Becket, personally and as the representative of papal authority in England, vehemently opposed the Clarendon clauses and his battle with Henry began in earnest. Later in 1164 he was summoned to trial at Northampton to answer for his public condemnation of the king's laws, thereafter he fled the country and for the next two years Henry was in fitful negotiation with the pope about his unseemly royal behaviour. In 1169 Henry and Becket met personally in France but this conference collapsed, whereupon Becket excommunicated the English clergy, though he fell short of excommunicating the king. It was not until the summer of 1170 that an uneasy reconciliation was effected and Becket returned to England. In December 1170 Henry, in one of his Angevin tempers, uttered his famous words, 'Why will no one rid me of this low-born clerk?', or alternatively, 'Why will no one rid me of this turbulent priest?'

As is well known, four loyal Anglo–Norman knights took him at his word, only too literally, and murdered Thomas à Becket in Canterbury Cathedral. Thereby a saint and a legend were created. It was generally accepted that Henry had not intended to have Becket murdered, and despite the wave of horror that swept through Christendom Henry survived the episode with his position remarkably unscathed. This perhaps says something for the contemporary view of Henry and Becket, as opposed to posterity's. In 1172 Henry and England were received back into the bosom of the

Church, albeit on certain terms. Henry was supposed to pay for a minor crusade to the Holy Land (though he never did), he had to return all the Canterbury lands he had appropriated and most of the offending clauses of the Constitutions of Clarendon were removed. In 1174 he did his public penance by travelling on the pilgrim's way from London to Canterbury, having himself scourged, and kneeling before the tomb of the martyred Becket. Incidentally, the word 'canter' entered the English language from the rate at which the more affluent pilgrims rode their horses to Canterbury.

Henry may have failed in his attempts at ecclesiastical reform but he was more successful in clarifying and overhauling the legal system. It was during his reign that the basis of English Common Law emerged – laws established by precedent and, through the king's writ and officers, made common to all, in theory anyway, if not always (and certainly not then) in practice. Henry did not introduce the jury system; it had existed in embryonic form in Anglo–Saxon England and even in Normandy. What he did was to clamp down on other forms of settling disputes such as the Anglo–Saxon trial by ordeal of hot iron and the Norman trial by combat, with the survivor as the successful litigant. He organized a 'jury of presentment', twelve witnesses to the facts who presented their versions to the king's officer who then judged on the evidence. Slowly, the givers of evidence turned into the judgers and a unique system evolved of trial by a jury of twelve good men and true, which has been one of England's major exports.

Henry spent a fair amount of time repelling invasions from or subduing England's turbulent neighbours, Scotland and Wales, as had his predecessors, but he gave Ireland more of his attention than they had. There had been an early Norman

Below The tomb of Henry II's wife, Queen Eleanor, at Fontevrault in France.

so comiti

n ayarm

enicus

31 m regno

prefata

no berm

nc?filius

er unisit

is corone

re sue

x orgni

rm ærone

tota cum

Henricus nacus ayardis reg
sub q̃ sacarr Thomas mucon

Henricus scorns genuit.

Above Henry II with Thomas à Becket, the Archbishop of Canterbury.

incursion into Ireland but thereafter the country had mainly been left to get on with itself. It had not got on particularly well, certainly not in the view of Pope Adrian IV who regarded with horror the reports he received from Ireland. It had alas regressed into a barbarian land and it was Adrian who in 1155 issued a Papal Bull which gave Henry of England the right to conquer and make Ireland a civilized country. At the time Henry was too occupied with other matters to bother about Ireland and it was not until 1169 that he organized an invasion force. The next year Dublin was under Anglo–Norman control and by 1172 part of Ireland – known as the Pale – was an appendage of the English crown, if a loose one, and the Irish Church had been brought into line with the English. In view of the later history of Catholic Ireland and Protestant England, it is ironic that it should have been by papal authority that England embarked on her first serious conquest of Ireland. However the Irish would assuredly note that the conquest was urged by the only Englishman, or more precisely Anglo–Norman, ever to have been pope, Nicholas Breakspear who became Pope Adrian IV.

By 1173 Henry's family problems had begun to ferment and soon brewed into open rebellion. Royal difficulties with sons and heirs were by no means confined to Henry II. What was unique about his brood was that they were Angevins infatuated with their own satanic legend, and they also had a powerful, politically involved mother. Before 1173 Eleanor and Henry had begun to lead their own lives, as her charms for him lessened (she was ten

Right Becket's murder in
Canterbury Cathedral.

years older) and their forceful temperaments clashed. Eleanor held glittering court in Aquitaine, while Henry charged round other parts of his domains. He was much given to 'fleshly lust' and had a series of mistresses the most famous of whom was the fair Anglo–Norman Rosamund de Clifford, his rose of the world. Henry's infidelities were comparatively unimportant, it was the exercise of power that his wife and children sought. The first-born son had died in infancy and the heir was Henry, born in 1155. His father tried to solve the dilemma of a restless heir and also the question of the succession, by having young Henry crowned King of England in 1170. Henceforward the two Henrys were known as 'the old King' and 'the young King', but the old king – he was thirty-seven – refused to give the young king any accompanying power. In 1173 young Henry rebelled, backed by his mother and her former husband, King Louis of France. One of Louis' daughters by his second marriage was the wife of young Henry, but the alliance had not healed ancient enmities. Louis was anxious to break up the Angevin empire, and backing the son against the father was a good way of achieving this aim.

The rebellion was not particularly successful and by the terms of the truce agreed in the autumn of 1173, the young king was to receive half the revenues of England and Normandy which he would inherit; his brother Richard was to inherit Aquitaine and his brother Geoffrey would have Anjou. Henry hoped by his share-out to settle his family differences, but he failed to include his youngest son, John. It was for this reason that John gained the name of Lackland which stuck to him all his life. For her part in the rebellion Eleanor was put under castle arrest, though she was always courteously treated. Henry had defined his sons' inheritances and given them more money, but he still refused to let them have any real hand in governing, particularly young Henry in England. For the rest of their lives his older sons were intermittently plotting against him, sometimes in concert, sometimes with other allies.

In 1183 the young king died suddenly and his father had to redistribute the inheritances. He proposed that Richard should now have Normandy, Anjou and England; Geoffrey should retain Brittany (he had married the daughter of the Count of Brittany), and his favourite son, the landless John, should have Aquitaine. This led to further trouble because Aquitaine was the country in which Richard had spent most of his life with his mother, and he stormed there for the second time saying he would never part with a hide of its land. (He had earlier quarrelled with young Henry about

Aquitaine).

The first few months of 1186 were the last peaceful ones that Henry enjoyed. Eleanor and he had by now become semi-reconciled and they held court in England in the early spring. The fair Rosamund de Clifford was dead which may have assisted the reconciliation, for if Eleanor had accepted the open liaison, she had not approved of it. Indeed in popular literature Rosamund's death was attributed directly to Eleanor, though this would have been a difficult feat even for the formidable Eleanor to achieve, as Rosamund died at Woodstock in Oxfordshire while Eleanor was under castle arrest at Chinon in Touraine. Later in 1186 Geoffrey, who had by now quarrelled with Richard, swore fealty to Philip the new king of France; Henry was saved from a two pronged Breton–French attack on Normandy only by the sudden death of Geoffrey. In 1188 the remaining

male Angevins – Henry himself, Richard and John – temporarily joined forces to repel further French threats, but soon afterwards Richard presented his father with an ultimatum. He demanded that his marriage to Princess Alice of France take place immediately (they had been engaged for fifteen years), and that his father recognize him publicly as his heir.

Henry refused to accede to these demands, whereupon the most vitriolic in the series of bitter family quarrels ensued. In a fury Richard swore fealty to King Philip for his future Angevin inheritance (though not for England, as that was a kingdom). By the early summer of 1189 Henry, who was now fifty-six and ageing fast under the stress of the last few years, was faced by the combined forces of his son Richard and King Philip. To cover his retreat he burned Le Mans, his birthplace, but he was nonetheless forced to submit

to his son and the French. The final blow was to learn that his beloved John, whom he had trusted, had deserted him and joined the victorious side.

Henry died in the great castle of Chinon on 6 July 1189 and was buried at Fontevrault in his native Anjou. Before his death he cried, 'Shame, shame on a conquered king.' His last years were sad and in the end he was defeated, but he left behind him a solid body of achievement in England at least, which assisted the fusion of Saxon and Norman and the development of the English nation. He handed over to his disloyal sons a larger empire than he had inherited, which was the aim for which all rulers schemed and fought. A contemporary chronicler summed up the general feeling about the departed King Henry 11: 'The man, who in his own times was hated by many, is now declared everywhere to have been an excellent and beneficial ruler.'

Above The great castle of Chinon in Touraine where Henry 11 died in July 1189.

Richard I

r. 1189-99

'A Prince born for the good of Christendom.'

Richard was born in England, on 8 September 1157 at Beaumont Palace near Oxford, when his mother and father were still on good terms and spending much of their time in their English kingdom. Richard looked like an Anglo–Saxon. He inherited his father's red-gold hair, though unlike Henry he was tall, and had a fair complexion (some Gascons are fair so the Anglo–Saxon appearance came more probably from his mother's ancestry). But Richard's interest in the land of his birth was at all times minimal. There is a joke in that light-hearted look at English history *1066 and All That* about his being known in England not as Coeur de Lion but Gare de Lyons because as soon as he arrived, he departed. There was of course no reason why Richard should have cared about England, certainly not before he became king. He was a younger son and he was brought up by his mother, mainly in Aquitaine. His father's domains were known as the Angevin empire, not the English or even the Anglo–Norman empire. England's value remained that she was a kingdom, which put her ruler on equal terms with the king of France, and she was rich; but she was not the heart of the empire – that was in mainland Europe.

Richard's life can be divided into three sections (his accession to the throne of England does *not* provide one of the breaks). The first phase covers his childhood under his mother's wing during which he learned the knightly arts of warfare and became an accomplished musician and linguist, though he never learned to speak the English tongue. Richard was a fair versifier too and several ballads attributed to him have survived. This was the era of romance and chivalry and Eleanor's court at Poitiers became a centre of the cult. (It is somewhat ironic that one part of the cult – the placing of women on inaccessible pedestals, as beautiful goddesses in need of male protection – should have been fostered by the powerful ambitious Eleanor).

Outside court circles Aquitaine was no more a

Richart roy dangle
terre eſtant de
mouite enaure bē
aut apres le dept
du roy phelippe ſe
iour eſtre venu que ſalhadin
deuoit rendre la vraye troꝛ
et ne lauoit fait. Non obſtāt
qͥl euſt eu de luᵗ et du roy
phle pluſieurs alongemens

pour ce faire fut tant pꝛe
qͥl fit trencher les teſtes
a plus de b.ᴹ turcꝗ et autꝗ
ſarrazins quͥl tenoit pꝛiſon
niers et le demourant des
autres miſt a raenꜱon. Ce
toſt apres ſe meuſt grant
diſſenꜱion entre lui et le duc
doſteriche. pour quoy il fit
getter en fange 𝇍 boe la bāne

land of romance and chivalry than anywhere else. It had more than its share of turbulent nobles and Richard spent a considerable part of his youth subduing them while the rest of his time was consumed by the Angevin family quarrels. Long before his father died Richard had acquired a formidable reputation and the contemporary comment that he cared 'for no success that was not reached by a path cut by his own sword and stained with the blood of his adversaries' indicated that he was a man and a soldier to be reckoned with. When the news reached Western Europe of the fall of Jerusalem to the Infidel and the virtual collapse of the Christian empire in the Holy Land – or Outremer, as it was known – Richard found his mission in life.

He entered phase two of his life as a Christian soldier who would reconquer Outremer. It is difficult now to be sympathetic towards the crusades, not because of the amount of blood spilled or the savageries committed (twentieth century excesses far outweigh those of the crusaders') but because everything was done in the name of Christ and the Christian soldiers failed so singularly to emulate the Christian virtues of compassion, charity or tolerance. Any age should be judged by its morality, ethics and standards and Christianity had become a militant, messianic religion. The heathen

were to be pitied and converted, by the sword if necessary, but those who espoused another religion and refused to be converted were to be slaughtered because there was only one true God. More mundane inducements were held out to the crusaders, but the impulse behind the majority, including Richard, was the gory, simplistic message of God.

Before Richard could organize his crusade, the final quarrel with his father erupted, then Henry was dead and Richard himself was King of England, Duke of Normandy, etcetera. His main Angevin empire was reasonably secure, apart from some negotiations with and payment to King Philip for his recent help (the payment was made from the English exchequer). But to become King of England Richard needed to be crowned. In August 1189 he duly crossed to the unloved land of his birth and the coronation took place on 3 September. The coronation evening was marred by a massacre of Jews who tried to enter the palace where the king was feasting to pay tribute to their new monarch. In the current wave of crusading fervour, the populace in other parts of the country turned on their Jewish communities as members of the race held responsible for the crucifixion of Christ. The blood-letting did not end until March 1190 with the massacre of the Jews of York. It was a fitting start to the great

Overleaf opposite Richard I.

Overleaf Richard I watching the beheading of the garrison at Acre on 20 August 1191.

Below Saladin's army besieges a crusader stronghold.

se antima manu cruciatum pmittir.

tande uenia petes ut absoluar

The captive Richard kneels at the feet of Emperor Henry VI.

crusader's reign, though Richard himself was furious at the anti-Semitic outbreak because the Jews, as money raisers and lenders, were under royal protection.

It was of course money that Richard wanted from England to finance his crusade. He milked the exchequer as dry as he could, he sold everything he possibly could and stated, 'I would sell London, if I could find anybody rich enough to buy it.' In his father's reign a traveller had noted, 'Among the noble cities of the world that are celebrated by fame, the city of London ... is one that spreads its fame wider, sends its wealth and wares further, and lifts its head higher than all others.' Richard managed to obtain the required amount of money without selling famed London city and in December 1189, his mission accomplished, he left England.

There were problems about who should govern the country in his absence. As Richard had no heir there were three actual claimants to the throne: his brother John, his bastard half brother Geoffrey and his nephew Arthur of Brittany (the young son of his legitimate brother Geoffrey). Richard had no wish to leave the adult John or Geoffrey in control, as he might return to find his throne usurped. He spiked Geoffrey's claim by making him Archbishop of York (no cleric could become king). John Lackland's ambitions he hoped to dampen by granting him the whole of the West Country, the counties of Nottingham and Derbyshire, the overlordship of Ireland and the Norman county of Mortain, but to hedge this uncertain bet he banished

John from England for three years. As Chief Justicair and Chancellor he appointed William Longchamps, an old and trusted friend from his days in Aquitaine. Longchamps was Papal Legate in his own right, so he was thus left in complete control of England.

Richard organized his crusade efficiently, as one would expect, but his course to the Holy Land was not rapid. First there were delays because Philip of France's wife died – he and Richard were jointly leading the Western crusade. They then spent the winter of 1190–1 in Sicily, storming Messina in the process. It was to Messina that the Dowager Queen Eleanor travelled, at the age of sixty-seven, to ensure that Richard's bride actually reached him. His bride was not Alice of France whom he had courted for some fifteen years but Berengaria of Navarre. (Richard had eventually rejected Alice on the grounds that she had been his father's mistress). It was not until after the crusaders had reached Cyprus that Richard finally married Berengaria, in the church at Limassol in May 1191; the excuse for this delay was that she had arrived in Lent when no good Christian could marry. Richard spent some time in Cyprus securing it for the crusaders and eventually made landfall near Acre in June 1191.

Richard's feats in the Holy Land have passed into legend. Much of his high popular reputation rests on his battles with the noble Saladin; his capture of Acre (the massacre of its surrendered garrison forgotten or excused); his magnetic leadership of the feuding crusaders; his march to

27

Jerusalem; and his final sad failure to capture the Holy City because of the desertion of King Philip and the stabs in the back delivered by his brother John. However, part of the internal feuding was caused by Richard's Angevin temper and King Philip returned to France because he was a wily statesman. Having made his crusading gesture Philip rightly considered that Jerusalem could not be held, even if captured, and that he would be better employed governing and extending his French realm. John's behaviour, though predict/able, was precipitated by the actions of Richard's appointed Chief Justicair.

William Longchamps had an apparently rapacious appetite for young boys and the barons complained that none of their sons was safe in the same building with him. His overbearing method of governing had aroused equal hostility and when John was allowed to return to England at the end of 1190 he became the immediate focus for the growing discontent, a position to which he had no objection. Richard received the disturbing news in Sicily in early 1191 and immediately sent Walter of Coutances to act as mediator between his brother's supporters and the hated Chief Justicair. Despite his Norman/sounding name Coutances was a Cornishman and he succeeded in averting the threatened civil war but in September 1191 Longchamps over/reached himself and was forced to flee the country. He departed in unseemly fashion as a chronicler described: 'Pretending to be a woman – a sex which he always hated – he changed his priest's robe into a harlot's dress.' Walter of Coutances became Chief Justicair in his place and, assisted by the indomitable Eleanor who had made the long journey back from Sicily, he managed to keep an uneasy peace.

By October 1192 Richard had finally conceded that he could not capture Jerusalem and that his return to Europe was necessary. Having concluded an equitable treaty with Saladin he sailed for home but his ship was caught in a storm and lost contact with the main English–Angevin fleet. Thereafter Richard encountered various difficulties which made him decide to travel home by the long overland route. This was a dangerous, even foolhardy decision as he would have to pass through the lands of several enemies. His small party reached Vienna without detection but in December 1192 he was recognized and promptly given into the custody of Duke Leopold of Austria, a gentleman he had managed to insult after the battle of Acre. The duke imprisoned his captive in the castle of Durnstein overlooking the Danube. It was there that the Blondel legend grew, the faithful minstrel warbling his way through central Europe until he located his master at Durnstein. Duke Leopold had landed a massive prize, though it was soon wrenched out of his hands by his overlord, the Emperor Henry VI, and the wheeling and dealing for Richard's release started.

Towards the end of 1192, when nothing had been heard of Richard for months, his brother John became busy. At first he genuinely believed that his brother was dead but when the rumours of his capture began to seep through, John decided he must strike. He rushed to France to gain the support of King Philip, swearing fealty for the Angevin empire which was not yet his; some said for England too, though this seems unlikely. He then rushed back to England and succeeded in raising support for himself as king and capturing some castles. However, by the early summer of 1193 contact had been established with the imprisoned Richard and a vast ransom sum – 100,000 marks – had been demanded by the Emperor for his release. Walter of Coutances and Eleanor persuaded John's supporters to sign a truce, while the task of raising the massive ransom for their lawful king was under/taken. The whole of the Angevin empire was bled but England, which already had the most wide/spread and efficient tax system, was bled the whitest.

Even when the money was raised, the haggling and plotting and counter/offers (particularly by Philip of France) for Richard's royal person continued. It was not until the beginning of 1194 that Richard was finally released, after payment of the larger sum of 150,000 marks – some thirty/four tons of silver, about three times the King of England's annual income. After a leisurely journey Richard landed in England in March: most of the barons welcomed him back and the only city he had to storm was Nottingham. Later that month Richard appeared at Winchester wearing his crown and full regalia to remind the barons that he was their lawful king. He then raised as much money as he could from England's strained exchequer and groaning tax/payers and in May 1194 left the country never to return. At least this time he left her in the hands of one of the ablest medieval administrators, Hubert Walter.

The last phase of Richard's life was spent in strengthening his Angevin domains, reconquering the land which Philip of France had appropriated during his imprisonment and executing alliances to isolate Philip. He also built the famous Château Gaillard, a fortress on a strategic bend of the river Seine into whose stones he poured all his military talent and knowledge. Richard died in an inappropriate manner for the greatest warrior in Christendom. He was besieging the small town of Chalus in Limousin because its lord had refused to

hand over some treasure found nearby. Local history asserts that the garrison of fifteen was defending itself against the great Richard with anything it could lay its hands on, including frying pans. Contemptuously Richard came to the siege unarmed but a crossbowman caught him with an arrow. His once magnificent body was now grossly overweight, the arrow was deeply embedded and difficult to extract, and gangrene set in. Richard summoned his mother to his deathbed, but not his wife, and named his brother John as his heir.

Why Richard became a legend as the lionhearted prince of Christendom is understandable, though it seems a trifle odd that a man who was almost certainly homosexual should have been given this particular mantle. Why Richard should have become and remained one of the most popular kings of England is less so. Judged from an English viewpoint he was a rotten king. His predecessors back to William the Conqueror had all shown some interest in the welfare of England and spent longer or shorter periods in the land. Richard's only interest in England was as a bank and he spent six months of a ten year reign in the country, but his popularity was established by the end of the sixteenth century because it was then that the story of Robin Hood was transferred to his reign. There *was* a Robin Hood who performed some of the feats and had some of the friends attributed to him, but this

Robin Hood was born in 1274, was outlawed by Edward II and the forest to which he escaped was Barnsdale in Yorkshire, not Sherwood. The story soon attracted the attention of the versifiers and was first published in 1489 as *A Lyttel Geste of Robyn Hode: Kynge Edward and Robyn Hode and Lyttel Johan.* Robin the famous archer makes sense in the reign of Edward II, when the English bowman was soon to be the scourge of the Continent, whereas it is nonsense in Richard's time. In reality, it was John round whom the discontented rallied against Richard's hated Justicair. To complete the picture, Nottingham – the legendary centre of pro-Richard, Saxon–English resistance to the hated Norman John – was the one city in England Richard had to take by storm on his return (though its citizens later claimed they had not known it was Richard, their lawful king, who was attacking them).

When people need a hero to propagate their causes they find one, but late sixteenth century England might have found a better *English* hero than Richard. He had some virtues as a medieval Christian soldier and towards the end of his life he was emerging as a cool diplomat. But as he lay dying in April 1199 at the age of forty-one, he commanded that his brain be buried in Poitou, his heart in Normandy and his embalmed body in Anjou at the foot of his father's grave. In death as in life Richard had nothing for England.

Above Chateau Gaillard, Richard's fortress on the river Seine.

John
r. 1199-1216

'His fortune was to be ever in action.'

John has received as consistently bad a press as his brother Richard has a good one, with Shakespeare's *King John* putting the seal of disapproval on it. Although it would be ridiculous to try to turn John into a hero, it is possible to cast a more dispassionate eye on his career. He was born at Beaumont Palace near Oxford on Christmas Eve 1167; his mother Eleanor was forty-five at the time and never showed much interest in her last child. Like his father he was small and he grew up as the youngest child of a large brood, sometimes indulged but more often ignored, in the shadow of three much older brothers. Some clues to his later character may be found in this information. John's first venture into the outside world was not a success, when in 1185 his father sent him to Ireland to re-establish the King's justice in the areas where it was supposed to run. It has been said that in eight months John managed to turn Ireland into a state of complete rather than semi-anarchy; it can also be said that he was not the last Anglo–Norman or Englishman to fail in Ireland.

Until the very end John was loyal to his father. The last minute change of allegiance, which broke his father's heart, was the first evidence of his flawed character but his behaviour while Richard, his lawful king was absent, was not unduly remarkable by medieval standards. In rushing to swear fealty to King Philip of France in return for the promise of support, he was merely following an Angevin family tradition. His brothers Henry, Richard and Geoffrey had all at various times sworn fealty to the French King to gain his support against their father.

The dying Richard nominated John, whom he had already pardoned for his treachery in England, as his heir, but there was the other claimant, Arthur of Brittany whom Richard had earlier nominated. Arthur was now thirteen and a man by early medieval reckoning; he also had one of those formidable mothers, Constance. Normandy and England opted for John, Eleanor was still alive so

Aquitaine stayed loyal to her and consequently to her son, but the heart of the empire – Anjou, Maine and Touraine – opted for Arthur.

John acted decisively from the moment he received the news of Richard's death and continued to do so. On 27 May 1199 he was crowned King of England and twelve months later had come to advantageous terms with Arthur and Constance – they retained Brittany but accepted him as their overlord – and was in a position to negotiate with Philip of France. By the terms of this treaty Philip recognized John as the Angevin ruler, though in return John made certain concessions, and there

were mutterings that neither Henry II nor Richard would have given away so much. But it seemed a fair bargain because France, under the immensely able Philip, had greatly increased her power and prestige in the last few years.

In the same year, 1200, John married Isabelle of Angoulême. It was an excellent diplomatic move, as Angoulême was one of the unruly areas of northern Aquitaine, and it was also a good personal move because his first wife, Isabella of Gloucester, had failed to bear children. To marry Isabelle of Angoulême he had to get his twelve-year marriage to Isabella of Gloucester annulled by the Pope but this was accomplished without difficulty, and his second wife fulfilled her function by producing the future Henry III.

Until 1202 all went reasonably well for John and he seemed to be holding together his vast empire as effectively as had his father or brother. But then the Lusignans used his marriage to Isabelle as an excuse to rebel against him (she had been previously engaged to a Lusignan noble); and Philip of France used their discontent as a pretext to invade Normandy and to recognize Arthur of Brittany as the rightful ruler of the Angevin heartlands. At the beginning of August 1202 John made a remarkable forced march from Le Mans to Mirabeau castle which his eighty-year-old mother was holding for him against the attacks of Arthur of Brittany (who was of course her grandson). John took the attackers by surprise, routed them and captured Arthur and then drove home his advantage by occupying the important towns of Tours and Angers. It was a campaign worthy of the mighty Richard.

Two years later his brother's supposedly impregnable fortress of Château Gaillard had fallen to the French and John had been driven out of Normandy. Before considering why his fortunes changed so disastrously there is the matter of Arthur of Brittany. Anybody who has seen or read *King John* will know that wicked uncle John ordered the little boy's eyes to be put out (and in the chronicler's version, on which Shakespeare based his play, little Arthur was to be castrated too.) Uncle John probably did murder Arthur, though it is doubtful that he had him blinded or castrated. Little Arthur was sixteen when he was taken captive while trying to storm a castle held by his eighty-year-old grandmother. He had also foresworn his oath to his uncle and was in open rebellion. Admittedly these were acts which John himself had performed but they were treasonable. John's probable action in murdering his nephew is not commendable, but neither was it remarkable in the circumstances, then or for many years thereafter.

The loss of Normandy was partly John's fault.

Below King John's tomb in Worcester Cathedral.

Arthur's disappearance was certainly laid at his door and turned the Bretons into bitter enemies, so he faced the dreaded two-pronged French–Breton attack when King Philip renewed the offensive. John also had a bad habit of quarrelling with people at the moment when he most needed them, but mainly it was circumstance and a changed mood that defeated him. England had been bled white by Richard but she was better placed, economically, socially and geographically than was Normandy which had suffered even more. Moreover the Normans were growing closer in spirit to the French and no longer wanted to pay homage to a king of England. Finally there was Philip, a man determined to reunite, slowly but surely, the France of Charlemagne. A better leader than John might have diverted the Norman tide but he could not then have stopped it coming in.

Philip laid the foundation stones of the later French nation and earned the name of Philip Augustus in consequence. Paradoxically, by the loss of Normandy, John helped strengthen the English consciousness because the Anglo–Norman barons had to decide which country they wanted to live in as they could not pay homage to two kings. The majority of them chose England, their links with mainland Europe were cut and their divided loyalties unified. In 1204 the redoubtable Eleanor

Below King John staghunting.

died at the age of eighty-one or eighty-two, and with the rest of his Angevin empire in such a fragile state John needed to impress himself on Aquitaine if he wanted to hold its rich lands. This he managed to do successfully and then concluded an uneasy truce with King Philip for the remaining Angevin lands. For the next eight years John remained in England.

The reason for this was his quarrel with the Pope which officially was about Hubert Walter's successor as Archbishop of Canterbury, but in effect related to the old question of the boundaries of power between Church and King. Walter died in 1205 and the quarrel dragged on partly because Innocent III was one of the most powerful of medieval popes, partly because John was so stubborn. In 1209 it culminated in John's personal excommunication which meant that his subjects were absolved from their vows of allegiance and entitled to rebel against him. It was not until 1213 that John and England were accepted back into the bosom of the church with the king's acceptance of the papal nominee as Archbishop of Canterbury, Stephen Langton, and acknowledgement of the pope as overlord of England and Ireland. One reason why John has always had such a bad press is that all medieval chronicles were written by churchmen and he had cocked a large snook at the pope for a considerable time.

Interestingly, the English barons did not then take the fully justified opportunity to depose their excommunicated king but supported John in his fight against the pope because it was in their interest, too, that the Church's power be curtailed. However the Welsh, the Scots and the Irish took advantage and John was engaged in subduing them. His quarrel with the pope and the excommunication meant he was unable to make the necessary alliances with other Christian rulers to embark on the re-conquest of Normandy. He was thus forced to concentrate his attention on England for eight years and concentrate it he did. John had inherited some of his father's energy and when he was not campaigning against the Scots, Welsh or Irish, he rushed around England. The North in particular saw more of its monarch than it ever had and the northern barons were not in the least pleased by the royal interference. John was not a creative administrator like his father but he was quite an able one, reorganizing the tax system, introducing an embryonic property tax (which made him unpopular with all the barons), and vitalizing civic life (many English towns owe their charters to King John). These measures were to raise revenue for the Crown but they contributed to the development of the State.

One other claim John has to English interest is

the attention he paid to the navy. King Alfred, Henry VIII and Charles II are all said to be the real founders of the Royal Navy but John can be added to the list. Since Alfred the rulers of England had paid remarkably little attention to sea power and when they needed ships they commandeered or borrowed them. After the loss of Normandy John had the intelligence to appreciate that sea power could be England's greatest weapon and that a more permanent fleet under the king's control was desirable. Such was his success in building one up that in 1213 his navy inflicted a heavy defeat on the French invasion fleet. (The French had been given papal permission to conquer excommunicated England and were extremely disappointed when John and Innocent III came to terms.)

By 1214 John's position was sufficiently strong for him to launch the long dreamed-of campaign to recapture all his Angevin empire. His main army would land in northern Aquitaine and march north, while a smaller English force with its allies would push the French south from Flanders where it would be squeezed like a nut between nutcrackers. John's part of the plan went reasonably well but his allies were defeated by the French at Les Bouvines. Innocent III then intervened and a treaty was agreed whereby each side retained what it had gained, but John had nevertheless been defeated.

The road from Les Bouvines led straight to Runnymede.

Baronial resentment against the King had been growing for some time. For most of the reigns of Richard and John the barons had been subjected to heavy taxation and they also disliked the man John had appointed as Chief Justicair, Peter Des Roches. He was an able administrator but a native of Poitou, and an element of Englishness was already developing. But the greatest resentment against John was the increased scutage money he had demanded to finance his French war and which some barons said flatly they would not pay. (Scutage was the already established method by which those who were liable for feudal military service but did not wish to leave England's shores, paid money in lieu.)

Had John returned from France the victor, the barons' resentment might have been assuaged in glory, booty and lesser taxation, but he returned the loser to face the barons arming their castles, and by May 1215 the country was in a state of civil war. By no means all the barons rebelled against him, though most of the northern ones did. Eventually, through the mediations of Stephen Langton whose appointment as Archbishop of Canterbury John had so stoutly resisted, a parley was arranged in a meadow known as Runnymede on the banks of the Thames. There, in the words of a chronicler, 'a sort

Below The English fleet sails into harbour. John has as good a claim as any English monarch to be called the founder of the royal navy.

of peace' was concluded, which is how the negotiations at Runnymede were regarded at the time and for many years thereafter. (Shakespeare has nothing to say about the famous Magna Carta in *King John*.)

Magna Carta was not discovered as 'the cornerstone of English liberties' until the seventeenth century; this view held for many years, then a reaction set in and the charter was viewed as a compact between robber barons and robber king. An accurate assessment lies somewhere in between. On the debit side the barons were not an attractive bunch and even their names are not remembered. If the credit for Magna Carta should go to anybody it is to Stephen Langton who brought the two sides together and worked hard to make the sixty-three clauses acceptable. It was only at the last moment that the vital amendment was inserted to make the charter applicable to 'any freeman' rather than 'any baron'. If all the charter had been implemented England would have regressed because some of its clauses were extremely reactionary and the Great Charter on which later historians and lawyers pounced so enthusiastically was the one issued by John's son Henry III in 1225.

On the credit side it was a comprehensive document which summarized the laws of England and redefined the king's rights. It tipped back the balance which had been seized by the king for several decades, without upsetting the unification of England. Most importantly it provided future generations with noble precepts on which they could rightly pounce, for example: 'No freeman shall be taken or imprisoned or disseised or exiled or in any way destroyed ... except by the lawful judgment of his peers', and 'To no one will we sell, to no one will we deny or delay right or justice.'

In effect neither side took too much notice of the clauses, though John ordered copies of the document to be sent to every shire in the land and his royal officers to swear loyalty to the twenty-five barons who had been appointed as guardians of the charter. But John also appealed to the Pope who was his overlord according to the settlement of 1213, and Innocent III roundly denounced the charter, excommunicating all the barons who continued to press its clauses. The mutual antagonism and distrust were thus inflamed and by September 1215 civil war had again broken out. Most of the western side of England stayed loyal to John and he spent the winter of 1215–16 marching through eastern rebel territory, to some effect because in the spring of 1216 the rebel barons felt the need to appeal to France for help. Prince Louis duly landed in England and had

The civil war – a scene from a contemporary manuscript.

himself proclaimed, though not crowned, king.

In September 1216 John again marched through eastern England with the aim of cutting off the northern rebels from the southern. He relieved Lincoln which had been stoutly held for him by another of those formidable medieval ladies, and advanced into King's Lynn. There he fell ill with dysentery but insisted on continuing his march and then aggravated the illness (according to the chroniclers) by gluttonously eating too many peaches and drinking too much cider. While crossing the Wellstream which flowed into the Wash, his baggage train containing all the royal jewels and treasures got lost in the treacherous mists and was swallowed by the quicksands. On 18 October 1216 John died at Newark aged forty-nine

and by his own wish was buried in Worcester cathedral, the first king in one hundred and fifty years to be born and buried in England.

John left the country in a chaotic condition, with Louis of France claiming the crown and about two thirds of the barons in arms against him. His reputation as the tyrant who murdered little Arthur, met his come-uppance at Runnymede and managed to lose his baggage in the Wash will probably always stick. Although he was not an attractive character, John had some virtues and when he died he remained in control of part of England; and sufficient men of calibre stayed loyal to ensure that the crown passed to his nine-year-old son Henry and to guide the boy through the tortuous years of a royal minority.

Above Worcester Cathedral where John is buried.

Robert Bruce

r. 1306-39

'Ah, freedom is a noble thing.'

Robert Bruce, Earl of Carrick, was born in 1274. At the time of his birth the borders of Scotland were much the same as they are today, except the Isles were not under the jurisdiction of the Scots kings. The ruling dynasty in 1274 was the House of Canmore which had been established in 1057 when Malcolm *Ceann Mor* (Gaelic for Big Head) had slain King Macbeth. (By courtesy of William Shakespeare, Macbeth is the most widely known of early Scottish monarchs, even if Shakespeare's character – driven by ambition, corrupted by power, stricken by guilt – probably bore scant resemblance to the actual man).

Scotland had been less affected by the Norman Conquest than England, but it had nevertheless felt the impact. Some Norman barons had pushed their way north and acquired estates in the Scottish lowlands, including Robert Bruce's ancestors, the de Brus, who had landed with Duke William of Normandy and fought by his side at the battle of Hastings. A form of feudalism had been introduced which fitted quite comfortably into the existing Scottish pattern of loyalty between clansmen and chieftains. The language had changed, too. By 1066 Gaelic had become the mother tongue; thereafter the inhabitants of lowland Scotland, some of whom were Anglo–Saxon refugees, started to speak the dialect of the north of England. Throughout the Middle Ages, lowlands Scots referred to their language as 'English', while 'Scots' meant the Gaelic still spoken in the Highlands.

The relationship between the two kingdoms was always strained, particularly as England became more unified and powerful under the Normans and Anglo–Normans. Scots kings were forced to pay homage to the kings of England. But there were also many links between the two countries, with inter-marriage at both royal and baronial level. Most of the lowland nobles owned lands on both sides of the border. Indeed for many years the kings of Scotland were themselves Earls of Huntingdon, the owners of vast estates in England. For two centuries an uneasy peace prevailed. From time to time the Scots kings would raid England. In return the Anglo–Normans would march into Scotland. But nobody pushed the issue too hard and even the question of homage was left vague, with nobody being quite sure whether the Scots kings were acknowledging the English king as their overlord for their English lands, or for their Scottish crown. The aim of each side was to secure its frontiers.

However, the centuries of comparative peace were based on the factor that lowland Scotland, which was where the bulk of the kingdom's activity occurred, was becoming more anglicized. There were always Scots who objected to this process, and even before Edward I ascended the English throne in 1272, a stronger sense of national identity and pride was growing, just as it was in England.

Edward I, John Lackland's grandson, was one of the most intelligent and dynamic of medieval kings (overweeningly ambitious and ruthless are other adjectives applied to him). He put his own house firmly in order and refrained from trying to reconquer the old Angevin empire. For Edward had another vision or ambition – whichever way one looks at it – which was to unite the kingdoms of England and Scotland and the ancient principality of Wales under one ruler – himself and his successors. He also had more than a touch of military genius and managed to conquer most of Wales, erecting a chain of castles to ensure his rule, as his Norman predecessors had done in England. It was in Wales that Edward's astute military eye noted the natives' use of the longbow, which he then adopted and adapted for English use.

Having conquered the disorganized Welsh by force, at first it seemed as if Edward might achieve a peaceful union between the crowns of England and Scotland when in 1286 Alexander III of the House of Canmore (whose wife had been Edward's sister) died suddenly. After a late council at Edinburgh,

ROBERT
THE
BRUCE
KING
OF
SCOTS

Alexander III set out to ride through a storm rather than spend the night away from his new young queen. His horse missed its footing on a cliff top and he fell to his death.

Predeceased by all his children, Alexander was succeeded by his infant grand-daughter Margaret, the only child of the marriage between his daughter and the King of Norway. By the Treaty of Brigham in 1290, Edward I contracted with the child's Scots guardians that she should eventually marry his own son and heir, Edward, whom he had created Prince of newly-conquered Wales. Despite the promises to respect Scotland's independence, Edward clearly hoped this marriage would give the English crown control over Scotland. But the plan came to nothing. Later in 1290, while sailing from Norway, Margaret died. Her death left the kingdom she had never seen to be contested by no less than thirteen claimants. Included among them was the older Robert de Brus or Bruce, Earl of Annandale.

As none of the claimants was powerful enough to take the crown by force, Edward found himself with a second opportunity to intervene in Scotland's affairs. Claiming the right of the English kings as overlords of Scotland, he offered to arbitrate between the rival claimants, providing they recognized that right and paid homage to him. Self-interest made all thirteen men agree. For them the

loyalties of feudalism were more important than patriotism; most of them still owned lands in England anyway and therefore already owed allegiance to Edward I. The claims were investigated by Edward with scrupulous honesty but the final decision, if just, also happened to be convenient. The rightful heir was John Balliol, a man with no other kingly quality than dignity; a noble, but not in the circumstances useful, attribute.

No sooner had Balliol been crowned than Edward set about humiliating him and provoking him to revolt. He allowed his own law courts to hear appeals from Scotland and even summoned Balliol to appear at Westminster to answer charges brought against him by his own subjects. In 1295 the exasperated John Balliol repudiated his allegiance to the English crown, signed a treaty with France and allowed some of his subjects to raid into Cumberland and Northumberland. Edward I, whose respect for the rule of law had already earned him the name of 'the Second Justinian', now had a lawful pretext for marching north with an army and taking the throne of Scotland.

Most of the Scots barons stayed loyal to Edward and although Balliol managed to raise an army, it was routed at the battle of Dunbar. Balliol was sent as a prisoner to the Tower of London, the Stone of Destiny was removed from Scone to Berwick and later to Westminster Abbey, the barons were made to recognize Edward as their king, and the Earl of Warenne was installed as viceroy. It seemed as if Edward's plan to turn Europe's largest island into a united kingdom was nearing completion.

But by trying to force his ambition or vision on Scotland, Edward set light to the incipient sense of Scottish identity. When the Earl of Warenne embarked on a campaign of heavy taxation, the light became a flame. It was clear that English rule would not be accepted without a fierce struggle. In Sir William Wallace the Scots soon found a guerrilla leader of genius. But though Wallace inspired a great mass of his countrymen and his spear-carrying clansmen defeated an English army in 1297 and even invaded England, he never had the majority of the nobles behind him. For them he was a lowly squire.

By 1297, the twenty-three-year-old Robert Bruce was already a prominent figure. But however justified his later reputation as a Scots patriot, in his early years Bruce was an opportunist, notorious for his savage temper. When John Balliol finally turned on Edward I, Bruce was in the English army at Dunbar. When Wallace's star was in the ascendant, he deserted Edward I and joined the temporary Guardian of Scotland. But he then quarrelled with John Comyn, another of the

thirteen claimants, and switched his allegiance back to Edward.

In 1298 Wallace was defeated at Falkirk, a victory the English won entirely through the fire-power of the longbow. Wallace then fled to the Continent and Edward placed Scotland under the rule of three Regents: Bishop Lamberton of St Andrews, John Comyn and Robert Bruce. When Wallace returned to fight in Scotland in 1304, Bruce assisted in storming his stronghold at Stirling. When Wallace was treacherously handed over to the English, it was Bruce who escorted him as a prisoner to London (where he was duly executed).

Yet throughout their regency, both Lamberton and Bruce had been parleying with the fervently anti-English elements. After Wallace's execution the Scottish cause was leaderless and Bruce had to decide where his loyalties lay. In 1306 he returned to Scotland and arranged a meeting with his co-regent John Comyn in the Greyfriars church at Dumfries. Whether Robert Bruce intended to persuade or negotiate or merely to question will never be known. It is unlikely that he would have arranged such a meeting if he had not intended to talk treason, but whatever his purpose, in the heat of the almost inevitable argument, Robert Bruce drew his dagger and stabbed 'the Red Comyn' to death.

Edward I was not likely to condone the murder of a co-regent and the pope would hardly overlook the fact that the murder had taken place on

Opposite top John Balliol King of Scotland.

Opposite middle The Stone of Destiny in Westminster Abbey.

Opposite bottom Edward I of England, the arbitrator in the Scottish succession dispute.

Above The English attack the Scots.

Above A message of defiance from Robert Bruce to Edward III.

consecrated ground. At last his own savage temper had forced Robert Bruce to commit himself. Before the news could spread, Bruce raced to Scone accompanied by his most ardent supporter, Sir James Douglas, and there on 27 March 1306 he was crowned Robert I of Scotland. But with his wife and children in the hands of the English and one of his brothers executed, outlawed by Edward I and excommunicated by the pope, the new king of Scotland spent the first year of his reign in hiding.

On 7 July 1307 fortune favoured Bruce and the Scots, for on that date Edward I died. His son,

Edward II, was quite incapable of consolidating his father's gains. While the new king of England was arguing with his barons and pampering his favourites, the king of Scotland started to reconquer his realm.

In 1308 Robert defeated the Earl of Buchan while his brother Edward reduced Galloway and in March 1309 he held his first parliament at St Andrews. In spite of his excommunication, the clergy recognized him as their lawful king and with the supporters of John Comyn silenced, Robert felt secure enough to set about the destruction of the English strongholds.

Linlithgow was taken in 1310, Dumbarton in 1311, Perth in 1312 and by the end of 1313 Roxburgh and Edinburgh had fallen, an army had been sent to liberate the Isle of Man and two raiding parties had crossed the border into England. Only Stirling, Bothwell and Berwick remained in English hands. But by 1314 Edward II was, at last, turning his attention to Scotland.

On 22 June 1314 an English army of 20,000 men arrived at Falkirk on its way to relieve Stirling which Bruce had been besieging with an army of 10,000. Along the old Roman Road which ran from Falkirk to Stirling Robert Bruce drew up his squares of experienced pikemen with five hundred cavalry behind them and waited for the English to attack. But Edward decided to make a surprise attack in the rear, working round Robert's flank under cover of darkness.

Throughout the night of 23 June, the English knights and archers waded through the streams and marshes of the Bannockburn but when dawn broke on the 24th, only the vanguard under the Earl of Gloucester was in a position to fight. Robert turned his army to face them and ordered the pikemen to charge. The English archers ran towards a hill beyond the marshes, but this was level with the rear of the Scottish army and before they could take up a position they were driven away by the Scottish cavalry. Disorganized and exhausted, hampered by the mud and unsupported by their archers, the English knights crumbled against the Scottish pikes. Finally, the battle became a rout and many of those who escaped the pikes drowned in the River Firth. Bannockburn was one of the most devastating defeats ever suffered by an English army.

By 1318 the last remaining English stronghold at Berwick had fallen to Bruce. If Edward I earned the name 'the Hammer of the Scots', Bruce can claim to have been 'the Hammer of the English'. But Bruce's mission was not completed. He wanted Edward II's recognition that he was the rightful king of an independent Scotland. In furtherance of this aim he pounded away, constantly raiding the northern

English counties. But recognition – from both England and the pope – was a long time a'coming.

In 1320 the Scottish barons sent the Declaration of Arbroath to the pope. Magna Carta became regarded as 'the cornerstone of English liberties'; the Declaration of Arbroath can justly be viewed as the foundation stone of Scottish nationalism. Its language was as stirring as any in Magna Carta: 'So long as a hundred of us remain alive, we will never be subject to the English king. It is not for glory, riches or honours that we fight, but for liberty alone, which no worthy man will lay down save with his life.'

It was not until 1328 that Robert Bruce achieved his legal victories. In that year the pope lifted the excommunication and recognized Robert I of Scotland. While in the Treaty of Northampton, Edward II's widow Isabella who was now ruling as regent for her son Edward III, also recognized the independence of Scotland and that Robert Bruce was her lawful king. A 'perpetual peace' was hopefully signed, with the friendship sealed by a marriage treaty between Edward III's sister Joanna and Bruce's son David. But as Bruce clebrated his triumph he was a sick man. As he lay on his deathbed, he confessed to his old friend Sir James Douglas that one dream remained unfulfilled. He had never had time to go on a crusade, and he made Douglas promise that when he was dead he would cut out his heart and carry it against the enemies of Christendom.

On 7 June 1329, at the age of fifty-four, ravaged by the dread disease leprosy, Bruce died. His body was buried at Dunfermline, but true to his word, Douglas cut out the heart and carried it with him to fight the Moors in Spain. Douglas died outside Granada and the heart was brought home by Sir William Keith who had commanded the cavalry at Bannockburn, and was buried in Melrose Abbey.

Before he died the legends started to grow around Robert Bruce. In particular there was the one about his watching a spider spinning its web, as he lived as a semi-outlaw during the first year of his reign. Generations of children were taught that the arrogant, black-tempered young man had thereby learned the virtues of patience and persistence and grown into one of Scotland's greatest heroes.

Bruce's achievements did not long survive him but his daughter Margery had married Walter Stewart, and her son Robert became the first ruler of the House of Stewart. Thus Robert Bruce was the common ancestor of the future kings and queen of Great Britain, an idea which may or may not have pleased him. For it was Scots liberty for which Bruce fought or, in the words of the epic poem *The Bruce*, 'Ah, freedom, it is a noble thing.'

Below Robert II and his first wife Elizabeth Mure of Rowallan. He was the first ruler of the House of Stewart.

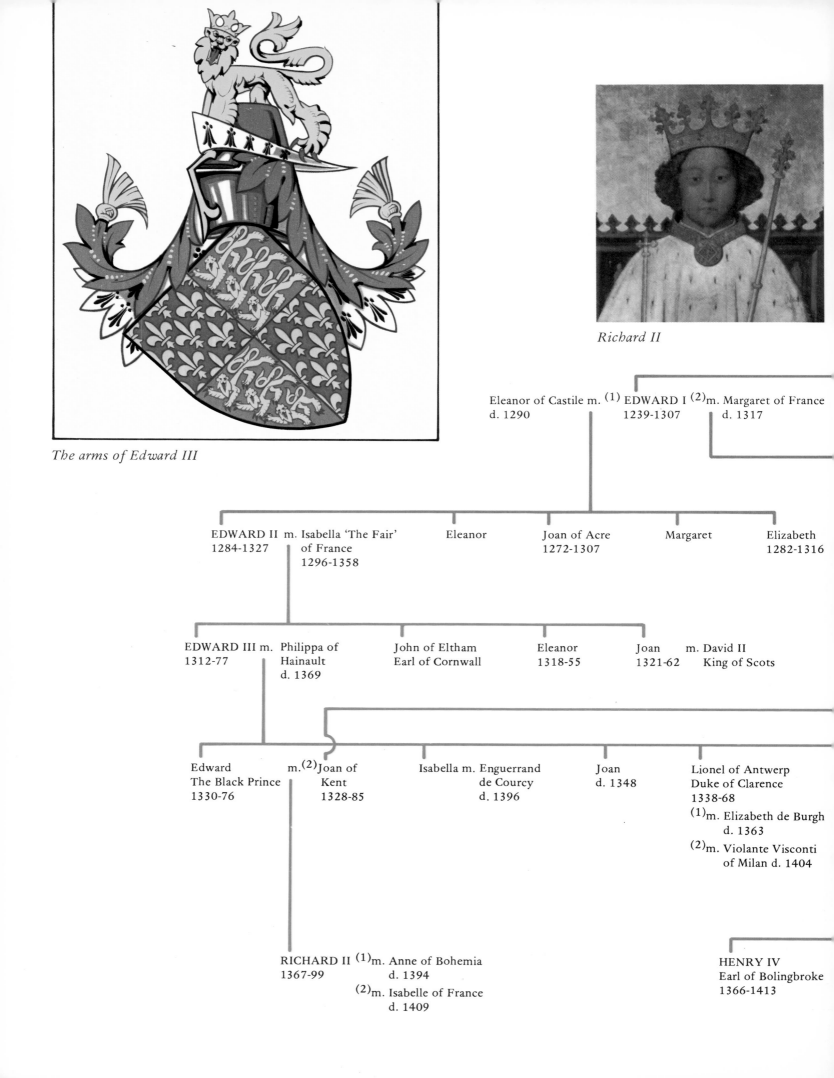

The arms of Edward III

Richard II

Eleanor of Castile m. (1) EDWARD I (2) m. Margaret of France
d. 1290   1239-1307   d. 1317

EDWARD II m. Isabella 'The Fair'   Eleanor   Joan of Acre   Margaret   Elizabeth
1284-1327   of France   1272-1307   1282-1316
          1296-1358

EDWARD III m.   Philippa of   John of Eltham   Eleanor   Joan   m. David II
1312-77   Hainault   Earl of Cornwall   1318-55   1321-62   King of Scots
        d. 1369

Edward   m. (2) Joan of   Isabella m. Enguerrand   Joan   Lionel of Antwerp
The Black Prince   Kent   de Courcy   d. 1348   Duke of Clarence
1330-76   1328-85   d. 1396   1338-68
                                                       (1) m. Elizabeth de Burgh
                                                         d. 1363
                                                         (2) m. Violante Visconti
                                                         of Milan d. 1404

RICHARD II (1) m. Anne of Bohemia   HENRY IV
1367-99   d. 1394   Earl of Bolingbroke
          (2) m. Isabelle of France   1366-1413
               d. 1409

The Plantagenets

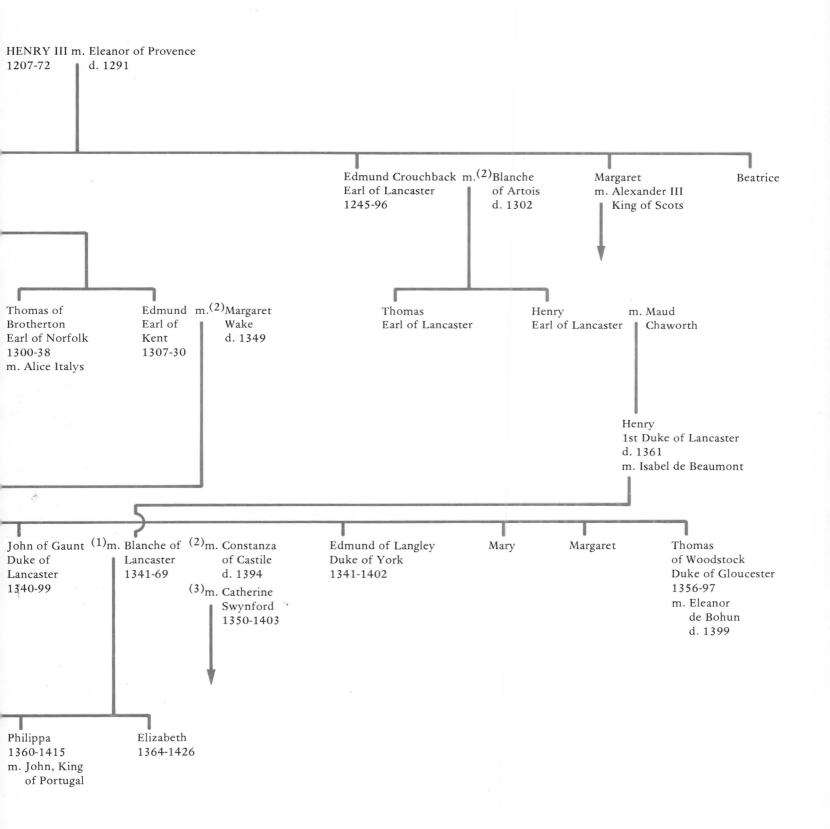

HENRY III m. Eleanor of Provence
1207-72   d. 1291

Edmund Crouchback m.(2)Blanche
Earl of Lancaster   of Artois
1245-96   d. 1302

Margaret
m. Alexander III
King of Scots

Beatrice

Thomas of
Brotherton
Earl of Norfolk
1300-38
m. Alice Italys

Edmund m.(2)Margaret
Earl of   Wake
Kent   d. 1349
1307-30

Thomas
Earl of Lancaster

Henry   m. Maud
Earl of Lancaster   Chaworth

Henry
1st Duke of Lancaster
d. 1361
m. Isabel de Beaumont

John of Gaunt (1)m. Blanche of (2)m. Constanza
Duke of   Lancaster   of Castile
Lancaster   1341-69   d. 1394
1340-99
                  (3)m. Catherine
                       Swynford
                       1350-1403

Edmund of Langley
Duke of York
1341-1402

Mary

Margaret

Thomas
of Woodstock
Duke of Gloucester
1356-97
m. Eleanor
   de Bohun
   d. 1399

Philippa
1360-1415
m. John, King
   of Portugal

Elizabeth
1364-1426

Pres que les pl?
des compaignons
de haynault se
furent partiz e
le seigur de beaumont se

Edward III

r. 1327-77

'Our cumly king.'

Edward III was born at Windsor Castle on 13 November 1312, the eldest son of Edward II and Isabella of France. His father was unfitted to be a medieval king, an unmartial, artistic man who loved his favourites not wisely but too well. He and his wife eventually parted company and early in 1325 Isabella was allowed to go to the Continent where she lived openly with her lover Roger Mortimer, and a few months later her eldest son was permitted to join her. These were bad mistakes on Edward II's part because his unregal behaviour, his military failures against the Scots and the stranglehold of his rapacious, inept favourites meant that discontent was already rife in England. By his actions he provided a base for a conspiracy centred on the heir to the throne (succession was now established by primogeniture, the inheritance of the eldest son.) In September 1326 Isabella and Mortimer landed in Suffolk, with young Edward in tow, the king's few supporters were routed and a revolution effected, with the only blood spilled that of the royal favourites.

Edward II remained alive and nobody was quite sure what to do with him. In January 1327 a massive Parliament was summoned to Westminster. Parliaments had met since the reign of Henry III, as baronial power and the king's need for money grew, and had been widened to include representatives of the shires. Its members petitioned, debated and advised the king but they neither governed nor legislated; that remained the king's job. However in 1327 Parliament acted; by the will of God and the people it indicted the lawful king of England for his failures, deposed him, and nominated his son as successor. It was an extraordinary action for an assembly of medieval barons, prelates and knights to have undertaken, but it was also already a peculiarly English one, because everything was done under a cloak of legality. Nevertheless, a live Edward II constituted a danger and later in the year the wretched king was secretly killed in Berkeley castle in one of the most hideous of medieval murders, 'with a hotte broche putte thro the secret place posterialle', so that his body would show no marks and his death seem natural.

For the next three years Isabella and Mortimer were the real rulers of England but they proved as inept and rapacious as Edward II's maligned favourites. Edward III was forced to sign a humiliating peace treaty with Robert Bruce at Northampton in 1328 (though Bruce failed to get back the stone of Scone, as promised, and that stayed in Westminster Abbey.) During these years one happy event occurred when, at York in January 1328, Edward married Philippa, a daughter of the Count of Hainault, Holland and Zeeland. For many years this was the happiest of royal unions. Philippa was not a formidable lady in the more masculine medieval tradition but she was shrewd, wise and generous. She bore her husband twelve children, travelled constantly by his side, counselled and cajoled him and was in every way a king's consort. Edward was one of the few monarchs not to have problems with his adult progeny, and this can be partly attributed to Philippa's love and tact.

Edward himself was extremely affable. Apart from the odd flash of Plantagenet temper he wanted to love and be loved, and was able to be familiar without losing his dignity. He looked like a king, tall and fair, with 'the countenance of a god' (as one admiring subject put it). If he was not the most intellectual of men, his equable character, together with an ability to listen and learn, counterbalanced any cerebral deficiencies. By the autumn of 1330 Edward had learned enough to know that he must strike or be submerged by the ambitious, arrogant Mortimer and probably share his father's fate. In a lightning coup he arrested Mortimer in his bedchamber at Nottingham castle, and he was subsequently tried and executed. But Edward made no move against his mother (who wisely retired

Opposite The coronation of Edward III.

Above The Great Seal of Edward II – Edward III's luckless father.

Right The nave of Exeter Cathedral.

from the centre of the stage); nor did he hound Mortimer's followers in the established manner and his wisdom and generosity were rewarded by their loyalty. By the end of 1330, at the age of eighteen, Edward was truly King of England.

For the next thirty years Edward cast his leonine shadow across Western Europe and raised England up to the highest peak she had reached. It was England that Edward raised up. The country was already developing a national identity which was strengthened during his reign, partly by his character and achievements, partly by an internal momentum, partly by outside circumstance. English literally became important when French was ousted as the official language. In the late 1350s proceedings in sheriff's courts were held in English, and in 1363 Parliament conducted its business in the native tongue for the first time. (Of the many dialects, that of the Midlands became the standard one.) The vernacular and an oral culture had survived the French domination, but with the triumph of English there was a burst of native literature, as exemplified by Geoffrey Chaucer and William Langland, the author of *Piers Plowman*. Architecture produced a style of its own, too. Now known as English Perpendicular, its graceful vaulting can be seen in such cathedrals as Gloucester, Exeter, Winchester and Ely. (Winchester owed much to William of Wykeham who also endowed its famous school. Edward III, like Henry II, was a good talent spotter and generous in promoting it, and Wykeham rose from comparatively humble beginnings to become one of the greatest, least liked men in the kingdom during Edward's later years.)

The arts, like many things, thrive in a warm, stable climate. The stability came from the top, with Edward's family life and the amicable relationship he established and maintained with the barons. An elaborate administrative system already existed, what would now be called the civil service, except it was the king's service. Edward introduced a new cog into the machine, the Keepers or, as they became known, Justices of the Peace who have played such a vital role in English government over the centuries. Keepers of the Peace were established in every shire, local men with local knowledge who acted as a two-way mirror of government between king and populace. Above all Edward was a great communicator; he believed in letting the people know what he was doing. The populace responded, the higher levels most actively, and civic life expanded enormously. There were, for example, nearly one hundred trade guilds in London by the end of the fourteenth century.

Edward's courts were the most lavish England

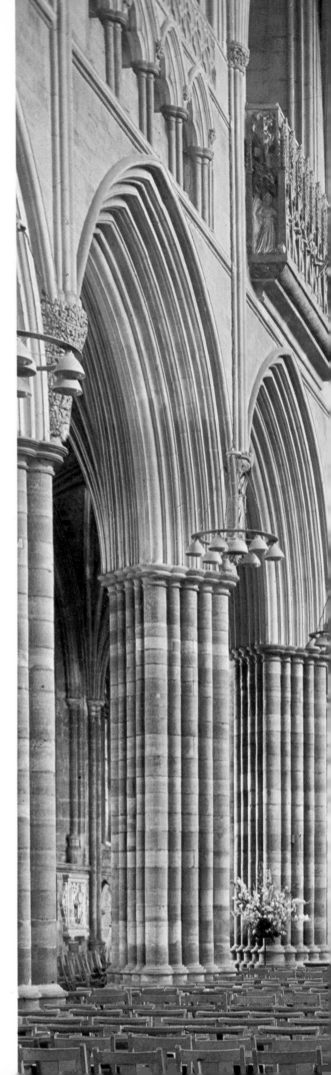

An de grace mil.iii.xxixe   Si fu respondu que

Above Edward III paying homage to the French king Philip VI in 1329; nine years later they were at war.

Right The Battle of Crécy 1346.

lart pitir du dit

had known. He fostered the cult of St George, which accorded well with the emerging national identity, and was of course responsible for creating the Order of the Garter. The story goes that Edward picked up a lady's garter at a ball and gallantly said, 'Honi soit qui mal y pense.' (In the spirit of emerging Englishness he might have said, 'Evil to him who evil thinks.') Thereafter a society of twenty-six gartered knights was founded on the basis of Arthurian Round Table equality, with Queen Philippa and ladies of the court as Dames of the Fraternity.

Even in Edward's golden years everything obviously did not run smoothly, happily and prosperously. In 1348 the first terrible outbreak of bubonic plague, the Black Death, struck Europe, and among the early victims was Edward's beloved daughter Joan. The first epidemic abated in 1349, though there were further outbreaks in 1361–62 and 1369. It left Europe numbed by a disease which had killed indiscriminately and swiftly in hideous vomiting, panting, pustule-ridden fashion. (There were actually three types of plague at work.) About one third of the total population of Europe died; villages were left with a handful of inhabitants, while mighty cities such as Florence, Paris and London seemed empty shells. It has since been observed that the Black Death solved a problem for Europe which had outstripped its capacity to feed itself: an accurate if callous piece of economic analysis. The Black Death also caused a social upheaval. Among other results there was no longer a surplus of labour and those at the bottom of the pile used their new bargaining power to break down old customs and ties. Edward and Parliament, at one in the face of this upset, tried to fix wages, prices and the movement of labour in the Statute of Labourers in 1351. They were not successful but paradoxically the efforts at enforcement, which included the strengthening of the Justices of the Peace, brought the populace, its king and his government into closer contact. Thereby, in England at least, national unity was increased.

To govern effectively at home and keep the country contented, medieval rulers still had to be successful in war. The ostensible cause of what became known as the Hundred Years War was Edward III's claim to the French crown. When he became King of England in 1327, his possessions in France had shrunk to the small area of Ponthieu in the north and part of Aquitaine. In comparison to the earlier Angevin empire this was trifling but the chunk of land in Aquitaine stretched from south of La Rochelle to the Pyrenees and included the vital Bordeaux vineyards. (The Bordeaux wine trade had long thriven and accounted for a good part of the King of England's revenue.) In 1328 the Capetian dynasty in France, of which Philip Augustus had been the most notable ruler, became extinct on the male side, and as France adhered to the Salic Law, Philip of Valois was crowned as Philip VI.

At the time England was under the weak regency of Isabella and Mortimer and did little more than protest that no King of England would pay homage for his Aquitaine lands to a mere count (which is what Philip Valois had been), though in fact Edward III did, with qualifications. By the mid-1330s England was ready to flex her muscles and Edward revived his claim to the French crown which lay through his mother. (The Salic Law disbarring females was not, so England argued, the immutable will of God.) The real causes of the Hundred Years War can be summarized briefly: fear of a French invasion of Aquitaine, of France's growing naval power which threatened England's trade, and of her designs on Flanders which was England's most important trading partner. On France's side it was fear of England's claims which lay in her Norman inheritance and Aquitaine possessions and of her growing power.

The first phase of the war settled the trading problem, when the English annihilated the French fleet at Sluys in 1340. (Edward, however, did nothing for the navy and relied on the old method of raising a fleet when he needed one.) This great victory enhanced Edward's reputation but did not solve the problem of Aquitaine; to do that he needed a decisive battle on French soil. Philip VI was, quite rightly, reluctant to give battle because he was in the ascendant position on the mainland. Eventually the two armies met at Crécy in 1346, the first, but by no means the last, time when the English longbowmen overwhelmed the French crossbowmen. The English were now the complete masters of the longbow and its difficult art was taught from boyhood, to such an extent that playing football and other games was officially banned so that men could concentrate on their archery practice. It was at Crécy that the king's eldest son, the Black Prince (so known because of his black armour), appropriated the plumed feathers and the motto of the slain King of Bohemia – 'Ich Dien'; 'I serve'.

In 1346 the English also inflicted a defeat on the Scots at Neville's Cross. The great Robert Bruce was dead but his successors decided to sieze the opportunity of invading England while the English were otherwise engaged, but Edward had left his northern 'postern gate' well guarded. 1346 was thus a notable year for the English, and the church bells rang throughout the land. Edward also utilized the clergy as a method of communication with the populace, and apart from the ringing of church bells to celebrate a victory, all sorts of royal messages were read in church. After Crécy Edward besieged Calais and there is the story – centuries later immortalized in Rodin's famous statue – that Queen Philippa interceded for the lives of the burghers after the city had fallen. By 1347 Edward had secured the Gascon lands of Aquitaine (which is what he really wanted) and established an English bridgehead round Calais. A French chronicler assessed England's new reputation when he wrote that previously 'nobody had thought much of the English. . . . Now, in the time of the noble Edward . . . they are the finest and most daring warriors known to man.' The chronicler Froissart noted another aspect, 'the great haughtiness of the English who are affable to no other nation but their own.' (Froissart came over with Philippa from Hainault and managed to settle among the haughty English, to their literary advantage.)

The next phase of the war was again settled to English satisfaction when the Black Prince, 'the flower of English manhood', defeated the French at Poitiers in 1356. In the Treaty of Brétigny which was eventually signed in 1360, Edward got exactly what he wanted, full sovereignty over the whole of Aquitaine and the northern French territories of Ponthieu and Calais, but he renounced his claim to the French crown. In theory the treaty should have lasted but the forces of nationalism were at work in France, too. They were more encumbered by the size of the country and considerably less unified than in England but they persisted. In the face of growing French nationalism, the last years of Edward's life were spent in a war of attrition, with savage raids to

subdue the rebel areas and discourage the others.

From 1364 it was not Edward himself who led the French raids because he went into a long, if slow decline. At fifty-two he was an old man by medieval reckoning, though others managed to retain their faculties longer (his forebear Eleanor of Aquitaine to name but one.) The campaign in the winter of 1359–60, leading to the Treaty of Brétigny, had been fought in appalling weather conditions – men and horses literally froze to death – and Edward's health never fully recovered. Also about 1364 Alice Perrers became the king's mistress. Although Edward had not been wholly faithful in thirty-five years of marriage, Mistress Perrers was his first serious open liasion and by 1366 she was installed as a lady of the queen's bedchamber which indicated that Philippa accepted the situation. But in 1369 the queen died. Edward was genuinely heartbroken and her death meant that he leant more on Alice Perrers. She was an intelligent lady, if a greedy one, and certainly enjoyed her role as the ageing king's mistress, but her exercise of wealth and power was increasingly resented by Lords and Commons.

It was during Edward's reign that the Commons grew in importance. Originally the commoners had been called to Westminster by the king to counterbalance the barons and the Church, but under Edward Parliament became divided into two segments, with the Commons assuming an identity of its own. In the Good Parliament of 1376 – in fact summoned to indict Alice Perrers and her faction – the Commons for the first time elected one man as their 'Speaker'. Edward allowed some transfer of power because of his own unquarrelsome temperament but equally because he had no wish to

Below Edward III swears to keep the Treaty of Brétigny in which he renounced his claim to the French Crown.

precipitate another clash such as had produced Magna Carta. (Though he made his Parliaments work for their privileges and in 1352 summoned one at dawn.) During Edward's reign a very English lack of definition which allowed room for interpretation, manoeuvre and compromise, developed.

Something else which grew under Edward III was anti-clericalism. Criticism of corrupt bishops and priests was neither new nor confined to England, but what was peculiarly English was the way in which the resentment focused on the pope as the alien responsible figure. It reflected the growth of an independent national identity, and various Statutes were passed in 1351, 1353 and 1356 which reduced the pope's power in England to doctrinal matters. Towards the end of Edward's reign the figure of John Wycliffe, the Oxford don and one-time ducal secretary, emerged on the scene. His arguments were to strengthen the national identity and help produce a social and religious change, though such were not altogether Wycliffe's intentions. For Wycliffe the truth lay in the Bible, not in the accumulated wisdom of the Church which voiced the views of fallible, frequently politically motivated churchmen. (Not that Wycliffe himself was uninterested in wordly power or infallible.) He translated the Bible into English so that men could judge for themselves, and has been called the father of English Protestantism. Initially Wycliffe received considerable support; John of Gaunt, Edward's most famous active son, was his protector. (The Black Prince had gone into an earlier decline than his father and died in 1376.) The dangers inherent in Wycliffe's teachings, the threat to the established order if lowborn men started to think and judge for themselves, did not become apparent until after Edward III's death.

Edward died in his palace at Richmond after a final stroke on 21 June 1377 and was buried in Westminster Abbey by the side of Queen Philippa. Malicious chroniclers said that as he died Alice Perrers stripped even the rings from his fingers, but at least she stayed faithful to the end. Edward's reign was the longest in medieval times, fifty years, and like many of his fellow rulers his declining years were sad. But he left England with a high reputation and in an apparently peaceful condition, and handed to his successor – Richard, the Black Prince's son – a larger empire than he had inherited.

Most modern assessments of Edward III admit that he was a charismatic figure, not an adjective known in his day when 'sweet', 'comely' and 'debonair' were the popular ones, but some historians accuse him of stupidity and over-ambition. By his stupidity Edward gave England fifty years of stability – there was no internal rebellion during his reign – and helped weld her into a nation. England might well wish for more such stupid leaders. As for his ambition, meaning the French ventures, that is to judge him by modern standards, not to mention hindsight. The French were just as eager to conquer; the Sluys fleet which Edward scattered in 1340 was aiming not only to capture the sea-lanes but to invade England. Conquest and war were as endemic in medieval society as rebellion. Edward was one of the more personally attractive monarchs, and by the standards of his day eminently successful.

Above The effigy of the Black Prince – Edward III's warrior son – on his tomb in Canterbury Cathedral.

James I of Scotland
r. 1406-37

'The Lawgiver.'

Above Henry IV of England, James's first 'gaoler'.

Opposite James I of Scotland.

In the years following Robert Bruce's death in 1329, Scotland was exhausted by her fight for independence. While England prospered under Edward III, Scotland found no peace-time Bruce to build on his victories. Intermittent fighting against England continued, internal disorder spread and for the last quarter of the fourteenth century, the country was in chaos. To quote a chronicler, 'There was no law in Scotland but he who was stronger opposed him who was weaker and the whole kingdom was a den of thieves.'

James I, who succeeded Robert III in 1406, was eventually to put an end to this period of lawlessness. But for the first eighteen years of his reign James was a prisoner in England. The ageing King Robert III suspected his brother the Duke of Albany of the murder of his eldest son, and to protect young James's life he decided to send him to Scotland's by-now traditional ally against the English, France.

In March 1406 the eleven-year old prince set sail. But in fleeing from one danger James fell straight into another. Off Flamborough Head his ship was captured by pirates and James was sent as a prisoner to the court of the King of England, Henry IV. Henry greeted his royal guest with good-humoured courtesy, but he did not release him. Although England and Scotland were officially at peace, to have the heir to the Scottish throne in his power was a political advantage which Henry was not prepared to relinquish. When on 4 April, Robert III died, grieving at the news of his son's captivity, the King of England's hostage became King James I of Scotland.

In the absence of the rightful king the scheming Duke of Albany assumed the title of 'Governor of Scotland' and ruled the kingdom in almost royal state. The documents he signed bore the date of his governorship, and not of James's reign. His aim was not to restore order and prosperity to Scotland, but to obtain the crown for himself and his descendants.

With that end in view, he set about ransoming another prisoner of the English – not James, but his own son, Murdoch Stewart, who had been captured in battle in 1402. Murdoch returned to Scotland, to learn the art of misgovernment from his father, while James I, the rightful king, remained a captive in London.

The place of his imprisonment varied. At times he was kept in the Tower of London, but he also spent time at Court and visited other royal residences such as Windsor Castle. A stocky, athletic young man, he occupied a good deal of his time in sport; skilful with the sword and the bow, he was also noted for his abilities in throwing the hammer and putting the shot. However, James's talents were not confined to physical activities. He had an aptitude for languages, he loved music, and he has left an enduring testimony to his interest in poetry. Influenced by the works of Geoffrey Chaucer, he composed 'The Kingis Quair', or 'The King's Book'. Written in 1423, the last year of his imprisonment, the poem describes his feelings on first catching sight of the woman he was later to marry, Lady Joan Beaufort, great-grand-daughter of King Edward III. 'The freshest young flower that ever I saw' was James's description of his future wife and queen. Soon, however, the pleasures of writing were to give way to the grimmer business of ruling. On the death of the usurper Albany his son Murdoch had assumed the government of Scotland. But he was not suited to the task, lacking even the driving ambition which had distinguished his father, and he agreed that James I should return at last to take possession of his kingdom.

During James's years of captivity King Henry IV had been succeeded by Henry V, and now the infant Henry VI nominally ruled England; the child-king's regents were happy to release the royal Scottish hostage on terms which included the condition that in future no Scots should fight for the French, a measure which effectively deprived France of thousands of valuable foreign mercenaries. For a ransom of sixty thousand marks James became a free man once more, and having married

IACOBVS I D GRATIA
REX· SCOTORVM

Lady Joan Beaufort in the church which is now Southwark Cathedral, he returned to Scotland in the spring of 1424.

The task of bringing order to Scotland was formidable, but James set about it with grim resolution. 'If God grant me life', he observed, 'though it be but the life of a dog, there shall be no place in my realm where the key shall not keep the castle and the bracken bush the cow'. Both the powerful and the humble were to feel the effects of his policy.

The independence of, and the in-fighting between, the Scots barons was a constant threat not only to the power of the king but to the stability of the realm. This was the first problem James tackled. He took immediate revenge on the House of Albany, executing Murdoch Stewart and two of his kinsmen, and he despatched two other possible claimants to the throne to England as hostages. Other noble houses, like the great clan Donald

whose chieftains for over fifty years had declared themselves 'Lords of the Isles', found their power curbed by the king's determination to reduce the violence and crime that had flourished for decades.

James displayed a real concern for his weaker subjects when establishing a new system of justice. In 1426 he founded the court which was to be known as 'The Session' to hear cases formerly brought before the King or Parliament. It consisted of the chancellor and certain discreet persons of the Three Estates. He also provided a 'poor man's advocate' to serve the interests of those who could not afford to pay for their own defence. This was a radical piece of legislation, the like of which did not exist in England.

In Scotland's constitutional development James's reign was a landmark. At the beginning of the fifteenth century the Scottish Parliament was still an assembly of feudal tenants-in-chiefs who derived their right to attend from the land they held from the king. In 1426 to improve the efficiency of his government James passed an Act requiring all his tenants-in-chief to attend Parliament in person. In practice this act proved unworkable and only two years later the king introduced a change which made the Scottish Parliament more like the English one. While the great magnates were still ordered to attend, the lesser barons and freeholders could be represented by 'two or more wise men' from each Sheriffdom.

Abroad a wary peace was maintained with England, whilst attempts were made to strengthen the 'auld alliance' with France, by the betrothal of James's daughter Margaret to the French dauphin. Of the twin sons born to James and his loving wife Joan, the elder, Alexander, died young, but the younger, James, survived to carry on the line.

As a place of both residence and government James preferred Perth to Edinburgh, and with good reason; whilst Edinburgh was more strategically placed for the constant negotiations with the unneighbourly English, Perth, by virtue of its more central position, kept the king in closer contact with his own unruly Highlands.

It was at Perth, in the Dominican priory, that James I met his death. By his reforms and attempts at a firm, but just system of government, James had given the nobles ample reason to hate and fear him. Towards the end of 1436, as he spent the Christmas season at the priory, a conspiracy was hatched. It came to fruition the following February, with the king's chamberlain, Sir Robert Stewart, at the centre of the plot. Stewart had a particular reason for disliking James, as his father had been one of the hostages sent into England (where he had died). Stewart also thought the rightful King of Scotland

Below Henry VI of England. It was during his reign that James was finally freed after seventeen years' captivity.

should be his kinsman the Earl of Atholl (another conspirator).

It was Sir Robert Stewart who dismissed the guards on the night of 20 February 1437, and allowed the assassins to enter the priory. In the royal bedchamber the intruders found the King in his nightgown, his queen beside him. A struggle ensued in which James, with characteristic determination, fought desperately, aided by queen Joan who was herself wounded. But the king and queen were too heavily outnumbered, and James died of multiple stab-wounds. He was forty-two years old.

Although the king had been killed according to plan, the conspiracy did not succeed. Instead of flocking to support the new ruler of the house of Atholl, the people mourned the Stewart king who had restored order to the realm and made justice available to all. It was said that Sir Robert Graham had cried that future generations would recognize the murder of the king as the destruction of an oppressor. But the reputation which survived was that of an able and resolute monarch. Huge crowds turned out to applaud the torture and death of his murderers, and in the memory of his people, James I ranked with the greatest of the kings of Scotland.

Above James's palace at Stirling.

James III and Queen Margaret

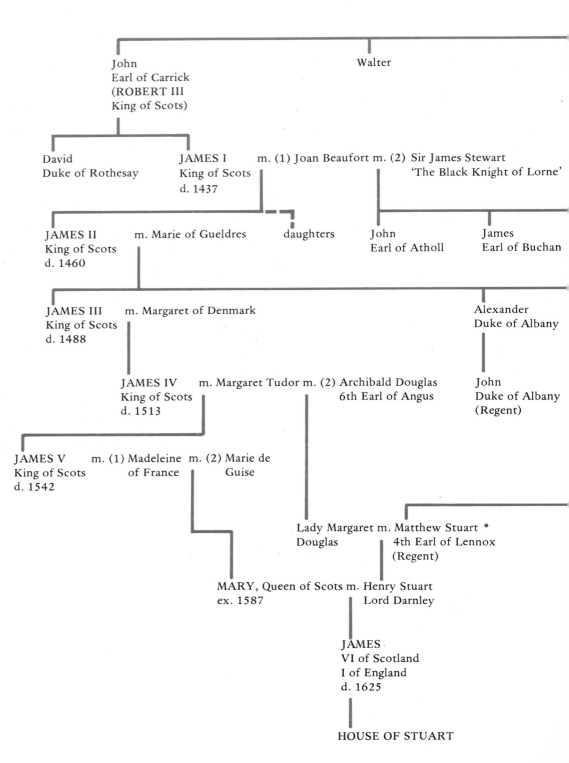

John
Earl of Carrick
(ROBERT III
King of Scots)

Walter

David
Duke of Rothesay

JAMES I
King of Scots
d. 1437

m. (1) Joan Beaufort m. (2) Sir James Stewart
'The Black Knight of Lorne'

JAMES II
King of Scots
d. 1460

m. Marie of Gueldres

daughters

John
Earl of Atholl

James
Earl of Buchan

JAMES III
King of Scots
d. 1488

m. Margaret of Denmark

Alexander
Duke of Albany

JAMES IV
King of Scots
d. 1513

m. Margaret Tudor m. (2) Archibald Douglas
6th Earl of Angus

John
Duke of Albany
(Regent)

JAMES V
King of Scots
d. 1542

m. (1) Madeleine m. (2) Marie de
of France   Guise

Lady Margaret m. Matthew Stuart *
Douglas   4th Earl of Lennox
                 (Regent)

MARY, Queen of Scots m. Henry Stuart
ex. 1587   Lord Darnley

JAMES
VI of Scotland
I of England
d. 1625

HOUSE OF STUART

The Scottish Succession

ROBERT I m. (1) Isabella of Mar   m. (2) Elizabeth de Burgh
'the Bruce'
1306-29

Margery m. Walter Stewart   DAVID II m. (1) Joan of the Tower
                                   1329-71   m. (2) Margaret Logie

ROBERT II, King of Scots m. (1) Elizabeth Mure m. (2) Euphemia of Ross
1371-90   of Rowallan

Robert   Alexander
Earl of Fife
(later Duke of
Albany and
Governor of
Scotland)

Murdoch
Duke of Albany

Andrew
Bishop of Moray

John   Mary m. (1) Thomas Boyd, Earl of Arran
Earl of Mar   m. (2) James, 1st Lord Hamilton

Elizabeth m. Matthew Stewart   James Hamilton
              2nd Earl of Lennox   1st Earl of Arran

John Stewart   James Hamilton
3rd Earl of Lennox   2nd Earl of Arran &
                                       Duke of Châtelberault (Regent)

*This Earl of Lennox took   John Stuart   James Hamilton
French nationality in 1537.   5th Lord d'Aubigny   3rd Earl of Arran
From him derives the French   d. 1609
spelling of the surname 'Stuart'
                                   Esmé Stuart
                                   6th Lord d'Aubigny &
                                   1st Duke of Lennox
                                   d. 1583

Mary Queen of Scots

Henry V
r. 1413-22

'Too famous to live long!'

Henry's fame as a great patriot king rests heavily on the battle of Agincourt and Shakespeare's exuberant play. But he was not born to be a king, heroic or otherwise, and historians have had difficulty establishing where and when he was born. The birth occurred at Monmouth castle some time in the summer of 1387 and if it was of no particular interest to the world at the time, Henry's lineage was illustrious. His mother was Margaret de Bohun, a daughter of the great Anglo–Norman family, and his father was Henry Bolingbroke, Earl of Derby. But it was his paternal grandfather who mattered because he was John of Gaunt, Duke of Lancaster, and in the years since Edward III's death he had become one of the mightiest figures in the kingdom. John of Gaunt was a remarkable man but he was also prudent and, considering the temptations and opportunities he had to seize the crown, astonishingly loyal to his nephew Richard II.

Richard II resembled his great-grandfather Edward II in many ways, being artistic, a bad judge of men and overfond of his favourites. He also had a particular belief in the divinity of kingship which did not accord with the reality of fourteenth century England. Froissart had earlier written, 'The King of England must needs obey his people and do their will.' While this was an exaggeration it had an element of truth and Richard's imperious attitude alienated many people. In 1398 he took the opportunity to rid himself of Henry's father Bolingbroke and Thomas Mowbray, by decreeing that the argument which had erupted between them should be settled in trial by combat at Coventry. But as the combatants entered the lists, Richard stopped the fight in regally dramatic fashion and made known his new decision. Bolingbroke and Mowbray were to be banished, the former for ten years, the latter for life. The next year John of Gaunt died and instead of pardoning his son Bolingbroke, which would have been the wise move, Richard extended the ten-year banishment to a life sentence and seized the vast lands of the House of Lancaster.

The nobles of England were aghast, for if the king could sequester his cousin's lands, whose would he not seize next? With a sublime confidence in his divinity Richard departed to quell a rebellion in Ireland, taking with him his supporters and young Henry of Monmouth whom he had not banished with his father but had treated like a son. In Richard's absence Bolingbroke grasped the opportunity to land in England, officially to reclaim his rightful Lancastrian inheritance. Much of the country rose to support him and when Richard returned from Ireland he was taken prisoner by the triumphant Lancastrians at Flint castle. Within three months Bolingbroke had raised his sights from reclaiming his lands to gaining the English crown, and in October 1399 he was crowned Henry IV.

At the age of twelve Henry of Monmouth found himself proclaimed Prince of Wales, the lawful heir to the throne. But there was nothing lawful about the way in which Henry Bolingbroke had seized the crown, and although he was a more able ruler than Richard II, for the rest of his life he was haunted by the guilt of having deposed an anointed king. (He had the double guilt of the king's murder because Richard, like Edward II, was a danger as long as he lived. He too was secretly murdered, though in Pontefract not Berkeley castle, and in a less hideous manner). The disposal of the man who had been kind to him did not affect young Henry in similar manner, and the element of iron in his character was shown by his singular lack of guilt.

The next ten years of Henry's life were spent fighting to retain his father's crown. In 1403 he fought by his father's side at Shrewsbury to subdue the most serious of all the rebellions which erupted, that of the great northern House of Percy, the Earls of Northumberland. It was led by the other Henry named 'Hotspur' who was in fact a contemporary of Bolingbroke, not young Henry as Shakespeare makes him. But Harry Hotspur and Harry

Opposite Henry V.

Above Henry Percy, Earl of Northumberland, presents a message from Richard II to Bolingbroke.

Opposite top The funeral of Richard II. Shortly after Henry V's accession the murdered Richard's remains were reburied as befitted a king in Westminster Abbey.

Opposite bottom Charles VI of France.

Monmouth knew each other, as the former had acted as the latter's guardian for a period after Henry IV had become king. At Shrewsbury in 1403 they faced each other as opponents, and it was young Harry Monmouth who helped win a bitter and bloody day, with the famed Hotspur killed in the battle.

Henry had already received his baptism of fire in his principality of Wales, though not in such bloody fashion as at Shrewsbury. (Pitched battles were rare in that bellicose age. The normal method of warfare was siege or the sudden raid.) The Welsh had been quiescent for a long period but when in 1400 Owen Glendower – or Glendwyr – broke into rebellion, they found their last great leader (to date anyway). Glendower was an elderly gentleman, already fifty in 1400, but he extended his power over the whole of Wales, had himself declared its prince and by skilful guerrilla warfare kept the English marching round in circles. But the heart went out of the rebellion when Harlech castle, the last of the great castles still in Welsh hands, fell in 1409, though Glendower and a small band fought on until 1412. In those ten years from 1399 to 1409, in Wales and at Shrewsbury, young Henry learned the

art and science of warfare in a hard school. He emerged at the top of his class, even if his early reports would have said he showed little signs of military genius or outstanding qualities of leadership.

Before the fall of Harlech castle, the pattern of Henry's life had changed. In 1405 Henry IV contracted some unnamed but nasty disease. He regarded it as God's punishment for his mortal sins and therefore had little will to resist, and in 1408 it seemed that he would die. In fact he lived until the beginning of 1413 but for most of those years his earlier fire and vigour were gone and the reins of government were frequently, if not always amicably taken over by his son. It was in this period from 1408 until his accession to the throne that Henry acquired his reputation as a roisterer which Shakespeare used to such good effect. The chronicles said that he 'intended greatly to ryot' and 'fervently followed the service of Venus as well as Mars.' Quite how great a womanizer or how riotous Henry was is open to doubt. He had too cool a head and his eyes too firmly set on his objectives to dissipate his energies or emotions overmuch, but at the age of twenty-one, after ten years marching round Wales, he seems to have unbuttoned himself when he came to London. The tales of his mis-spent youth add humanity to an otherwise single-minded character and life.

When his father died in March 1413 Henry's objectives were clear. He, the son of a usurper, would prove his right to the crown of England by ruling her justly and regaining her former glory. But if Henry was cool-headed and single-minded, he was not a machine; he was usually merciful to his enemies and one of his early acts as king was to remove the remains of Richard II, meanly interred at King's Langley, and have them reburied in Westminster Abbey. He was loyal and generous to his friends, and had Shakespeare's marvellous character of Falstaff existed he would not have been cast off by his former friend and told to get to his prayers. Like all good leaders Henry recognized talent and chose his friends and advisers well. He surrounded himself with one of the ablest administrative teams in medieval times, with his brother John, Duke of Bedford and the Earl of Warwick among its most trusted members.

One of the first matters with which Henry had to deal was the continuing militancy of the Lollards. They were the followers of John Wycliffe (himself dead). Their challenge to authority was now recognized and links were seen between the Lollards and those who had inspired the peasants into revolt in 1380, particularly John Ball, a priest who had posed the revolutionary question, 'When

Adam delved and Eve span, Who was then the gentleman?' The peasants' rebellion had been smashed but Lollards still roamed the countryside. They had lost any chance of becoming a powerful reforming or revolutionary movement when Wycliffe's reputation was destroyed at Oxford and men, such as John of Gaunt, realizing their possible threat rejoined the established ranks. But a few aristocrats stuck to their Lollard creed, the most notable of whom was Henry's old comrade-in-arms from the Welsh days, Sir John Oldcastle, later Baron Cobham.

As a devoutly orthodox Christian, Henry had little compunction in sending to the stake those Lollards who refused to recant their heretical views. (It was to combat the Lollards that death by burning was introduced into England, though such purging of heretical bodies and souls was already established on the Continent.) Henry was loath to move against Oldcastle and when he was arrested later in 1413 and sentenced to death, Henry commuted the sentence for forty days. During this time Oldcastle managed to escape from the Tower of London and at the beginning of 1414 there was a general uprising. The plan was that the Lollards of England would assemble at Temple Bar in London and then capture the royal family at Eltham. Precisely what they were to do next was none too clear, as they were not anti-royalist, but it did not matter as the plan was betrayed and Henry himself headed the force which met the ill-armed Lollards at their rendezvous. Thirty-eight victims were dragged through the streets on hurdles and hanged in batches on St Giles's Field and that was the end of serious trouble from the Lollards for the rest of Henry's reign. But the Lollard creed of individual thought and challenge to authority did not die, even if it went underground for many years. Oldcastle himself was not recaptured until 1417 by which time Henry was in France. It was left to his brother Bedford to have Oldcastle tried before Parliament which sentenced him to death by partial hanging and final burning.

England's body politic and religion was secured by the suppression of the Lollards, but the regaining of her former glory was another matter. That lay overseas and of course centred on the reconquest of her former French lands. If England had known 'a scrambling and unquiet time' for much of the reigns of Richard II and Henry IV, the conditions in France in that period had become disastrous. Two powerful factions had grown up, the Burgundians and the Armagnacs, each prepared to fight and murder the other to remain the most influential in the land. At the centre, where power should have been, there was a vacuum. Charles VI of France had always been a weak monarch but from 1392 onwards he spent much of his life actually insane, with periods of lucidity when he would try to exert himself, ally himself with the Burgundians or Armagnacs and make the situation worse.

Apart from ravaging each other and the land of France, both Burgundians and Armagnacs angled increasingly for the support of a stabilized England. Presented with such a heaven-sent opportunity Henry played his cards adroitly. He not only demanded that the clauses of the Treaty of Brétigny be implemented in England's favour, but he reactivated the claim to the French throne which lay in his Plantagenet blood through his great-grandfather Edward III (even if Edward had renounced the claim at Brétigny). By the beginning of 1415 Henry had tied up the loose ends of his diplomatic war and was ready to embark on his invasion of France. He had allied himself with the Burgundians, whose star was currently in the descendant in France, and they had tacitly agreed not to resist his claim to the French throne. The Armagnacs had enough problems without going to war with England and had fallen over backwards to be conciliatory, but Henry had made such outrageous demands that they had finally baulked. Henry was thus able to make his invasion preparations with the assent of part of the French nation, with the other part having broken off diplomatic negotiations, cloaked in the legality which was becoming popular on the Continent as well as in England.

In England itself Henry had support for his claim and the prospective invasion from everybody who mattered, together with the enthusiastic backing of the populace. By 1415 Parliament had become intensely English, not to say chauvinistic, in its outlook. The spirit reflected by Shakespeare in his 'God for England, Harry and Saint George' speeches was manifest in Henry who himself said, 'This people is God's people' and that they would pull down the might of France. The organization of the invasion was directed by Henry and his brother Bedford, and an excellent job they made of it, strengthening the muster, the supply lines and the fleet. (Henry is another monarch whom admirers call the founder of the Royal Navy.)

On 11 August 1415 Henry sailed for France, landing at Harfleur without opposition, and by 22 September he had taken the town. Another continental bridgehead had been established but it was hardly a resounding victory and Henry decided to march his army through hostile Normandy to show the flag in his one remaining northern French possession, Calais. It was a defiant, some said foolhardy gesture but against a run of near-disasters,

Le premier chapitre de monstre coment le roy se en ala a Rains pour faire couronner quelque emps dement il eust...

D nom du peir du filz du saint esperit De la glorieuse vi...

cerge marie de mon seigneur sainct Denis patron de frace et de toute sa beatitude ce seste. cy commencent les croniques et gestes du temps De tres crestien roy de france Charles vij De ce nom fai tes et compilees par moy frere Jehan churtier religie[x] et chantre De leglise monsi...

Our King went forth to Normandy,
With grace and might and chivalry,
Then God for him wrought marvellously,
Whereof England may call and cry:
    Deo gracias,
    Deo gracias Anglia,
    Redde pro victoria.

Henry was accorded a fantastic welcome home and the battle of Agincourt established his personal reputation as a soldier of genius and reestablished the English as the greatest warriors in Europe. These were important factors but in concrete terms the battle achieved little. The French had suffered a severe blow to their prestige and many casualties, but France remained a large, unconquered country.

For the next five years Henry was engaged in the real campaign to conquer France, building up another invasion force which sailed in 1417, moving slowly through Normandy until he was within sight of the gates of Paris. All the time his brilliance as a commander was assisted by the plotting and counter-plotting and the enmity not only of the Armagnacs and the Burgundians but of the Queen of France and the various dauphins. Faced by the success of 'Henri le Conquérant', the Armagnacs and Burgundians finally agreed to a truce to defend Paris. But as their emissaries met to parley, the Armagnacs murdered the Duke of Burgundy with a great hole in his skull, and the hatred that had gone before was as nothing to that which now consumed the two factions. It has often been said that Henry entered Paris and cemented his claim to the French crown through the hole in the Duke of Burgundy's skull.

By May 1420 Henry was in a position to impose his will and wishes on France. In the Treaty of Troyes Henry was recognized as the heir and regent of France, with the bargain sealed by his marriage to Princess Katherine, a daughter of Charles VI, so that their children should be the future rightful kings of France. Henry became heir and regent, rather than immediate ruler, because the French signatories to the treaty did not wish actually to depose Charles VI (unlike their counterparts in England who had lesser qualms about deposing more qualified monarchs.) The snag was that though the signatories included the mad Charles, his sane queen and the Burgundian nobles, it excluded the dauphin and the Armagnacs. They were now ensconced in Bourges and Orléans and held all the lands south of the Loire – with the exception of Gascony which remained an English possession – but that still meant the larger part of France.

Henry's last campaign in 1421–22 was to

Above The marriage of King Henry V and Princess Katherine of France which aimed to cement the peace treaty between the two countries and to unite the two Crowns.

Overleaf The Battle of Agincourt, 23 October 1415.

assisted both by Henry's brilliant leadership and tactics and the incompetence of the French commanders, it was a stunning success.

On 23 October 1415, St Crispin's and St Crispinian's Day, the depleted, hungry, exhausted, fever-stricken English army met the might of France near the hamlet of Agincourt. The English line held against the first massive French attack and within half an hour the longbowmen and knights of England had annihilated the French. Apart from the thousands of uncounted peasant bodies, the flower of French chivalry died in that muddy cornfield. It was a staggering victory against enormous numerical odds, the church bells rang throughout England and the first Agincourt Song was written:

establish his rule over the remainder of France, assisted by the Burgundians. In the main it was successful and a few more towns were won, but when he died Orléans had not fallen and the Dauphinist–Armagnac hinterland held firm against him. By the summer of 1422 Henry was desperately ill, probably of dysentery, he could no longer even sit on his horse and had to be carried on a litter to the château of Vincennes outside Paris. There he died on 31 August 1422, naming his brothers Bedford and Gloucester as the regents of France and England and his friend Warwick as the guardian of the infant son which Katherine had borne him, now Henry VI of England and France. Henry's body was brought home, crossing northern France and southern England in scenes of unparalleled mourning splendour, to be buried in Westminster Abbey.

Henry's popular reputation remains high, but there are those who now flatly accuse him of being a jingoistic, chauvinistic warmonger. There are those who more soberly can see that the growing force of nationalism doomed Henry's attempts to conquer France even more strongly than it had Edward III's. Their arguments say that Henry's foolish expansionist policy led England into a futile struggle which, with the emergence of that most formidable of medieval ladies Joan of Arc, culminated in his son's loss of all French lands except Calais. Henry has also been berated for producing that son, Henry VI, who inherited his grandfather Charles VI's insanity and thereby plunged England into much the same state as France, with two factions battling for power. While Henry has not exactly been condemned for dying at the age of thirty-five, it has been suggested that he was extremely lucky to have died young and not had to reap the whirlwind he had unleashed. Despite the criticism and the fact that fortune was with Henry V as it was with William the Conqueror, he was an exceptionally gifted soldier, leader and diplomat, as near an heroic figure as medieval England produced.

Below Henry V's tomb in Westminster Abbey.

Edward III: ancestor of the houses of Lancaster and York

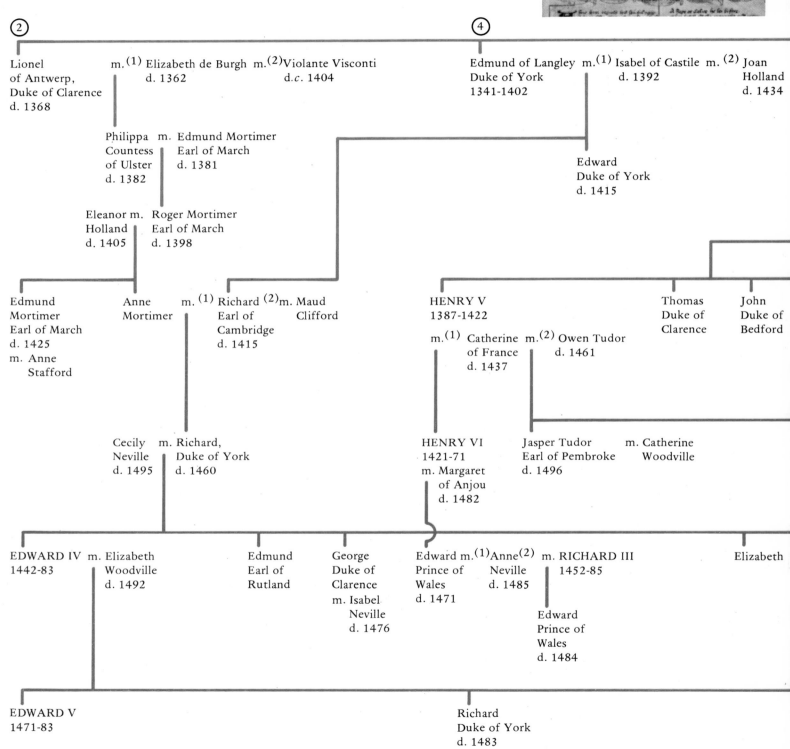

② ④

Lionel
of Antwerp,
Duke of Clarence
d. 1368

m.(1) Elizabeth de Burgh m.(2) Violante Visconti
d. 1362 d.c. 1404

Edmund of Langley m.(1) Isabel of Castile m.(2) Joan
Duke of York d. 1392 Holland
1341-1402 d. 1434

Philippa m. Edmund Mortimer
Countess Earl of March
of Ulster d. 1381
d. 1382

Edward
Duke of York
d. 1415

Eleanor m. Roger Mortimer
Holland Earl of March
d. 1405 d. 1398

Edmund
Mortimer
Earl of March
d. 1425
m. Anne
Stafford

Anne
Mortimer

m.(1) Richard (2) m. Maud
Earl of Clifford
Cambridge
d. 1415

HENRY V
1387-1422

m.(1) Catherine m.(2) Owen Tudor
of France d. 1461
d. 1437

Thomas
Duke of
Clarence

John
Duke of
Bedford

Cecily m. Richard,
Neville Duke of York
d. 1495 d. 1460

HENRY VI
1421-71
m. Margaret
of Anjou
d. 1482

Jasper Tudor m. Catherine
Earl of Pembroke Woodville
d. 1496

EDWARD IV m. Elizabeth
1442-83 Woodville
d. 1492

Edmund
Earl of
Rutland

George
Duke of
Clarence
m. Isabel
Neville
d. 1476

Edward m.(1) Anne (2) m. RICHARD III
Prince of Neville 1452-85
Wales d. 1485
d. 1471

Elizabeth

Edward
Prince of
Wales
d. 1484

EDWARD V
1471-83

Richard
Duke of York
d. 1483

The Houses of Lancaster and York

showing their descent from Edward III and the Tudor claim to the throne

EDWARD III m. Philippa of Hainault
1312-77   d. 1369

③   ①

Blanche   m.(1) John of Gaunt   (3)m. Catherine   Edward,   m. Joan of Kent
of Lancaster   Duke of Lancaster   Swynford   The Black   d. 1385
d. 1369   d. 1399   Prince
                                                               d. 1376

Mary   m. HENRY IV   John   Henry   Thomas   RICHARD II   (1)m. Anne of Bohemia   (2)m. Isabelle of France
de Bohun   1366-1413   Beaufort   Cardinal   Beaufort   1367-1400   d. 1394   d. 1409
d. 1394   Marquess   Beaufort   Duke of
                             of Dorset   Exeter
                             m. Margaret
                               Holland

Humphrey   Henry   John
Duke of   Beaufort   Beaufort
Gloucester   Earl of   Duke of
              Somerset   Somerset
              1401-18   1403-44
                             m. Margaret
                               Beauchamp

Edmund Tudor   m. Margaret
Earl of Richmond   Beaufort
d. 1456

Margaret

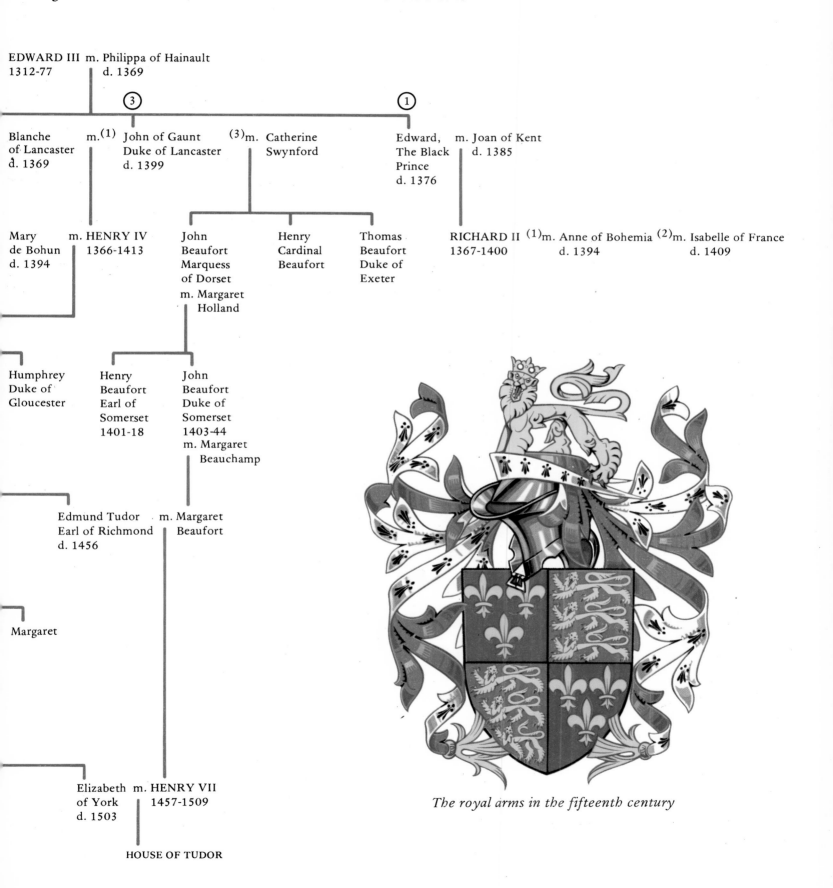

Elizabeth m. HENRY VII
of York   1457-1509
d. 1503

HOUSE OF TUDOR

The royal arms in the fifteenth century

Richard III
r. 1483-85

'Loyalty binds me.'

Richard III has had the misfortune to attract the attention of two men of literary genius, Sir Thomas More and William Shakespeare. The former held Richard up for examination in the light of the new Renaissance learning, as a model of what a king should *not* be, while Shakespeare drew on More (and other Tudor chroniclers) to produce a piece of propaganda which also happened to be a vastly entertaining work of art. Although the two illustrious authors' motives were not the same the end result was and Richard emerged from both portraits coloured pitch black. To discover how evil a genius he really was the known facts of his life and the available evidence have to be weighed as soberly as possible.

Richard was born on 2 October 1452 at Fotheringhay castle, Northamptonshire, the youngest son of Cicely Neville – famed as the 'Rose of Raby' – and the Duke of York. In the year of his birth England lay on the brink of the Wars of the Roses, the power struggle symbolized by the red rose of the House of Lancaster and the white rose of the House of York for the crown held by the always incompetent and frequently insane Lancastrian Henry VI. The opposition claim to the throne centred on the Duke of York and his sons because they were descendants of Edward III's third son, whereas the Lancastrians were descended from the fourth son, John of Gaunt. Richard was brought up at Middleham in Yorkshire, one of the many castles belonging to his powerful Neville uncle, the Earl of Warwick. In 1459, when he was seven, he was suddenly removed to the supposedly greater safety of Ludlow castle where shortly afterwards he and his mother were taken prisoner by the Lancastrians. In the middle of 1460 the Yorkists retriumphed and the Duke of York became Protector of the Realm, but by the end of the year his father and an older brother had been slain and Richard had to be smuggled out of the country. By the spring of 1461 the Yorkists were emphatically

on top again and Richard's brother was crowned Edward IV. Eleven-year-old Richard was created Duke of Gloucester and his life entered another period of comparative tranquillity in Yorkshire.

In 1469 the last agonizing phase of the Wars of the Roses erupted. Edward IV and his powerful ally the Earl of Warwick – rightly known as the Kingmaker – had quarrelled. Warwick tried to make another York brother, the Duke of Clarence, king but Clarence was a weak reed so Warwick allied himself with his previous bitter enemy Queen Margaret, the exiled wife of Henry VI. Edward IV and his brother Richard were forced to flee the country, the sad mad figure of Henry VI was briefly readopted as King and it was not until the battles of Barnet and Tewkesbury in 1471 that the Yorkists emerged as absolute victors. For at Barnet the Earl of Warwick was killed, at Tewkesbury Prince Edward – the one son Henry VI and Margaret had managed to produce – likewise, and Margaret was taken prisoner. Later in the year the victorious Yorkists captured and murdered the imbecilic Henry VI.

By this time Richard was a young man and in the last struggle he fought loyally by his brother Edward's side. Indeed Richard adopted the motto 'Loyauté me lie' – loyalty binds me – and appeared to have emerged from his turbulent, traumatic childhood as unscathed as any of his predecessors from theirs, better than some. (If the childhood events of most medieval monarchs, and many later ones, were presented as case histories to modern child psychiatrists they would assuredly comment, 'Highly disturbed and deprived; bound to lead to adult maladjustment.' Attitudes to children have certainly altered over the centuries.)

In 1477 the machinations of the oft-pardoned Duke of Clarence became too much even for his tolerant brother Edward. In January 1478 Clarence was sentenced to death on a charge of high treason and when Edward IV hesitated about implementing

Opposite Richard III.

RICARDVS · III · ANG · REX ·

almighty mars · that with

Left Richard's brother Edward IV.

Above The Battle of Barnet 1471.

was so overcome by grief that, 'Thenceforth Richard came very rarely to court. He kept himself within his own lands. . . . The good reputation of his private life and public activities powerfully attracted the esteem of strangers.'

The good contemporary reputation of Richard's private life is in stark contrast to Shakespeare's version in which his wife laments for 'that wretched Anne thy wife, That never slept a quiet hour with thee.' Richard had married Anne Neville in 1472, a daughter of the dead and disgraced Earl of Warwick, with whom he had grown up at Middleham, and it seems to have been a happy, if not very fruitful union. Anne was able to bear only one son, an always sickly child, but thoughts of having the marriage annulled – an easy matter as they were first cousins – seem not to have entered Richard's mind. The rectitude of his married life was also in sharp contrast to that of his brother Edward IV who was perhaps the most lascivious monarch ever to sit on the English throne. Early in 1460 Edward had succumbed to the charms and steely will of Elizabeth Woodville and in the one maladroit political act of his career had married her. By 1480 the king's grip was faltering, while that of the Woodville clan was increasing.

The picture of Richard which can be gleaned from the records and comments *before* he became king and *before* the Tudor writers went to work on him is by no means fully rounded, but a reasonably clear outline emerges. It is that of a good soldier – he fought well by his brother's side in the last battles of the Wars of the Roses and in the North to subdue potential rebellions and Scottish incursions – and a hard-working administrator. The impression is also that of a man who did not care for intrigue and was very loyal to his immediate family. Richard kept well away from the court, the queen and the rival factions and nobody then imputed his loyalty to Clarence or Edward IV. The outline further suggests a withdrawn, self-contained man of puritanical views (even if the word did not exist in his day) who detested the permissiveness of Edward's court.

What strikes one most about Richard is how much of a north countryman he was. He wielded great power in the North which he governed on his brother's behalf, with his home base at Middleham, his administrative centres at Barnard and Pontefract castles. But he was also at home there among people he understood and who understood him, and his reserve, puritanism and hard-headed attention to business affairs were to become north country characteristics. To complete the pen portrait of Richard as he appears to have been, if the paintings

the sentence it was the Commons who petitioned the king, urging that it be carried out forthwith. It seems likely that Clarence was drowned in the butt of malmsey wine as celebrated in Shakespeare's *Richard III*, if not in the way so graphically depicted by the playwright. Edward IV was recorded as offering his brother a choice of death, and Clarence elected to depart in the best of all possible manners, drowning in his favourite wine. According to the few contemporary chroniclers – as opposed to the many Tudor ones – Richard's was the only voice to speak up for Clarence. After his brother's death he

71

Left Richard III with his wife Anne Neville.

Below Barnard Castle in County Durham. Richard used this castle as an administrative centre while he ruled the North for his brother.

of him are examined and the tale they tell is accurate, he looks an extremely worried gentleman rather than the arch-intriguer of legend. Physically he had not inherited his mother's or his brother Edward's good looks and body but there is no mention in contemporary accounts of the misshapen, crooked, hunch-backed figure portrayed by the Tudors. The growth of this legend appears to rest on the comment that one of his shoulders was slightly higher than the other.

Edward IV died in April 1483 at the age of forty-one, leaving two legitimate sons, twelve-year-old Edward and ten-year-old Richard, as well as several legitimate daughters. In his will he made Richard, Duke of Gloucester, the Protector of the Realm and of the young King Edward V and Prince Richard, rather than their mother Elizabeth Woodville. The reaction of the Woodville clan to this posthumous denial of power was fast. With the new Lord Protector still in the North, they proclaimed a regency council to rule the country until Edward V was crowned and, as Edward's mother controlled the council, they hoped to rule for several years thereafter. It was the Woodvilles, not Richard, who took the first aggressive step towards further civil strife and usurpation of the crown.

As Richard made his way south, another kingmaking figure appeared, the Duke of Buckingham. He joined forces with Richard at Northampton and they appropriated the person of the young King Edward who was being brought to London for the Woodvilles by his uncle Lord Rivers. On 4 May the two dukes escorted the boy king into the capital. They were received with popular acclamation and, thanks to the intervention of Lord Hastings one of the late king's most trusted friends,

by the support of the majority of the nobles. Richard was established as Protector and a date was set for Edward V's coronation. But by June Lord Hastings had switched allegiance and was negotiating with the Dowager Queen Elizabeth who had fled, with her daughters and younger son Richard, to the sanctuary of Westminster Abbey. Why Hastings changed sides is a matter of argument; according to the Tudors it was because he had already appreciated Richard's villainous intentions and was suffering from remorse. It was not a surprising move; most members of the English nobility had turned their coats with monotonous regularity during the last thirty years, either from motives of revenge or self-interest.

Richard's reaction was as fast as the Woodville attempt to seize power had been. He had Lord Hastings summarily executed. It then became clear that he had raised his sights and was aiming for the crown with the assistance of the Duke of Buckingham. Prince Richard was removed from the sanctuary of Westminster Abbey and installed in the Tower of London with his brother Edward (though the Tower was still regarded as a royal residence and had not yet acquired its sinister reputation as a royal prison). The Lord Protector resurrected the old story that Edward IV's marriage to Elizabeth Woodville had been invalid and therefore his sons were bastards. Technically in medieval law it probably had been but Richard was only giving a cloak of legality to his seizure of power. However, with Richard's northern supporters pouring into London and a general dread of the renewed civil warfare which might be provoked by another child on the throne, the technicality was accepted by Lords and Commons. With the greatest reluctance and surprise Richard acceded to the Commons' petition to accept the crown. At the moment he was reluctantly acceding, in the north his Percy ally the Earl of Northumberland was removing further opponents from the scene. At Pontefract castle four leading members of the Woodville clan were executed, including their one talented and popular figure Lord Rivers.

On 6 July 1483 Richard was crowned in Westminster Abbey in a ceremony of particular sumptuousness. Three months after his brother's death he was king, with no great noble or popular enthusiasm except in the North, but with equally little opposition or resentment. It was now up to him to prove that he could subdue the obvious dissidents thirsting for revenge, and give England peace and prestige. Immediately after the coronation the new king and queen set off on a grand tour of their realm. They had reached Lincoln when the news reached them that the Duke of Buckingham

had suddenly switched *his* allegiance and was now backing the Woodville–Lancastrian alliance which focused on the figure of Henry Tudor.

The reason why Buckingham changed sides was, according to the Tudors, because he too was overcome by remorse and realization of Richard's true character. But Buckingham was an ambitious kingmaker, his own claim to the throne was good (he was a direct legitimate descendant of Edward III's sixth son) and most kingmakers saw themselves eventually as king. It seems more likely that Buckingham decided he had backed the wrong horse and that the shadowy figure of Henry Tudor offered better prospects. Henry Tudor's claim to the throne was less good and stained by bastardy. Through his mother he was descended from John of Gaunt's long liaison with Catherine Swynford; when Gaunt's son by his first marriage, Henry IV, seized power he recognized his Swynford half-brothers and sisters as legitimate but disbarred them from the crown. On his father's side Henry's

descent was from Henry V's widow Katherine who had set up house with an obscure Welshman called Owen Tudor. The Tudors said that Owen and Katherine had married but unfortunately were unable to produce the proof. However, the claim was considered sufficiently strong to ensure that after the Lancastrian defeat at Tewkesbury in 1471, fourteen-year-old Henry Tudor was whisked to the safety of Brittany. Henry Tudor was now twenty-seven and from Brittany had his eyes firmly set on the English crown.

What gave the Woodville–Lancastrian–Tudor alliance such potency were the rumours which began to circulate in England. The rumours said that Richard III had either spirited young Edward and Richard away from the Tower to the fastness of his northern domains from which it was unlikely they would emerge alive or, more sinisterly, that he had already had the two boys murdered. Thus one comes to the most heinous of Richard's alleged crimes over which gallons of ink and oceans of print

Above A romantic Victorian painting of 'The little Princes in the Tower'.

the evidence and the inconsistencies Richard III still emerges as the strongest candidate for the murders.

However, the rumours were not at the time sufficiently strong to swing the nobility against Richard. (His enthusiasts claim that the rumours were initially circulated by the Tudor faction because *they* knew the princes were dead.) Henry Tudor's first attempt to invade England in the autumn of 1483 was a failure and Richard was able to suppress without difficulty the Duke of Buckingham's rebellion which was supposed to link with Henry's landing. Richard's reaction was the same as to Hasting's disaffection; he had Buckingham summarily executed. For the rest of his brief reign Richard was faced with the knowledge that sooner or later Henry Tudor would invade the country again. The factor which swung much of the nobility, if not into active opposition to Richard, at least into a more ambivalent, uncommitted position, was the death of his only son in April 1484. Richard with a legitimate heir was a reasonably attractive proposition, Richard without one could lead England back into civil war.

Their son's death sent both his parents half-mad with grief and Richard then sustained a further loss when his wife Anne died in March 1485 after a long illness whose symptoms sound like tuberculosis. Anne's death became a further weapon in the vicious propaganda war being waged between Yorkists and Tudors. According to the Tudors, Richard had poisoned his wife because she had long been barren and had his eyes fixed on an incestuous marriage with his niece Elizabeth, Edward IV's eldest daughter. The Tudors and Woodvilles had already sealed a pact whereby when Henry gained the crown he would marry Princess Elizabeth, thus healing ancient wounds and strengthening the Tudor claim. To live up to his villainous, Machiavellian reputation, Richard should indeed have got rid of Princess Elizabeth, though he could hardly have married her since his claim to the throne rested on her (and her brother's) supposed illegitimacy.

Richard's administrative record during his brief reign was good. His most important act was to set up the Council of the North which gave the northern counties their own government based on the Westminster system. By this innovation Richard dealt the old feudal power of the northern barons a crippling blow, while giving the North a sense of identity which at the same time incorporated it more firmly in the centralized state. Richard also encouraged printing and the dissemination of books. William Caxton had printed the first book in England during Edward IV's reign but it was during Richard's that Sir Thomas Malory's *Morte*

have already been spread. Later Richard had tacked on to him the personal murder of Prince Edward of Lancaster after the battle of Tewkesbury, of Henry VI and the Duke of Clarence, as part of his long-term strategy to attain the crown. There is no foundation for these allegations; Prince Edward was slain in battle according to all contemporary sources, and it was Edward IV who ordered the killing of Henry VI and Clarence. But the rumours about Richard's involvement in the disappearance of the two princes were contemporary.

Fighting one's way through the mass of arguments and counter-arguments about the little princes in the Tower is not easy. It is quite true that Henry Tudor and the Duke of Buckingham had as good a reason as Richard for wishing to dispose of the children. As long as either lived, the legitimate heirs of Edward IV, both were a menace to any incumbent or claimant of the crown. The known facts are that Edward and Richard went into the Tower under their uncle's aegis in 1483 and were never seen alive again; in 1674 the skeletons of two children were found in a chest near the White Tower by workmen; in 1933 the skeletons were examined scientifically and it was established that they had belonged to a ten-year-old and twelve-year-old child respectively. Although the case is now unlikely to be proven any way, despite the gaps in d'Arthur was published. Malory had assembled all the oral stories about Arthur, the Knights of the Round Table and their ladies and shaped them into a dramatic, narrative form, thus providing England with a permanent legend and an inspiration for generations of poets and writers yet unborn.

On 7 August 1485 Henry Tudor finally landed at Milford Haven, drawing on his Welsh roots for initial support. Once he had crossed the border into England there was no welcoming rush such as had greeted Henry IV. When the Yorkist and Tudor forces eventually met near Bosworth on 22 August 1485, the most notable feature of the battle was the lack of enthusiasm for either leader. Each man had his loyal supporters but the Earl of Northumberland set the tone of the proceedings when he refused to commit his army for Richard, and, until the very last minute, Lord Stanley his for Henry Tudor. In an indecisive battle it was Richard who precipitated his own doom by personally leading a charge of some eighty devoted followers straight at the figure of Henry Tudor. The rash charge nearly succeeded but finally Richard's small force was overwhelmed and he was hacked to death. In the melée the crown was said to have fallen from his head and rolled into a gorse bush from which it was later retrieved by the victorious Tudors.

Richard's body was taken into Leicester where it was displayed for two days in naked ignominy before being buried unceremoniously in a nearby chapel. Richard was thirty-two years old but according to legend he had packed more planned villainy into a short life and even shorter reign – one of the briefest ever, just over two years – than any man in English history. The impression gained by approaching Richard's life without strong feelings either way is how bad a plotter and how little of a Machiavellian diplomat he was. Once his ambition had been stirred – there is no evidence that it was before his brother Edward died and the Woodvilles moved against him – he leapt from action to action with all the impulsiveness of a normally cautious north countryman faced by a situation beyond his dreams. A cleverer man would have pardoned Hastings, Rivers and even Buckingham, at least until he was in a position to ensure their loyalty or to destroy them in battle; or a more ruthless man would have made a cleaner sweep of executions. This was the path followed by his brother Edward in his dealings with dissidents and kingmakers. Richard pardoned the unreliable, showered favours on the less powerful and spent too much time wooing the Commons and commoners. In this last action he can be called far-sighted because the commoners – the middle classes – were the emerging power, but they had not yet emerged and more of his

Above Henry Tudor.

time should have been devoted to those who actually held power. Perhaps Richard's motivating factor was a strong sense of loyalty to his Yorkist inheritance, based on sound north country principles, against the decadent southern influence of the Woodvilles. By turning him into the arch-villain who plotted from misshapen youth with fiendish foresight, through a trail of bloody murders to gain the crown of England, the Tudors assured Richard III an unwarranted position in the forefront of English history.

Henry VIII

r. 1509-47

'*The handsomest potentate I ever set eyes upon.*'

Henry VIII was born at Greenwich Palace on 28 June 1491 of the union which Henry Tudor had indeed made with Elizabeth of York after the battle of Bosworth, but it was not until his older brother died in 1501 that he became heir to the throne. Henry also inherited his brother's wife, Catherine of Aragon, when in 1503 a second marriage treaty was sealed between England and Spain. The theological strictures on a man marrying his brother's wife which loomed so large in the future, played little part in the negotiations. Although it was hardly considered necessary – Catherine's first marriage had been brief and almost certainly unconsummated – a papal dispensation was obtained for the eventual second marriage.

In April 1509 Henry VII died unmourned by his subjects though he left the exchequer in an extremely healthy state. He had also, as a Welshman, started the process of incorporating Wales into England without anybody really noticing. The process was completed by his son in 1536 when English law became current in Wales and the Welsh sent MPs to Westminster.

Henry VIII bounded on to the throne in a burst of enthusiasm which was partly a reaction against his father's sour gloomy reign, partly due to young Henry's obvious attributes. His features were never strictly speaking handsome but he was tall, well-proportioned, with a fine swaggering gait which warranted the description of 'the handsomest potentate'. Moreover he was a good linguist, a passionate theologian, a talented musician and lover of the arts. Above all Henry had an extrovert self-confidence and that priceless ability of which Sir Thomas More commented, 'the King has a way of making every man feel that he is enjoying his special favour.' Henry's less pleasant characteristics – his ruthlessness, capriciousness, lack of principle, self-will bordering on megalomania and a callous cruelty – were not then too apparent.

When Henry succeeded to the throne, English and Spanish diplomats were still wrangling about the terms of the marriage settlement with Catherine of Aragon. The new broom swept them aside and on 11 June 1509 Henry and Catherine were married when he was a few weeks short of his eighteenth birthday, she five years older. Shortly afterwards the obviously happy and loving newly-weds were crowned in Westminster Abbey. In the first phase of his reign Henry concentrated his attention on trying to make England the most influential European nation, by incursions into France and by being involved in diplomatic alliances. In reality England's day had not yet arrived and power lay between the sprawling Hapsburg empire and the Valois kings of France, while the actual country emerging as the most powerful was Spain.

Henry had a few moments, when from his off-shore position, he could lay some claim to being 'the arbiter of Europe'. The most splendid occurred in 1520 when he and Francis I of France, accompanied by the flower of their respective nobility, met on the borders of the English bridgehead near Calais. For a fortnight the two kings and their nobles foreswore their ancient enmity in jousting, wrestling, singing, dancing and one High Mass. Contemporaries called the magnificent rendezvous the 'Field of the Cloth of Gold' and said it was the eighth wonder of the world. It was less durable than the ancient seven wonders and within two years of the golden orgy of brotherly love England and France were at war.

For most of the first phase of Henry's reign, the man who did the king's wheeling and dealing abroad and ran the country for him at home was Thomas Wolsey, the son of an Ipswich cattle-dealer and butcher. The old feudal aristocracy in England had abdicated its responsibilities and torn itself to pieces during the Wars of the Roses and the Tudors gave it little time to recover. For the able and intelligent who also possessed courage and ruthless-

Opposite Henry VIII at about the age of twenty.

77

Above The betrothal of Prince Arthur and Catherine of Aragon.

ness, it was a glorious hour to be alive. Wolsey was a perfect example of the new breed of Tudor men, ambitious, hard-working, efficient, greedy, earthy, sophisticated and loyal to his king. The French ambassador later said of Henry VIII, 'He is a wonderful man and has wonderful people around him, but he is an old fox.' Henry was a young fox, too. Wolsey did all the work – though this was also because Henry had an indolent strain and lacked powers of prolonged concentration – but the king never allowed real power to slip from his grasp. By picking men of ferocious ability, letting them know who was master but hiding behind their actions, Henry ensured that he personally never became too unpopular.

For several years Henry's marriage was happy and he was faithful to Catherine of Aragon. His posthumous reputation, because of his six marriages, is of a monarch who rivalled Edward IV or Charles II in lasciviousness. But although Henry possessed healthy male instincts, it seems doubtful that he was a prodigious lover. His obsession, for which he had good reasons, was not with women as such but with siring at least one male heir while he was still a young man. The fate of the previous usurping Houses of Lancaster and York was not one anybody wanted to follow, least of all an usurping Tudor. Children on the throne led to

disaster, so, it was believed, did women. (The example of Matilda and twenty years of civil warfare was quoted.) Apart from his own dynastic dreams, Henry genuinely wanted to save his country from the dangers of a weak succession.

Had Catherine of Aragon managed to produce a living son, the events which changed the face of England would probably not have occurred. But though Catherine tried to bear a son, producing four boys who were either still-born or died within weeks, as well as similarly fated baby girls, with miscarriages in between, the only child to survive was a girl born in 1516 and christened Mary. Henry still admired his wife and remained hopeful that she would produce the desired son, but he was no longer faithful and in 1519 one of his mistresses, Bessie Blount, bore him a son. From then onwards Henry's dynastically obsessed mind began to wonder. Had he offended against God? Was His wrath apparent in the peculiar circumstances that his fertile wife had failed to produce a male heir, while his mistress had succeeded at the first attempt? Henry's elastic conscience and passion for theology then went to work. The answer they came up with lay in the Bible, to be precise in Leviticus chapter 18, verse 16 and chapter 20, verse 21. There in God's own book it stated that if a man uncovered his brother's wife's nakedness it was an unclean thing and the sinful couple would be childless. It needed some contortions to fit Leviticus to Henry's case as he and Catherine had not been childless, but the salient fact was that he had married his brother's wife. Although this had been by papal dispensation he had nonetheless sinned and the failure to have a son was God's punishment.

The idea of his sinfulness and having his marriage annulled had crossed Henry's mind before he became enamoured of Anne Boleyn. But had he not been enraptured by a young lady of such iron will and ambition, it is more than possible that the erratic, indolent Henry would have settled for the inheritance of his bastard son or waited until Catherine of Aragon was dead before making a second marriage. Totally infatuated by Anne's bold black eyes and luxuriant raven hair – her only good features according to unkind commentators – maddened by her steely refusal to become his mistress, already half-convinced of his sinfulness, desperate to have a legitimate male successor, Henry came to his irrevocable decision. He would divorce Catherine and marry Anne who would bear him the son to carry forward the Tudor dynasty.

Initially the annulment of his marriage did not seem too difficult a task, even if it came as a shock to most of the inhabitants of England who loved Catherine of Aragon. Despite its Lollard background and habit of taking quirky independent action, England was regarded as an untroublesome, orthodox Catholic country. When Martin Luther had launched his thunderbolts against the Catholic Church, who in 1521 had written a trenchant tract in *Defence of the Seven Sacraments* which had become a best-seller throughout Europe? None other than Henry of England, and he had been duly rewarded in 1524 by the papal title *Fidei Defensor*, Defender of the Faith. (This still appears on Britain's coinage as F.D., though it was incorporated by Henry in 1544 after England was on the high road to Protestantism.) There should therefore have been few problems about persuading the pope to annul the marriage of one of his most devoted kingly subjects.

What became known as 'the King's Great Matter' in fact dragged on for six years from 1527 to 1533. In the first two years it was prolonged by the reluctance of some powerful Englishmen, by Queen Catherine's steadfast, skilful defence of her marriage, by the power of her nephew the Hapsburg Emperor Charles V and by the weakness of the pope. By 1529 the anti-clericalism which had long existed in orthodox Catholic England was growing stronger, with its focus on the corrupt power exercised by Cardinal Wolsey. Henry was always ready to throw the first mate overboard in order to save the captain's skin, but Wolsey's initial failure

to take the matter seriously and then to obtain the divorce, together with Anne Boleyn's hatred of him, also led to his disgrace in September 1529. Had he not died two months later he would probably have been executed.

After 1529 what had started out as a diplomatic tussle to obtain a not unusual annulment of a noble marriage changed course. It became a direct challenge to the pope's authority and his right to dictate anything to a King of England. Wolsey was replaced as chancellor by the reluctant figure of Sir Thomas More. To posterity More became known as the noble martyr who went to the block for his Catholic faith, but to his contemporaries he was a radical intellectual who had written one of the most original and startling books, *Utopia*. He was a friend of Erasmus and John Colet, one of the new Renaissance scholars who questioned and criticized the Catholic Church and man's relationship with God. His appointment thus seemed a sign that the king was preparing to fight Rome but More – the 'man for all seasons' – always had reservations about the course Henry was following, foreseeing in a clearer intellectual light than the king where it might lead.

With a reluctant, uncommitted Thomas More as his chancellor, for the next two years it was an invigorated, energetic Henry who battled against

Above Anne Boleyn, Henry's second queen and mother of Elizabeth I.

the pope. He summoned Parliament which had been virtually ignored while Wolsey had held the reins; its consequently disgruntled members responded with virulent anti-clerical sentiments. The texts from Leviticus were upheld, and a text from Deuteronomy chapter 15, verse 5 which stated that when a brother died childless, his surviving brother should take up his wife and raise seed, was stonily ignored. Henry's supporters scoured the libraries of Europe to produce precedents and authorities favourable to the annulment; they dug out Edward III's Statutes of Praemunire and charged recalcitrant, pro-Catherine clergymen with overmuch allegiance to Rome and insufficient to their king. It

Right The 'Field of the Cloth of Gold', the meeting of Henry VIII and Francis I of France in June 1520.

was all very exhilarating, England shaking its fist at Rome, but in the face of Queen Catherine's steadfastness, the Emperor Charles's power and the pope's impotence, it was not bringing the divorce any closer.

By 1532 another of the new breed of Tudor men was on his way to becoming chief minister, Thomas Cromwell. Like Wolsey, in whose household he learned the art of politics, Cromwell was of humble origin, the son of a Putney blacksmith. Unlike Wolsey he was not interested in personal glory; it was the exercise of power and administration of the State that fascinated Cromwell. For sheer efficiency he has had few equals and was one of the most subtle and original, if least loved politicians and fiscal reformers England has ever known. With Henry's 'Great Matter' in Cromwell's hands everything moved forward with the inevitability of the incoming tide. In May 1532 Henry demanded the Submission of the Clergy in allegiance to him rather than the pope and with few exceptions he obtained it; though Sir Thomas More, who could see which way the ship of State was now sailing, promptly resigned as chancellor.

At the end of 1532 the matter was given the final impetus when Anne Boleyn, now as certain as More that the tide was with her, finally submitted to the king's demands and became pregnant. In January 1533 she and Henry were secretly married. In February the pope, with an incredible misunderstanding of what was happening in England, sanctified the appointment of Thomas Cranmer as the new Archbishop of Canterbury. (The old Archbishop Warham, who had opposed Henry, had conveniently died. Cranmer had decidedly Protestant leanings and had been assiduous in his support for the king.) In April Catherine of Aragon was informed that the king had taken a new wife and she was no longer queen. In May Archbishop Cranmer convened a special court which ruled that the king's marriage to Catherine had been invalid, therefore his new one was legal. On the last day of May the pregnant Anne Boleyn was crowned queen.

Rome had been more than defied, she had been ignored. Without anybody in England having any clear revolutionary aims, a major revolution had been effected whose repercussions reverberated throughout Europe. Reversing normal revolutionary practice, it was left to Thomas Cromwell to work out the revolution's principles and put them into effect. The lynch-pin was the quickly passed Act of Appeals which stated: 'This realm of England is an empire ... governed by one supreme Head and King.' The following Act of Supremacy hammered home the fact that England now owed its allegiance to a king who was head of the Church as well as the State. The Act of Succession gave the monarch the right to nominate his successor in his will. Further Acts started to define the limits of power claimed by the king and left to his Church in this hastily cobbled regime and its religion.

Above Thomas Cromwell.

because it was led by a literally one-eyed, starry idealist, Robert Aske, who trusted the king's word. With the main Pilgrimage disbanded, a less starry-eyed but ill-equipped gentleman led another rebellion. Henry and Cromwell immediately seized the opportunity to kill all the leaders and a selected batch of lowly victims in another spasm of blood-letting.

By 1540, against the odds, the Henrician Reformation was secured. The odds had included the massive Dissolution of the Monasteries, an action which was a political and economic necessity. In the new State, the clergy had to be stripped of the power which lay in their wealth; Henry was also broke. The task of laying bare the monastic institutions of England was undertaken with maximum efficiency by Thomas Cromwell. England was still not officially a Protestant country but her breach with Rome and her own enactments were now so complete there was no other road along which she could travel. Perhaps the major reason why England achieved the change from Catholicism to Protestantism so smoothly is that few people, including its architect Henry, knew what they were doing. Other factors which assisted the easy transition were the Lollard tradition of independent thought, the long-standing antipathy to the alien pope and a sense of national identity stronger than in other European countries. Then there was the supineness not only of the majority of the Catholic clergy in England but of Rome itself. Henry was not even excommunicated in the early years, and those who stood and died for their Catholic faith received precious little support, moral or otherwise, from the pope. Finally there was a man with a touch of genius at the helm during the crucial years, Thomas Cromwell, who ensured that the steering of the new State stayed firmly in the hands of the king and his ministers and operated efficiently.

To back-track now to the fatal year of 1533: on 7 September Anne Boleyn bore the long-awaited child who would justify all Henry's actions. It of course turned out to be a girl who was christened Elizabeth. On 27 January 1536 Anne miscarried a baby boy, and with hideous irony it was the day on which Catherine of Aragon was buried. Nobody needed to tell Henry that his passion for Anne, now as dead as his first wife, had been futile and unnecessary. By the miscarriage Anne's fate was sealed and on 19 May 1536 she went to the block on the charge that she had committed adultery – and therefore treason – with five men, including her brother. Henry's callous obsession with dynastic matters was never more clearly exhibited than at this moment. The day after Anne's execution he

The revolution occurred with the minimum of horror and bloodshed, certainly in contrast to what happened on mainland Europe where France and Germany swam in Catholic and Protestant blood and Spain reeked with burning heretical flesh. There was opposition to Henry's revolution and some cruelty on his side. Many of those who refused to take the new Oath of Supremacy were dragged on hurdles, hanged, drawn and quartered or left to die of starvation, loaded with lead weights, in the streets of London. John Fisher, the Bishop of Rochester and Henry's oldest councillor, and Sir Thomas More were spared these horrors but they were executed nonetheless. More spoke for their consciences when he went to the block, 'I die loyal to God and the King. But to God first of all.' In 1536 a rebellion broke out in Lincolnshire, though this was suppressed with comparative ease. However, the one which erupted in Yorkshire and spread to other loyal Catholic northern counties was more serious and could have brought the Henrician Reformation to a speedy end. It became known as the Pilgrimage of Grace, and while protesting their loyalty to the king the pilgrims demanded the restoration of the pope's authority and of clerical power. Henry had no standing army with which to suppress such a massive eruption of popular northern sentiment and the Pilgrimage failed

married Jane Seymour, a shy prim young lady of whom he was genuinely, if not passionately fond. Seventeen months later in October 1537 Jane actually produced the desired objective, a healthy son christened Edward. But to ensure the safe delivery of the baby, Jane was subjected to a barbaric Tudor version of a Caesarian section from which she never recovered. At least Henry showed some grief at her death.

His next wife was chosen for urgent diplomatic reasons, though another son would be useful. In 1538 the pope finally stirred himself and issued a Bull which absolved Christian Englishmen from allegiance to their king, and further called upon good Christians throughout Europe to unite in the destruction of Henry VIII and the re-establishment of the true Church. Also by 1538 Charles V and Francis I had temporarily settled their quarrels (which had greatly assisted England during the early years of the Reformation). Suddenly England was faced by the very real threat of concerted invasion, and Cromwell urged Henry to seek an alliance abroad by marrying again.

Several foreign princesses were wooed but apart from England's diplomatic isolation, few of the ladies were eager to marry a coarsened middle-aged man who had divorced one wife, executed another and buried a third. Eventually Princess Anne of Cleves declared herself willing; Cleves was a useful ally because it was a Protestant domain on the lower Rhine, which could be a thorn in the side of Charles V when England was invaded. (In fact she never was as the Catholic allies quarrelled again.) Henry accepted the princess on the strength of a portrait painted by Hans Holbein and attested as beautifully accurate by Thomas Cromwell. The glowing portrait bore little resemblance to the

actuality and Henry got rid of his 'Flanders Mare' as quickly as he could. Six months after the unconsummated wedding they were divorced, though Anne of Cleves stayed in the country which had given her such scant welcome and managed to remain on good terms with Henry and his children, dying safely in her bed in 1557.

In popular history the reason for Thomas Cromwell's downfall is attributed to his mishandling of the Anne of Cleves affair, but though Henry was furious with his chief minister there were subtler reasons. The Dissolution of the Monasteries had produced continuing discontent, particularly in the North, the area in which the monasteries had still performed one of the functions for which they were founded, the care of the poor. Henry needed a scapegoat and Cromwell was also suspected of being too radical and too much of a Protestant. It was he who suggested that Miles Coverdale's English translation of the Bible be placed in every church, an action which ensured the spread of Protestant thought. What ultimately unseated Cromwell was an aristocratic backlash and a renewal of Henry's lust. The Duke of Norfolk had a beautiful young niece, Catherine Howard, whom he introduced to the king. Henry fell for her with the thump of the ageing, obese, capricious tyrant he had become. The Duke of Norfolk and his aristocratic faction had visions of being the power behind the throne in the manner of Anne Boleyn and her relations. However they should have remembered that Anne Boleyn had been executed for alleged adultery, particularly as Catherine Howard already had a stained reputation. In July 1540 Cromwell was executed; in the same month the nearly fifty-year-old Henry married the teenaged Catherine Howard. Henry got a poor bargain in

Top Holbein's flattering portrait of Anne of Cleves.

Above Catherine Howard, Henry's fifth queen.

Below The famed Nonesuch palace.

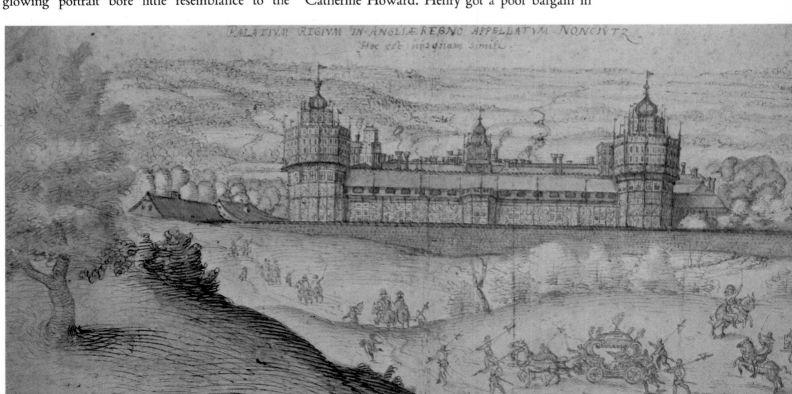

return for the brilliant loyal Cromwell and by the end of 1541 even his infatuated eyes had to accept the evidence of Catherine's continuing affairs. She and her lovers were duly executed.

The last five years of Henry's reign were almost as gloomy as his father's had been. Henry had long suffered from severe headaches and an ulcerous leg which caused him excruciating pain and both were growing worse; he was now so gross that he was virtually immobile. He obtained some consolation from his last marriage in 1543 to the twice-widowed Catherine Parr, an intelligent woman who soothed and nursed her ailing spouse and provided some semblance of the family life he had enjoyed only once in his life, then briefly, with Jane Seymour. Catherine Parr persuaded her husband to have all three of his children at court, Mary and Elizabeth as well as the beloved Edward.

In his declining years Henry tried to clear the path for his son by purging anybody who could lay claim to Plantagenet blood, though he was not entirely successful. He also made another incursion into France but this merely drained the English exchequer of the money so skilfully accrued by Thomas Cromwell. Henry died on 28 January 1547, a hulking shell of the shining prince who had ascended the throne. He left England virtually bankrupt and with little of the glory or prestige for which he had striven. (The resounding martial victory of his reign, over the Scots at Flodden in 1513, had been achieved when he was in France.) However Henry had recognized England's insular position and her dependence on sea power and the fleet had expanded from half-a-dozen small ships to some three-score, well-armed vessels. Despite his excesses and failures, Henry improved England's status and never entirely lost his popularity.

The tangible results of Henry's reign can be seen in the ruined monasteries which stretch across the countryside from Fountains to Glastonbury, and in the squat, eminently practical castles he had built to counter the threatened invasion in 1538. Two excellently preserved ones still guard the Carrick Roads in Cornwall, St Mawes and Pendennis. Not a trace remains of the great palace of Nonesuch which, as its name implies, rivalled any in Europe and the main surviving Henrician palace, Hampton Court, was built by Cardinal Wolsey. Less tangibly, Henry brought immeasurable religious and social change to England. He himself lived and died protesting that he was a Catholic but by the end of his reign many of his subjects were genuine Protestants, including his widow Catherine Parr and the Archbishop of Canterbury, Thomas Cranmer. It can be truly said of Henry VIII that 'he goes furthest who knows not whither he goes.'

Opposite An imaginary portrait of Henry VIII with his third wife Jane Seymour, who died in childbirth, and their son Edward.

Below The deathbed of Henry VIII.

IACOBVS 5 · D · GRA
REX · SCOTORVM

James V of Scotland

r. 1513-42

'A good poor man's King.'

In 1503 James IV married Margaret Tudor, the older sister of Henry VIII. One of the few good things to emerge from the marriage was William Dunbar's famous, celebratory poem, *The Thistle and the Rose*. Otherwise, although Margaret bore her husband six children, it was an unhappy union which did little to foster good relations between England and Scotland.

James firmly refused to abandon the 'auld alliance' with France and in 1513, while Henry VIII was himself fighting in France, war broke out between the two kingdoms. In August James IV invaded England and on 9 September, at Flodden, he met the English army led by the Earl of Surrey. The battle of Flodden field went down in the annals of Scottish history as the greatest defeat ever suffered at English hands. James IV was himself killed and the Scottish losses were appalling. (William Dunbar may have been among those killed at Flodden).

James's son, who became James V, was only 17 months old at the time of his father's death. But two weeks later, on 21 September 1513, he was crowned King of Scotland in the Chapel Royal of Stirling.

The years of James's minority saw a struggle for power between the pro-French and the pro-English factions at Court. In accordance with the terms of James IV's will, the widowed Queen Margaret was named 'tutrix' or guardian of the infant king, but as the sister of Henry VIII and natural ally of the English she could hardly have been a less popular choice for the office. She was an unstable woman, and her remarriage in 1514 to the ambitious Earl of Angus did nothing to increase her suitability in the eyes of the Scottish nobility. They turned instead to their old ally, France. At their request, John Stuart, Duke of Albany, arrived in Scotland in 1515 to administer the realm during James's minority.

One of his first actions was to expel Queen Margaret and her pro-English supporters. Half French by birth, brought up in France and married to a French heiress, Albany naturally sought to

strengthen Scotland's links with France. The 'auld alliance' inspired by the common hostility to England had by now endured for over two hundred years, and as well as bringing political advantages to Scotland it had also left its mark on Scottish culture. Scottish churchmen received their higher education in France; Scottish universities were modelled along French lines; Scottish literature used French words and forms of expression; and much of Scotland's finest architecture drew its inspiration from France.

Albany ruled Scotland for nearly ten years and proved a diligent and responsible governor. But in 1525, while he was away in France serving his own king, the Earl of Angus, Queen Margaret's second husband, brought off a successful *coup d'état* which gave him control of his thirteen-year-old royal stepson. When James came officially of age, in the following year, his formal investiture as king was no more than an empty ceremony. It was Angus, now divorced from Queen Margaret, who ruled Scotland.

It said much for James's strength of character that he succeeded in breaking away from his stepfather's dominance. Angus had tried to corrupt and weaken the boy, encouraging him in sexual adventuring from an early age and neglecting the more important aspects of his education, but James displayed a resolute sense of his own royal birthright. In the summer of 1528, on the pretext of going hunting, he escaped in disguise from Angus's custody. Supporters flocked to his cause, and in a matter of months he rid Scotland of the usurper, who found shelter in England. James V then took command of the kingdom that he had inherited sixteen years before.

With his oval face, aquiline features and auburn Stewart colouring, James was a handsome young man. He had a lively personality, and the number of his bastards testifies to his powers of attraction where women were concerned. But he did not use charm or conciliation in dealing with his nobles. His bitter childhood experiences had convinced him that ruthlessness was the secret of power, and the Scottish nobility had to be taught to fear, not love him.

His policy met with success during the early part of his reign. In the lawless Highlands and borders he imposed some order. He successfully put down a rebellion in the north-west regions in 1539, when the chief Donald Gorme of Sleat claimed the Lordship of the Isles. To reassert his royal authority, James embarked on a personal tour to the outposts of his kingdom, arriving on Orkney in 1540 and returning to Dumbarton in triumph, bringing with him numerous prisoners as security. Thereafter the title of Lord of the Isles was annexed to the Crown.

James V was greatly loved by 'the people'. He displayed an interest in their daily lives and a concern for their hardships which earned him the name of 'King of the commons'. The stories which circulated of his dressing up as a farmer and going amongst his people disguised as 'The Goodman of Ballangeich' added to his popular appeal. Among the nobles obviously his actions met with no such approval. As John Knox later put it, 'He was

Overleaf opposite James V of Scotland.

Overleaf James IV of Scotland, James V's father.

Below Margaret Tudor, James V's mother and regent.

called of some a good poor man's king; of others he was termed a murderer of the nobility and one that had decreed their whole destruction'.

Alienated from his nobility, James looked to the clergy for support. Unfortunately for him, the Scottish clergy were no great force within the kingdom at this time. Protestantism was gaining ground – in England Henry VIII had already broken away from the authority of Rome. James, however, chose to adhere to Catholicism and by retaining papal support, he was able to levy the Great Tax of £10,000 a year on his Scottish prelates. The sum was officially raised for judicial purposes, but it actually went into James's private purse. Likewise the appointment of five of his bastard sons to remunerative clerical jobs enriched the House of Stewart's personal pockets.

As a child of eight, during Albany's governorship, James had been betrothed to a daughter of the King of France, under the Treaty of Rouen of 1521. That treaty was at last fulfilled in 1537, when he visited France and married François I's daughter Madeleine. The French princess was a highly desirable wife, not only on account of the size of her dowry and the power of her father, but also because of her delicate beauty. Tragically, the climate of Scotland took its toll of her frail health, and within two months of their marriage James V found himself a widower.

James appears to have grieved for his pretty and unfortunate first wife, but it was his duty to the Stewart line to remarry and produce heirs. He therefore embarked on another round of matrimonial negotiations with France. This time a more robust young woman was chosen to become his wife. Widowed at the age of twenty-two, Marie of Guise had already proved her childbearing abilities.

She found no great happiness with James V. Despite his liking for France and Frenchwomen, it was said that he 'set not much store by the queen', and his womanizing continued. Not surprisingly, Marie was homesick for her native country. However, in May 1540 a son was born to them, and another followed a year later. Then, in the spring of 1541, tragedy struck when both the infant princes died, within two days of each other. There were rumours of poison, and talk of divine retribution for James's notorious sins of the flesh.

The death of his sons made James V's own safety doubly important. When in the autumn of 1541, his uncle Henry VIII proposed a meeting in Yorkshire, James deemed it unwise to attend. The Tudor king duly arrived in York, but his nephew did not. Henry was not only furious at the slight to his royal majesty, but finally became convinced that the policy of reconciliation with Scotland was

JACOBVS QVINTVS SCOTTORVM REX
ANNO ÆTATIS SVE

MARIA LOTHORINGIA ILLIVS IN SECVNDIS
TIIS VXOR ANNO ÆTATIS SVE 24

hopeless. With England's current isolation in Europe, Henry was badly in need of allies and had tried quite hard to woo James to his side.

In the summer of 1542 Henry decided to teach the Scots a lesson, and English troops crossed the border. Initially they met with defeat at Berwick, but James's alienation of the nobility and reliance on the clergy now proved his undoing. Many of his nobles in any case approved of Henry's Protestantism, and favoured England rather than France. They were doubly furious when James put his favourite Oliver Sinclair in command of the Scots army to harry the retreating English, and they refused to serve under him.

On 24 November 1542, Sinclair's army was routed by the English at Solway Moss. An already ill James collapsed into a state of mental breakdown. He embarked on an aimless progress from palace to palace, spending a few days with Queen Marie (who was far-gone in pregnancy) at Linlithgow, ending up at the French-inspired residence at Falkland. There he took to his bed, alternating between meloncholic despair and furious railing against his cruel fortune. When the news was brought that Oliver Sinclair had been not only defeated but captured, he cried, 'Oh fled Oliver! Is Oliver taken? Oh fled Oliver!' Six days later, on 14 December 1542, in the words of a chronicler, 'he turned his back unto his lords, and his face unto the wall', and died, a broken man at the age of thirty.

Above James V with his second wife, Marie of Guise, the mother of Mary Queen of Scots.

Mary Queen of Scots

r. 1542-67

'The Daughter of Debate.'

Top Marie of Guise.

Above James Stewart, Mary's regent and later trusted adviser.

Opposite Mary Queen of Scots.

'It came with a lass, it will pass with a lass.' Such was James V's despairing comment when he learned that his wife had given birth to a girl at Linlithgow on 1 December 1542, as he lay dying at Falkland. He was alluding to the crown which had come to the House of Stewart through Margery Bruce's marriage, though his prophecy did not prove correct as far as his daughter was concerned.

The child was christened Mary, her nearest kinsman, James Stewart, Earl of Arran, was named as regent, and almost immediately he set about the important task of selecting her husband. That a woman should rule alone seemed unthinkable; the question was which alliance would bring the greatest benefit to the kingdom. James Stewart's choice was the heir to the English throne, Henry VIII's little son Edward. In 1543 the marriage-treaty which, it was hoped, would unite the crowns of Scotland and England, was signed.

But Marie of Guise had other plans for her daughter's future. With the support of her adviser Cardinal Beaton she had the treaty repudiated, and though the wrathful Henry VIII retaliated with the 'rough wooing' of two invasions, she turned to her own country of France for aid.

It was agreed that Mary Queen of Scots should be sent to the French court and brought up there until she was of age, and then she would marry not a Tudor but a Valois prince – the Dauphin François, eldest son and heir of Henry VIII's rival King Henri II of France.

In 1548, as a child of six, Mary set sail for France. Already an exceptionally pretty girl, she was received with great warmth at the French court; under the care of her relations and tutors she blossomed into a lively, sophisticated and beautiful young woman, fond of poetry and dancing. When the time came for her marriage to be celebrated, ten years after her arrival, the youthful dauphin was adoringly in love with her. He was, indeed, fortunate in his bride. Apart from her celebrated beauty and other charms of person, Mary brought with her the crown of Scotland, which she agreed should pass to France if she should die without children, and the hope of a yet greater prize, the throne of England.

In Scotland Marie of Guise succeeded James Stewart and ruled her absent daughter's kingdom as a pro-French, Catholic regent. Frenchmen were put in charge of finance and of the Great Seal and the French ambassador even on occasions attended meetings of the Scots Privy Council. When the young Mary became Queen Consort of France as well as Queen of Scotland, it seemed as if the 'auld alliance' might end with Scotland being absorbed by the French, not the English, crown.

During the French Catholic domination, indeed in part inspired by it, Protestantism grew apace. In 1557, urged on by the preaching of John Knox, great nobles and lesser men signed the first formal Covenant, binding 'the congregation of Christ' to resist 'the congregation of Satan'. When in 1558 a Protestant was burned at the stake, the anti-French, anti-Marie of Guise, Protestant ranks swelled in number and strength. In 1559 they managed to obtain help from the newly-crowned Elizabeth of England (albeit reluctantly on her part as she had no wish whatsoever to become embroiled in Scotland).

By 1560 the Reformers had routed the French, and signed the Treaties of Edinburgh and Leith. In the first they recognized Elizabeth I as the rightful Queen of England, and in the second they sent the French packing. Shortly afterwards a newly assembled Parliament passed three Acts which destroyed the Catholic Church in Scotland. Thus the 'auld alliance' came virtually to its end, and thus entered the lion of Calvinistic Protestantism.

Also in 1560 both Marie of Guise and her daughter's husband François died, and Mary's brief reign in France was over. No longer a Valois queen, but an eighteen-year-old widow, she left the land she had come to regard as her home, and

Above James Hepburn 4th Earl of Bothwell, Mary's third husband.

Below Mary with Henry Darnley, her second husband.

Henrie Stewart Duke of Albanye and Marie Quem of Scotland 1566

returned to her wild northern kingdom of Scotland.

The Scots received their newly-returned queen with considerable mistrust. She spoke the language with a foreign accent, and in her dress and manners was entirely French. Her youth and inexperience did not inspire confidence, while her devotion to the Catholic faith seemed a major stumbling block. Mary in her turn faced a Calvinist establishment and the thundering denunciations of John Knox against her own person and 'the puddle of papistry'.

However, the beautiful young queen succeeded in overcoming much of her subjects' initial antipathy. Despite her pleasure-loving nature she showed herself to be suitably grave in her attitude towards matters of state, and initially she had the wisdom to allow herself to be guided by good ministers, chiefly James Stewart, whom she created Earl of Moray, and her Secretary of State, William Maitland of Lethington. In accordance with their advice, she obeyed her own conscience by attending Mass as her sovereign privilege, while giving official recognition to the Reformed religion.

In one matter Mary refused to obey her ministers' wishes. She said she would not ratify the Treaty of Edinburgh unless Elizabeth named her as successor. Elizabeth had no intention of naming anybody, least of all a rival Catholic queen. Equally, Mary could not officially recognize Elizabeth as the rightful English monarch, for if she did her own claim to the Tudor crown would be nullified. Even while she temporarily prospered in Scotland, Mary never lost sight of the greater objective, which was the inheritance (or usurpation) of the English crown. It was with that great prize constantly in mind that she considered the rival merits of the princes and nobles who sought to become her second husband. One whom she especially favoured was the young Don Carlos, son and heir of Queen Elizabeth's mighty rival Philip of Spain. However, it was upon an Englishman that her choice finally alighted. The tall, 'lady-faced' nobleman Henry Darnley had both Tudor and Stewart blood in his veins, and the combination of his claim to Elizabeth's throne with Mary's made their match an advantageous one, not only for themselves but for any children they might have. It was a marriage in which political strategy and personal feelings were united, for Mary fell passionately in love with the effeminately good-looking 'long lad'.

Queen Mary and Lord Darnley made a handsome couple, but their marriage proved disastrous. Darnley's attractive face hid an ugly nature. Corrupt, arrogant and self-seeking, he soon found himself at odds with his wife's ministers and nobles and ultimately with Mary herself. His brutal murder of Mary's favourite, the Italian David Riccio, a musician suspected of being a foreign agent, was an act for which the young queen could never forgive him. She was pregnant at the time of Riccio's murder, and after the birth of her son and heir Prince James, in June 1566, it was obvious that Mary longed to be free of her depraved husband.

It has never been conclusively proved whether or not Mary consented to the violent events which took place on the night of 10 February 1567, when the house of Kirk o'Field, in which Lord Darnley was staying, was blown up and his body found mysteriously strangled outside in the garden. However, there could be no doubt of Mary's relief at finding herself free of the consort she had grown to hate. Less than five months later, she married for the third time.

Mary may have been innocent of complicity in Darnley's death, but she was guilty of grave folly in her subsequent actions. On 15 May 1567, she married, by Protestant rites, James Hepburn, Earl of Bothwell, a man newly divorced from his wife and widely suspected of having played a leading part in the Darnley murder. Bothwell had abducted Mary and may have made her pregnant; the marriage may have been a diplomatic necessity. But it gave the Queen of Scotland's enemies the evidence they required.

An army was raised in the name of the infant Prince James, and on 15 June, one month after her fateful third marriage, Mary met her son's supporters on the field of Carberry Hill, near Musselburgh. The queen's troops deserted, and her cause was lost. Under guard she was taken to Edinburgh, where the crowds called for her blood with shouts of 'Burn the Whore!'; she was then removed to the island stronghold of Lochleven. There, on 24 July, she was forced to sign away her kingdom to her baby son.

Mary was still only 25 years old. She was a young woman of courage and resource, she believed herself unjustly treated, and she had powerful allies both at home and abroad. In England, Queen Elizabeth displayed some sympathy towards her plight. When, early in May of the following year, Mary succeeded in escaping from her island prison, it seemed that freedom was hers again. Within a short space of time she had gathered supporters, and on 13 May 1568 she joined battle against the kinsman who had formerly been her trusted adviser, the Earl of Moray. But again she met with defeat. She left the battlefield of Langside, near Glasgow, and fled across the Solway Firth into England. There she hoped that she would find not only shelter but aid for her cause.

The hope was in vain. Mary was kept in confinement, with increasing severity, for nineteen years. Time and time again she begged Queen Elizabeth to grant her an interview, believing that if she could only plead her cause in person her royal cousin would look more leniently upon her, but the request was never granted. Elizabeth was courteous to the captive queen, but reminded her that there were grave charges against her which must be fully investigated. In the English Parliament Mary was fulminated against as a 'vile and naughty woman'; others, however, regarded her in a very different light. There was considerable Catholic activity on behalf of the beautiful Scottish prisoner. While Mary passed the long days with needlework, music, or conversation with her devoted attendants, plans were made to free her from her imprisonment, reinstate her on her Scottish throne, and acquire for her the long-desired crown of England.

It was not surprising that Mary should have longed for the success of such schemes and willingly

participated in them. But nor was it unnatural for the Queen of England to be deeply concerned by the danger which Mary presented. 'The Daughter of Debate, that eke discord doth sow', Elizabeth called her in verse, and with justification. As long as Mary remained alive she would be a focus for Catholic plots, a constant threat to the peace of England and the safety of the childless Elizabeth.

The Queen of England had no wish to execute her cousin. But with the discovery of the Babington Plot in 1586 Mary's fate was sealed. Elizabeth continued to hesitate, and put off the act of signing the death warrant as long as she could. But on 8 February 1587, Mary was finally led to the executioner's block in the great hall of Fotheringhay Castle.

She died nobly. The phrase 'In my end is my beginning' which she had embroidered, during her early imprisonment at Sheffield, might have stood as her epitaph. Though she never inherited the English throne which she had so long desired, it was her son and thereafter her descendants who were to succeed Elizabeth and thus unite the crowns of England and Scotland, down to the present Queen Elizabeth II. Surrounded still by the romance and enigma which characterized her lifetime, Mary Queen of Scots, remains, after four centuries, the 'Daughter of Debate'.

Above Mary's rosary and prayer book which she carried to her execution.

Elizabeth I

r. 1558-1603

'Yet this I account the glory of my crown, that I have reigned with your loves.'

Elizabeth's childhood and adolescence lived up to the traumatic royal tradition. Before she was three her mother Anne Boleyn's head had been severed on her father's orders, and at the age of four, with the birth of her half-brother Edward, she was declared illegitimate as her half-sister Mary had already been. Until Henry VIII's death which occurred when she was thirteen, Elizabeth was shunted from place to place, occasionally in her father's favour but more often not, but her life was not in danger, at least not more than any member of the royal family's was. Because she was of royal blood, if currently disgraced, Elizabeth received a first-class education in the hands of a highly intelligent lady Kate Champernowne (better known by her married name of Kate Ashley), and then two of the most famous tutors of the day, Sir John Cheke and Roger Ascham. Elizabeth emerged deeply versed in Latin and Greek, fluent in French and Italian so that in later years she could exchange quips in Latin with ambassadors and deal with them in their own languages. By all her childhood tutors Elizabeth was educated as a Protestant, trained to repudiate ecclesiastical authority and to study and enquire for herself.

With Edward VI, a precocious if somewhat callous child, Elizabeth got on well but her life was nevertheless endangered during his reign. In his last will Henry VIII had nominated Edward as his successor, followed if necessary by the Princesses Mary and Elizabeth. Thus Elizabeth had become a prize and the man who tried to win her was Thomas Seymour, the ambitious brother of the Lord Protector Somerset. First he married the thrice-widowed Catherine Parr in whose household Elizabeth was then living and proceeded to indulge in sexual romps with his young step-daughter, hugging, slapping and tickling her and jumping on her bed in the early mornings. When Catherine Parr died in childbirth Seymour announced that he would marry Princess Elizabeth, with an added plan to kidnap the boy King Edward VI and marry him to Seymour's ward, Lady Jane Grey. His antics were too much for the Lord Protector; Seymour was arrested early in 1549 and duly executed. Elizabeth's name was implicated in his plots and only by keeping a very cool head did she escape a similar fate.

Much has been made of this episode in Elizabeth's young life, particularly in our post-Freudian era with its interest in sexual influences and motivations. Her adolescent heart almost certainly was touched by the handsome, witty if imprudent Seymour. It has been suggested that his amorous advances and swift execution and her awareness of the danger produced for both of them even by such a tentative affair, froze something within the fifteen-year-old Elizabeth and made her physically and emotionally incapable of committing herself to any man. It may also have taught Elizabeth that if men could use *her* to advance their ends, she could use *them*. In 1553 the consumptive Edward VI died at the age of sixteen. The Duke of Northumberland tried to ensure a Protestant succession and his own retention of power by persuading the fanatically Protestant, dying Edward to nominate Northumberland's new daughter-in-law, Lady Jane Grey, as successor rather than the fanatically Catholic, next-in-line Mary. Princess Elizabeth was summoned to court but wisely pleaded illness, the country as a whole opted for the legitimate, not the Protestant succession, and Mary became Queen.

During the six years of her half-sister's reign Elizabeth received a gruelling training for the onerous task of ruling England. She survived the rebellions and plots which true-born English Protestants focused on her, and the queen's suspicion and jealousy, by developing many of the characteristics which made her such a great queen: self-reliance, prudence, patience, flexibility but above all intelligence and courage. Elizabeth may

Opposite Elizabeth I.

have wept when she was taken by barge to the now-dreaded Tower of London but as she landed at the water-gate in the pouring rain she defiantly proclaimed that she was no traitor. In her forty-third year Queen Mary died, an embittered, lonely, intelligent, high-principled Tudor who unfortunately for her country lacked judgement and any understanding of the national spirit. In the last months of her unhappy reign and life the childless Mary became reconciled to her frequently imprisoned half-sister, recognizing Elizabeth as her successor and allowing her to go to the congenial tranquillity of Hatfield. It was there on the morning of 17 November 1558 that Elizabeth received the news that she was, at the age of twenty-five, Queen of England.

The literally burning issue which faced Queen Elizabeth was religion. England had become an avowedly Protestant country during the short reign of Edward VI. The counter-reformation which the

Below Princess Elizabeth at about the age of twelve.

devoutly orthodox Mary had tried to effect by returning the country to the bosom of the Catholic Church and sending so many heretics to the stake, had made England even more Protestant. The resounding words of Hugh Latimer as he went to the fire had already proved true, 'Be of good faith, Master Ridley, and play the man. We shall this day light such a candle, by God's grace in England, as I trust shall never be put out.' The last message the dying Mary had sent to Elizabeth had been a plea to keep England true to the old faith, but that was out of the question. The majority of the country did not want it and Elizabeth was by upbringing and temperament a Protestant.

Elizabeth was also a passionate moderate; if that sounds paradoxical the whole of her career bears it out. In the 1559 Acts of Supremacy and Uniformity Elizabeth started on her tenaciously moderate path by establishing the Protestant Church of England as the State Church, with herself as 'governor' rather than 'supreme head' (a subtle change of wording) on the broadest possible, least doctrinal base; a church for all seasons, except the extremes of mid-winter or blazing summer. Elizabeth expressed her viewpoint in the early days, 'Let it not be said that *our* reformation tendeth towards cruelty', and later she said she had no intention of making 'windows into men's souls'. Perhaps an apocryphal story sums up her non-sectarian, pragmatic view best. Shortly after her accession the citizens of Oxford were concerned how and where they should rebury the bones of disinterred Catholic saints and recently burned Protestant martyrs. Elizabeth's terse reply was allegedly, 'Mix them.'

When she ascended the throne the state of England was described with equal succinctness: 'The Queen poor, the realm exhausted, the nobility poor and decayed. The people out of order, Justice not executed, All things dear.' Poor exhausted England was also beset by enemies, with both France and Spain waiting to pounce at the first opportunity, while Elizabeth herself was beset by claimants to her throne. The major one was of course Mary Queen of Scots. Her claim was based on her being the legitimate grand-daughter of Margaret Tudor who had been Henry VIII's older sister. While, as far as Catholics were concerned, Elizabeth's birth had been illegitimate because the pope had never recognized her father's marriage to Anne Boleyn, and Henry VIII himself had declared Elizabeth illegitimate for much of her childhood (even if he had recognized her in his last will). For some devout Catholics Elizabeth had no rightful claim to the English throne, and if Mary could secure it, then England would be returned to the true church. As William Cecil told Elizabeth, 'The Queen of Scots is and shall always be a dangerous person to your estate.'

Elizabeth's room for manoeuvre was extremely limited by England's current poverty and lack of power. One false step and she was doomed, but from the start she had an invaluable if intangible weapon, an almost mystical feeling for England and the English to which her subjects responded in full measure. Its lineage had deeper roots than some Elizabethan enthusiasts allow and can be traced through the Yorkists – foreign observers even in Richard III's day commented on how special the English thought they were – back through Henry V to Edward III's haughty Englishmen. After her coronation Elizabeth announced, 'I am already bound unto a husband, which is the Kingdom of England.'

However, this statement was accepted as a pretty conceit and it was believed by everybody, except Elizabeth herself, that she would marry. The second half of the sixteenth century was the age of queens, with Mary and Elizabeth in England, the other Mary in Scotland and Catherine of Medici all-powerful in France, but one thing the Protestant religion had not introduced was an improvement in the status of women. In Germany Martin Luther had declaimed, 'Let them bear children until they die; that is what they are made for', while in Scotland John Knox was thundering against 'the Monstrous Regiment of Women.' Obviously, like all other queens, Elizabeth must marry. The Spanish ambassador said, 'Everything depends on the husband this woman takes.'

As it turned out everything depended on the husband Elizabeth did not take. There may have been psychological and physical reasons why she was averse to matrimony but there were also resounding reasons of state. With consummate skill Elizabeth manipulated the ambition and ardour of a string of home-grown suitors from Robert Dudley onwards; though to Dudley she once revealed her passionate independence, 'God's death, my lord, I will have but one mistress and no master.' Likewise she kept dangling foreign suitors from the Hapsburg Archduke Charles of Austria in the early days to the French Duke of Alençon when she was in her mid-forties. At times her indecision drove her ministers to distraction and William Cecil once threatened resignation, but though procrastination may later have become the proverbial thief of time, for Elizabeth it was salvation. By refusing to commit herself to any marriage, or even any clear policy, slowly Elizabeth built up her country's security and power.

Elizabeth selected extraordinarily able, upright ministers and if she sometimes drove them to desperation, she also earned their unswerving devotion and admiration. Her most notable minister was William Cecil (later Lord Burghley) who served on her first council in 1558 and died in harness exactly forty years later. Elizabeth rightly

Below Hatfield. It was here that Elizabeth received the news that her sister was dead and that she was Queen of England.

said, 'No prince in Europe had such a counsellor as she had of him.' Cecil was a member of the new Tudor middle class which had emerged since Henry VIII's day; by and large Elizabeth went for the new or newer men and her court was as open to ambitious talent as her father's had been. But pursuing her path of moderation she kept a balance with the old nobility and there was no serious aristocratic backlash in her reign. Another man who later served her with the utmost skill and loyalty was Sir Francis Walsingham who developed a vitally necessary intelligence network unrivalled in Europe.

Elizabeth's court became a galaxy of shining talent which she dominated by being as Robert Cecil (William's son) ruefully commented, 'More than a man, and, in troth, sometimes less than a woman.' Despite having an intellect to rival any man's and swearing like a trooper, Elizabeth never pretended that she was a man. On the contrary she used her femininity skilfully, sometimes ruthlessly. She was never a beautiful woman; even the stereotyped, ageless portraits she insisted on having painted do not show her as such, with the eyebrow-

Below William Cecil, Lord Burghley.

less face and aquiline Tudor nose, but she had her gorgeous auburn hair and particularly elegant hands (all her portraits show her hands prominently). Dispassionate or unfriendly foreign eyes were forced to admit that she had an immense vitality and fascinating personality. In a not over-hygenically minded age she was famous for her personal fastidiousness, the cleanliness of her linen and the sweet scent of her perfumes.

Among the many stars who glittered at Elizabeth's court an early one was Robert Dudley, later Earl of Leicester, the man whom the queen perhaps came nearest to loving and marrying. Leicester was not the greatest intellect or talent but anybody who survived at Gloriana's court needed considerable wit and ability; though athletic good looks, which he possessed, were no handicap. Leicester weathered several storms, political and personal, including the scandal of his wife Amy Robsart being found dead at Kenilworth castle; this at a time when it was seriously believed that if he were free the queen would marry him. To her dying day Elizabeth kept 'his last letter' locked in a casket by her bedside (Leicester died in 1588). There was Christopher Hatton who attracted Her Majesty's attention because of his dancing skill but eventually rose to be Lord Chancellor; of all those who professed undying love for Gloriana, Hatton was the only one who actually remained unmarried. There was Walter Raleigh, the Devonshire outsider who shot to the winning post in the middle years and whom a Jesuit called 'the Darling of the English Cleopatra'. Raleigh is associated with the story of throwing his beautiful new cloak across a puddle so that Her Majesty should not soil her dainty feet and robes. It is probably untrue but it is the sort of action the bold, inventive Raleigh could have performed.

Less intimate favourites, though not lesser talents, included Sir Philip Sidney who, as he lay mortally wounded after the battle of Zutphen, gave his water-bottle to a dying soldier with the words, 'Thy need is yet greater than mine.' There was Edmund Spenser who dedicated *The Faerie Queen* to his fairy queen but received small thanks and was one of the few Elizabethans to decide that court life was not worth the candle and humble men should stay at home. In the mixture of intimacy and imperiousness that Elizabeth blended so well, she had nicknames for all her close friends and favourites. William Cecil was her Spirit, Walsingham her Moor, Leicester her Eyes, Hatton her Lids and Raleigh her Water (a play on Raleigh's Devonshire pronunciation of his christian name.)

The everlasting glory of Elizabeth's reign was its literature, and not just Shakespeare's, in many ways untypical because he was a towering genius (though he was a typical Elizabethan in his interest in acquiring good solid land and property in Stratford-on-Avon.) Christopher Marlowe's plays are wholly Elizabethan because nobody asks questions about motives; everybody already knows the answers, the pursuit of personal power, glory and gratification, albeit in the lushest language. Melancholia was admitted in Elizabethan society but introspection was not, and Elizabeth was not alone in refusing to make windows into men's souls for any sort of inspection. But music and writing were part of life, things everybody did or could do, not peculiar aspects undertaken by peculiar people called artists, and for a brief period England was not divided into artistic 'us' and 'them' camps. When Francis Drake sailed to raid Spanish America it was natural that a group of musicians should accompany him.

Under the Tudors England was a musical nation and produced genuinely original composers such as William Byrd and John Dowland but for some reason the musicality withered away and it was the love of language which rooted. Nearly all literate Elizabethans wrote well and more of the country's inhabitants were becoming literate as more grammar schools were endowed for the sons of the poor. (The death of the monasteries had left an educational gap but the Tudors, particularly the Elizabethans, saw that it was filled.) Elizabeth's speeches contain phrases which most writers would give their right arm to compose. In the heat of the Armada battles Drake and Lord Howard of Effingham tossed off despatches filled with felicitous phrases and imagery. In words the Elizabethans expressed their exhilarating new confidence in the wholeness and possibilities of life. But already fairly clamorous in the wings were 'the diligent barkers agains the popish wolf', the Puritans who, for all their many admirable qualities, helped turn England into a largely philistine nation in which art was at best an adornment, at worst an unnecessary abomination. Elizabeth herself suffered from the Puritans who were strong in Parliament and for whom she was not Protestant enough by half, but she kept their barking within bounds.

However confident most Elizabethans were in their own minds and estimation, though their prestige had crept upwards under their queen's tortuous guidance, their actual strength was not great. The threat to England centred on its being the one established, comparatively powerful Protestant kingdom in Europe. In 1570 the pope had finally excommunicated Elizabeth which meant that her Catholic subjects were absolved from their

allegiance and Catholic monarchs could invade England with papal blessing. There was remarkably little home-brewed Catholic rebellion, partly because until 1580 Elizabeth's policy of toleration worked well, partly because most were Englishmen first and Catholics second. The fomenters of rebellion were the Catholic exiles in France and Rome who had little idea what was actually happening in England but believed

Top Robert Dudley, Earl of Leicester.

Above Sir Christopher Hatton.

implicitly that 'whoever sends her (Elizabeth) out of the world with the pious intention of doing God service, not only does not sin but gains merit.' The exiles' hope was that either or both of the kings of Spain and France would launch what was called 'the Enterprise of England', namely its forcible re-entry into the Catholic Church. In the meantime the focus of their plots was the imprisoned Mary Queen of Scots.

Although Elizabeth had given her the protection she desired in 1568 from the Scots baying for her blood, Mary was always the most unwelcome guest. For nineteen years Elizabeth avoided a decision refusing to heed Parliament's demands that Mary be executed for treason or more confidential advice that she be secretly murdered. What Elizabeth hoped would happen is difficult to gauge. Perhaps that Mary would renounce her claim to the English throne and somehow regain her Scottish crown and rule in sisterly love, or simply that she would stop plotting and become forgotten. The King of France knew better when he commented, 'Ah, the poor fool will never cease until she loses her head.'

After Mary had indeed lost her head at Fotheringhay castle in 1587, there was surprisingly little reaction from her fellow Catholic monarchs. Among them the feeling was that Elizabeth had been given no option but would have done better to go for the secret murder, rather than parade the English mania for legality in official trial and execution.

From the 1580s the previously lax enforcement of anti-Catholic laws become stricter and people were persecuted and executed for their faith. Some of the priests who had been smuggled into England and caught, rightly claimed that their mission was solely to minister unto fellow Catholic souls and went to their deaths like Sir Thomas More proclaiming their loyalty to God and the queen. But many of the priests were engaged in 'the Enterprise of England' and Elizabeth equally rightly claimed that for her the question was not about religion but the stability of the kingdom. In the forty-five years of her reign three hundred Catholic martyrs died for their faith; her half-sister Mary had managed to kill the same number of Protestant martyrs in a six-year reign. In an age of bitter religious hatred the figure speaks for Elizabeth's moderation.

By 1588 Philip of Spain was finally ready to embark upon 'the Enterprise of England'. Elizabeth had long provided a base and refuge for Philip's rebellious Protestant subjects in the Netherlands but by the 1580s, with the Spanish assassination of William of Orange, she had become actively (if reluctantly) involved. English soldiers were now fighting by the side of the Dutch and Philip needed

to subdue England to regain control in the Netherlands. Once faced with the hated crunch of war Elizabeth proved that she could act decisively. The Spanish Armada, of which it was deliciously said 'the ocean sighed under the burden of it', was sighted off Cornwall on 19 July 1588 and the warning beacon-fires flamed along the coast of

southern England, alerting every true-born Englishman to the defence of his native land. The naval defence was in the hands of Howard of Effingham, Drake, Hawkins and Frobisher and their plan was daring and novel. Instead of sailing out to meet the mighty Armada they would let it come to them, destroy it on their home seas and thus

prevent the rendezvous with the Duke of Alva's land force waiting in Flanders. No decisive battle was fought off the English coast and it was Drake's inspired improvisation that saved the day. As the Armada anchored off Calais for the night Drake sent in fire-ships, vessels loaded with anything inflammable that could be found. The Spanish fleet

Below Elizabeth I with her courtiers.

N SINE SOLE
IRIS.

Left The Rainbow Portrait of Elizabeth I.

Below The fireship attack on the Spanish fleet on 28 July 1598.

panicked and was dealt a considerable, if not mortal blow off Gravelines. In fact much of the Armada remained intact but the link with the Duke of Alva had been denied and the commanding Duke Medina of Sidonia made the fatal decision to sail his ships northward where they were slowly decimated by harrying English and storms. It was while England waited to learn the outcome of the naval battles that fifty-five-year-old Elizabeth rode down to Tilbury to review her troops and deliver the speech which resounded throughout the country, 'I know that I have the body of a weak and feeble woman, but I have the heart and stomach of a king, and of a king of England, too.'

It was during Elizabeth's reign that the foundations of the future British Empire were laid but she herself had no great interest in colonization. As she told Parliament, 'My mind has never been to invade my neighbour, or to usurp over any. I am contented to reign over mine own, and to rule as a just prince.' She was willing to accept the title Queen of Virginia – though Sir Walter Raleigh's first attempt at American colonization in 1584 was a failure – but her main concern was to ensure a share of the booty her sea-dogs stole from the Spaniards. However, the European discovery of America had radically changed England's position from an off-shore island into an admirable jumping-off point for the New World, and Elizabeth appreciated that a large part of her country's interest now lay westward.

In her last years, unlike other long-lived monarchs, Elizabeth did not lose her grip. Even her infatuation for the Earl of Essex, a beautiful boy of seventeen when he first came to Court and thirty-four years her junior, fell short of being total. Essex was nicknamed Wild Horse by his loving queen and he was a proud, headstrong boy who never really grew up. Elizabeth said, 'I warned him that he should not touch my sceptre', but in 1601 he did just that, leading a London-based rebellion against Her Majesty. Although Essex, unlike previous royal favourites, was immensely popular with the people, in the event they showed their loyalty to their ageing queen, not to the young upstart, and Essex paid with his life. Less than three months after his execution, on 30 November 1601 Elizabeth went to the House of Commons for what proved the last time. An earlier speech had been described by a member of her loyal, argumentative Commons as worthy of being written in gold; this one became known as Elizabeth's 'Golden Speech'. In it she said, 'And though God has raised me high, yet this I account the glory of my crown, that I have reigned with your loves', and then towards the end, 'And though you have had, and may have, many mightier and wiser princes, yet you never had, nor shall have any that will love you better.'

At the beginning of 1603 Elizabeth, now in her seventy-first year, was in excellent health and spirits but by the beginning of March she was feverish. She sank into melancholy but defiantly refused to go to bed and when Robert Cecil said that for her own sake she must, she told him, 'The word *must* is not to be used to princes ... little man, little man'. With equal defiance she refused to name her successor, though the story went that before her death Robert Cecil asked whether it should be Mary Queen of Scots' son James and she grudgingly responded with a nod. On 24 March 1603 Elizabeth died at Richmond and what a contemporary called 'the clear and lovely sunshine of her reign' was ended.

Few have denied Elizabeth's greatness. By her genius she left the poor exhausted country she had inherited, if not the richest and most powerful in Europe, yet imbued with an exuberant self-confidence. Perhaps the last word on Elizabeth should go to her bitter enemy the pope who in the year of the Armada said, 'She is a great woman', though he added the sixteenth-century rider, 'and were she only Catholic she would be without match.'

Henry VIII

James VI and I

Arthur
Prince of Wales
1486-1502

m.(1) Catherine (2) m.(1)HENRY VIII (2)m. Anne Boleyn (3)m. Jane Seymour (4)m. Anne of Cleves (5)m. Catherine Howard
of Aragon   1491-1547   d. 1536   d. 1537   (divorced)   d. 1542
d. 1536   d. 1557   (6)m. Catherine Parr
(divorced)   d. 1548

MARY I
1515-58
m. Philip II
of Spain

ELIZABETH I
1533-1603

EDWARD VI
1537-53

James V (1)m. Madeleine (2)m. Marie of
King of   of France   Lorraine-Guise
Scots   d. 1537   d. 1560
1512-42

François II
King of France
d. 1560

m.(1)Mary
Queen
of Scots
1542-87

(2)m. Henry Stuart
Lord Darnley
1545-67

(3)m. James Hepburn
4th Lord Bothwell
d. 1578

Anne of Denmark m. JAMES I
d. 1619   (VI of Scotland)
                    1566-1625

Henry Frederick
Prince of Wales
1594-1612

CHARLES I m. Henrietta Maria
1600-49   of France
                1609-69

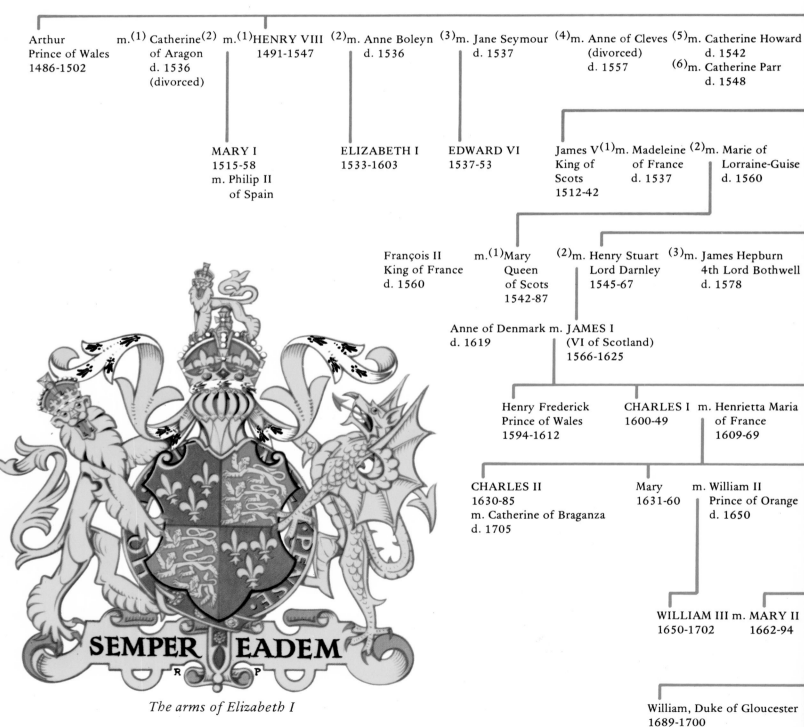

SEMPER EADEM

The arms of Elizabeth I

CHARLES II
1630-85
m. Catherine of Braganza
d. 1705

Mary
1631-60

m. William II
Prince of Orange
d. 1650

WILLIAM III m. MARY II
1650-1702   1662-94

William, Duke of Gloucester
1689-1700

The Tudors and Stuarts

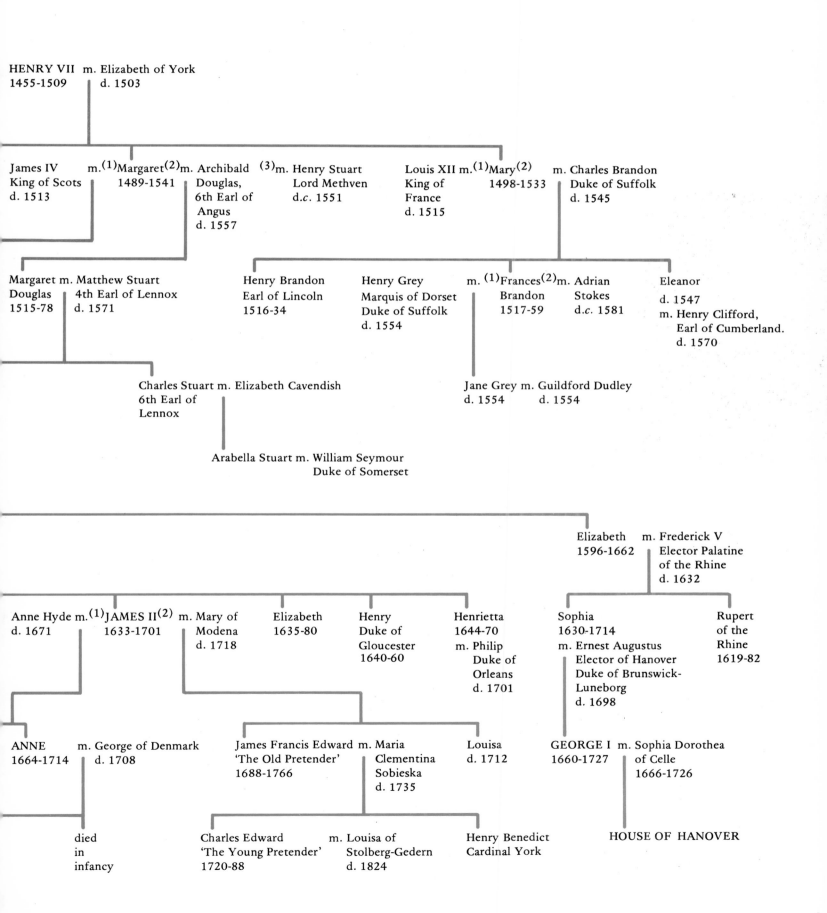

HENRY VII m. Elizabeth of York
1455-1509   d. 1503

James IV   m.(1)Margaret(2)m. Archibald   (3)m. Henry Stuart   Louis XII m.(1)Mary(2)   m. Charles Brandon
King of Scots   1489-1541   Douglas,   Lord Methven   King of   1498-1533   Duke of Suffolk
d. 1513   6th Earl of   d.c. 1551   France   d. 1545
     Angus   d. 1515
     d. 1557

Margaret m. Matthew Stuart   Henry Brandon   Henry Grey   m. (1)Frances(2)m. Adrian   Eleanor
Douglas   4th Earl of Lennox   Earl of Lincoln   Marquis of Dorset   Brandon   Stokes   d. 1547
1515-78   d. 1571   1516-34   Duke of Suffolk   1517-59   d.c. 1581   m. Henry Clifford,
     d. 1554   Earl of Cumberland.
       d. 1570

Charles Stuart m. Elizabeth Cavendish   Jane Grey m. Guildford Dudley
6th Earl of   d. 1554   d. 1554
Lennox

Arabella Stuart m. William Seymour
Duke of Somerset

Elizabeth   m. Frederick V
1596-1662   Elector Palatine
     of the Rhine
     d. 1632

Anne Hyde m.(1)JAMES II(2) m. Mary of   Elizabeth   Henry   Henrietta   Sophia   Rupert
d. 1671   1633-1701   Modena   1635-80   Duke of   1644-70   1630-1714   of the
     d. 1718   Gloucester   m. Philip   m. Ernest Augustus   Rhine
     1640-60   Duke of   Elector of Hanover   1619-82
       Orleans   Duke of Brunswick-
       d. 1701   Luneborg
       d. 1698

ANNE   m. George of Denmark   James Francis Edward m. Maria   Louisa   GEORGE I m. Sophia Dorothea
1664-1714   d. 1708   'The Old Pretender'   Clementina   d. 1712   1660-1727   of Celle
     1688-1766   Sobieska   1666-1726
     d. 1735

died   Charles Edward   m. Louisa of   Henry Benedict   HOUSE OF HANOVER
in   'The Young Pretender'   Stolberg-Gedern   Cardinal York
infancy   1720-88   d. 1824

James VI and I

r. 1567-1625

'The Wisest Fool in Christendom.'

Above James VI as a child.

Opposite James VI and I.

The son of Mary, Queen of Scots and her consort Lord Darnley was born at Edinburgh Castle on 19 June 1566. Less than fourteen months later the baby prince was crowned King James VI of Scotland. His father was dead, his mother was a dethroned prisoner, and the kingdom which he was to rule was in turmoil.

During the troubled years of his minority, four successive regents governed Scotland, while the boy king pursued the lessons and pastimes designed to equip him for his role as a Protestant monarch. Under the care of the Earl of Mar and his stern wife, James underwent a rigorous programme of education, which included studies in Greek, history, Latin, cosmography and rhetoric; by the age of eight he was already performing remarkable feats of scholarship. At the same time it was the task of his tutors to mould the boy's attitudes towards the political and religious issues of the day. James was taught to regard his mother as an adulteress, a murderess, and above all an enemy. As a Catholic, her interests were in direct opposition to those of the Calvinistic Scottish Church in which James was being brought up, and throughout his boyhood her supporters represented a constant threat to his security.

The upheavals of his childhood left James with a lifelong dread of violence and a craving for affection. Slight and ungainly in appearance, he had inherited none of the charm or beauty of his parents, and the precocious brilliance of his intellect was not matched by any great qualities of character. As he grew towards maturity he was a vulnerable figure both personally and politically, and at the age of thirteen he proved an easy target for the schemes of ambitious men.

The last of James's regents, James Douglas, Earl of Morton, was still in office when the handsome young French nobleman Esmé Stuart d'Aubigny arrived in Scotland. Though sent by the Guises to win James over to Catholic interests, and thereby revive the old French–Scottish alliance, Esmé Stuart soon began to work on his own behalf, with notable success. James fell passionately in love with him, creating him Duke of Lennox, and with the aid of his henchman the Earl of Arran, Esmé ousted and eventually executed Morton. In 1582 the dominance of the Frenchman was ended when the ultra-Protestant Earl of Gowrie kidnapped the boy king and forced him, heartbroken, to banish his beloved Esmé. However, a year later, James, now seventeen and of age, escaped and began to rule Scotland effectively as King James VI.

Once established on his Scottish throne, James occupied himself increasingly with the pursuit of the crown of England. As the senior surviving descendant of the first Tudor king, Henry VII, he had a strong claim but Elizabeth refused to name any successor during her lifetime. However, the conclusion of a league between England and Scotland in 1586, and the grant of a pension of £4,000 a year, gave James good reason to hope he would be the eventual successor.

When, in February 1587, Elizabeth finally signed the death-warrant for the long-imprisoned Mary, Queen of Scots, James offered only nominal protests. The execution of the estranged mother whom he had scarcely known could not be allowed to jeopardize his prospects of gaining the English crown. Later, however, he vindicated his mother's memory, and built her a suitably magnificent tomb in Westminster Abbey.

Despite his shortcomings of physique and personality, as King of Scotland James VI proved in many respects an able and successful ruler. In the all-important issue of religion he forsook the Calvinistic theological principles which had been instilled into him as a boy, in favour of a Kirk in which bishops should act as instruments of royal authority. The principle of the divine right of kings, which James argued in his publication entitled *True Law of Free Monarchies* was one from which he

Top James Douglas, Earl of Morton, the last of James's regents.

Above Esmé Stuart, Duke of Lennox.

would not waver. It was in vain for the arch-Calvinist Andrew Melville to declare that the king was merely 'God's silly vassal' – God's simple subject, like any other man. James's famous response was 'No Bishop, no King', and James's will prevailed.

By 1589 Scottish affairs were sufficiently settled for James to venture to leave his kingdom for several months while he journeyed to meet and marry Princess Anne of Denmark. His golden-haired bride was a frivolous stupid young woman, but she represented a suitable Protestant alliance. Despite his homosexual preferences James fulfilled his dynastic duties conscientiously and fathered seven children by her, of whom two sons and a daughter survived. Not for generations had the future of the Stewart line seemed so well assured.

Continued religious discontent and a series of plots failed to shake King James from his northern kingdom. By 1603, when his cherished ambition was fulfilled and he succeeded to the throne of England, he had achieved a reputation as a successful ruler as well as a scholar. It was with considerable anticipation that the English awaited his arrival.

Their first impressions of the new ruler who was to style himself 'King of Great Britain' were not favourable. James had never been good-looking, and his pallid countenance and limping figure were growing less prepossessing with age. His broad Scots accent was difficult for his new courtiers to understand, while his clownish manners and lavatorial sense of humour which frequently reached 'a fluorescence of obscenity', caused great astonishment.

An Englishman commented, 'He is wonderfully clever', though he added, 'and has an excellent opinion of himself.' To an extent James's self-congratulation was justified. He had managed his turbulent Scottish kingdom efficiently, and therefore regarded himself as 'an old experienced king, needing no lessons.' What he failed to understand was that England was not the land flowing with milk and honey of his imagination; on the contrary she remained far from rich. And England also had a much rowdier, more demanding Parliament than Scotland had recently possessed.

For the first few years of his reign, James was carried along by Elizabeth's old ministers, notably Robert Cecil (whom he created Earl of Salisbury in 1605). The king had left Scotland promising to return every three years, but it was a pledge he did not honour. James followed the example of William Dunbar, one of whose most beautiful poems was written in praise of London; opening with the lines, 'London, thou art of towns *A per se*,

Sovereign of cities, seemliest in sight, of renown, riches and royalties . . .', it ends, 'London, thou art the flower of Cities all.'

Similarly enamoured of London city, James wrote, 'Here I sit and govern with my pen, and by the Clerk of the Council I govern Scotland now, which others could not do by the sword.' In 1607, via the Clerk of the Council, his more amenable Scottish Parliament passed an Act of Union, but the English Parliament could not be prevailed upon to follow suit. The best James could achieve was a compromise whereby Scots born after 1603 were given dual nationality.

The role of the Church in relation to the Crown in England was very much to James's liking. However, his religious policies met with opposition from both Catholics and Protestants. Only two years after his accession to the English throne a group of Catholic conspirators concealed gunpowder beneath the Houses of Parliament. They would have 'blown up all at a clap', including the king, had the plot not been discovered. The incident, and one of the conspirators Guy Fawkes, is still remembered in England on 5 November each year. Towards the Puritans James showed equally little sympathy, threatening to harry them out of the kingdom. However, James's most enduring achievement was nonetheless in the sphere of religion. He commissioned a translation of the Bible; published in 1611 it became known as the Authorized Version, famous for the beauty of its language.

After Lord Salisbury's death, James's relationship with the English Parliament became increasingly acrimonious. As a fervent believer in the Divine Right of Kings whose responsibility lay only unto God, his attitude towards England's Parliament can be summed up in the observation, 'I am surprised that my ancestors should have permitted such an institution to come into existence.' Nobody particularly objected to James's interest in young men – that was his business – but everybody objected to the way he slobbered over them in public, to the liberality with which he showered money and titles upon them and, most importantly, to the political power he gave them.

James was by nature pacific and he kept his new kingdom out of any serious wars. However, this policy did not appeal to all his subjects, notably in the case of Bohemia. James's daughter Elizabeth, known as 'the Queen of Hearts', had married the Protestant Elector Palatine in 1613. In 1619 the Elector accepted the proffered crown of Protestant Bohemia (the incident which triggered off the thirty years religious wars and devastated central Europe). When the Catholic monarchs fell upon

Bohemia, and Elizabeth and her husband were driven from their realm – earning the names of the Winter King and Queen in the process – James was exhorted to send English aid. But Parliament was in no mood to grant him the money for such a momentous undertaking, even if James had been desirous or capable of mounting it. His failure to react decisively to the defeat of his daughter and the Protestant cause did not enhance his reputation.

Increasingly, contemporary writers depicted James as a figure of fun, bandy-legged and scanty-bearded, his doublet padded against the knives of possible assassins, his lips dribbling over some handsome favourite. His intellectual powers did not, alas, enable him to understand the political situation in England or how smouldering a keg of parliamentary gunpowder he was lighting for his son and heir. Nor did they make him choose wisely among the young men his nature craved.

His last favourite George Villiers, his 'dear wife and son, sweet Steenie gossip', whom he ennobled as Duke of Buckingham, was particularly detested. (Buckingham was given the pet name of 'Steenie' because of his supposed resemblance to portraits of St Stephen). It was with some justification that Henry IV of France labelled James VI of Scotland and I of England 'the wisest fool in Christendom'.

James died in March 1625, a prematurely senile figure at the age of fifty-nine. He was not a popular

or beloved King of England. Nor, in some quarters, was he a popular King of Scotland, though overall he succeeded better in his northern realm. But for some Scots he was the great betrayer who sold their birthright to the English. For others, who did not object to the union of the two crowns, his betrayal lay in settling in London, rather than Edinburgh, and thereby reinforcing the eminence of the English capital and English domination.

But generally, it was agreed that the unlikely James had succeeded where his more illustrious forebears – and English cousins – had failed. If he was not in fact the King of Great Britain, he had peacefully united the two crowns into a dual monarchy.

Above Anne of Denmark, James's wife.

Left The King and his family listening to a sermon at St Paul's Cross.

Charles I

r. 1625-49

'That so good a man should be so bad a king.'

Above Prince Charles.

Opposite Charles II by Sir Anthony van Dyck.

Charles I was born at Dunfermline castle on 10 November 1600 before his father had become James I of England. He was a weak, sickly child who experienced great difficulty in walking and talking. When his elder brother Henry, who had seemingly been the robust, brave, promising member of the family, died suddenly in 1612 and Charles became the heir to the two thrones, he could still barely walk. However, he had managed to overcome the worst of his speech problems, though all his life he had a pronounced stammer.

As an adolescent Charles detested his father's favourite, 'sweet Steenie gossip'. While the Duke of Buckingham lacked real intelligence, he had a beady eye for the main chance, and by 1618 Charles had become as devoted to Buckingham as was his father, though in his case there was no sexual involvement. On the contrary Charles had a rigid moral code.

Indeed everything about Charles was fairly rigid. His long melancholy face rarely relaxed into a smile, and he always walked badly (though he rode well) and used his disability to hold his small figure – he was 5 feet 4 inches tall – with stiff dignity. Perhaps to counteract his innate lack of confidence Charles imbibed deeply of his father's pronouncements about the Divine Right of Kings. Unfortunately, Charles was not by temperament a genuine autocrat, nor genuinely self-reliant, nor did he possess his father's touch of buffoonery. His choice of 'Steenie' to fill the post of royal friend and councillor demonstrated a characteristic which was both personal and peculiar to most members of the later Stuart dynasty; a disastrous inability to select good friends and be influenced by the right people.

Just before Charles ascended the throne he and Buckingham were involved in a dash to Spain to try personally to persuade the Infanta to marry the heir to the English and Scottish thrones. The hare-brained episode showed the strain of romantic unreality that Charles also possessed. When James I died in 1625, the accession of his more attractive, twenty-five-year-old son proved no occasion for rejoicing, for it was immediately apparent that nothing had altered and power remained in Buckingham's hands. Once Charles had become king, Buckingham changed his mind about the Spanish marriage, a new alliance with France was negotiated and Charles married Henrietta Maria, the sister of Louis XIII. Initially, the marriage was not a success. Henrietta Maria was only fourteen, physically and emotionally immature, and her husband remained in Buckingham's glittering thrall.

The quest for foreign glory in which Buckingham indulged cost money and with that Charles was not over-endowed. For a long time the welfare of England and the raising of money by taxation had depended on some sort of balance being maintained between monarch and Parliament, something that neither James I nor his son ever began to understand. Charles informed the first assembly that lack of money forced him to call in 1625, 'Remember that Parliaments are altogether in my own power for their calling, sitting, and dissolution.' Technically Charles was right, but it was unwise of him to tell its members quite so arrogantly that they were his servants, there to do his bidding. Early in 1628 he was presented with a Petition of Rights by an angry Parliament and was saved from a major showdown only by the murder of the Duke of Buckingham. The assassin was the half-crazed John Felton who had no parliamentary axe to grind but overnight he became the most popular man in England.

In 1629 the famous scene occurred in Parliament when three resolutions hostile to the king were proposed but the Speaker refused to put them, whereupon he was forcibly held blubbering in his seat while a favourable vote was passed by acclamation, with Black Rod thundering on the door of the House demanding admission and

Charles threatening to send in his royal troops. But the militants, led by the fiery figure of Sir John Eliot, had gone too far in their demands and behaviour. There was a moderate reaction in the king's favour and Charles was able to dissolve Parliament without difficulty. For the next eleven years he ruled as an autocratic monarch, with a council but without any assistance from Parliament.

The eleven years from 1629 to 1640 were the happiest of Charles's life. The murder of Buckingham could have been his political salvation had he possessed the wit to accept reality, but it was at least his personal salvation because in his grief he turned to his wife. Henrietta Maria was now a mature seventeen-year-old and their mutual love and devotion became a by-word. The first-born Charles arrived in 1630, followed by further children in 1631, 1633, 1635, 1636, 1639 and 1640. During these years Charles enriched English culture by bringing Van Dyck, Rubens and Inigo Jones to court and buying the treasures of the Duke of Mantua (though he was criticized for 'squandering millions of pounds upon rotten old pictures and broken nosed marbles'). However, the court remained a formal frigid place for if Charles was a loving husband in private, he never unbent in public.

Politically these eleven years were not the calm before the storm because it was brewing all the time. There was increasing resentment of the king's methods of raising money, of his use of the personal courts such as the Star Chamber against his opponents, and of his religious policy. To obtain money Charles extended a tax known as Ship Money, previously levied for the defence of the realm, and in 1637 this matter came to a head when John Hampden courageously went to law in his refusal to pay. But the religious question roused even deeper passions. Charles, himself a devout Anglican, had come under the influence of William Laud who favoured a more ritualistic, authoritarian version of Protestantism. Laud viewed the Puritans, not as a body barking at the popish wolf, but as the wolf itself which must be 'held by the ears.' When Charles appointed Laud Archbishop of Canterbury in 1633 he doubled his efforts to suppress Puritanism, and the fears grew of renewed clerical power and of England's being re-Catholicized. The fact that Charles's wife was a Catholic who openly held Mass at court did nothing to lessen the fears. The storm finally broke when Laud tried to impose a revised Prayer Book on Scotland.

The Scots signed the Covenant in defence of their dour Presbyterianism and Charles lost the so-called first Bishops' War against them. He realized that unless he could impose himself on Scotland,

which was after all his Stuart kingdom, he might also lose control of an increasingly restless Puritan England. He therefore recalled his strongman from Ireland, Thomas Wentworth whom he created Earl of Strafford. A Yorkshireman by birth, Strafford can be called the last of the barons because while Charles was a theoretical autocrat who believed in the Divine Right of Kings, Strafford was an actual despot who believed in personal government

Above George Villiers, Duke of Buckingham.

ruthlessly enforced. He had put his precepts successfully into practice in Ireland, earning a savage reputation as Black Tom, and he told Charles to recall Parliament and get them to vote the money for a further war against the Scots. When Parliament met in April 1640 it refused to vote any money and the attitude of both Houses was ominously hostile to the king. Strafford then urged Charles to dissolve Parliament and rule by force; it was duly dissolved in May 1640, earning the name of the Short Parliament. Even Strafford's driving energy and mini-reign of terror could not produce an army to defeat the Scots and after the Second Bishops' War a destitute Charles was forced to recall Parliament in November 1640.

This Parliament earned the name of the Long Parliament because it was not formally dissolved until March 1660. But in 1640 only one issue united its divided members, hatred of Strafford. Charles's agreement to Strafford's execution was morally the most inexcusable act of his career and in one way his most politically inept. He had recalled this man to govern for him and if he wanted to push England into a kingly despotism, Strafford was the man to do it, but Charles shillied and shallied and finally threw Strafford to the baying parliamentary hounds. His sacrifice, like Buckingham's murder, could have been Charles's salvation had he had the wit to compromise, produce any constructive plan of his own or to woo the moderates who were faintly appalled at the judicial murder and even more aghast at the militancy of Parliament led by the reforming John Pym.

With his Grand Remonstrance of November 1641, listing Charles's misdeeds, Pym raised the question whether this particular monarch was fit to rule at all unless he agreed to some parliamentary control. Urged on by Henrietta Maria who had taken over Strafford's mantle of tough tactics and no surrender, but without any consultation with his council, Charles decided to impeach five leading Members of Parliament for high treason, including John Pym. At the beginning of January 1642 he made a leisurely progress to the House of Commons with his personal troops but not unsurprisingly arrived to find, in his own words, 'all the birds had flown.' Virtually the whole of London was now against him, not just its rowdy mob but its solid respectable citizens. A few days later the royal family fled the capital, Henrietta Maria and the younger children then left for France, while Charles and his older sons Charles and James stayed to defend their kingdom.

The first Civil War officially broke out when the king raised his standard at Nottingham in August 1642. Basically it was a power struggle between the

Above Charles I and Queen Henrietta Maria.

Below The three eldest children of Charles I.

King and Parliament, between two kinds of religious and political thought and two ways of ruling the country, but issues, loyalties and aims were confused and divided on both sides. There were not two monolithic structures – one representing an old traditional loyalty to a benign cultured monarch and ruling aristocracy, the other a more ruthless, philistine Puritanism – on the lines of romantic Cavalier and Roundhead literature or paintings such as 'When did you last see your father?' Initially Charles had the advantage of being king (despite his defects), of a superior cavalry and a good general, Prince Rupert, the son of his older sister Elizabeth; while Parliament had the advantage that it controlled London, most of the ports and the more densely populated areas. What was in hardly anybody's mind when the Civil War started was the idea of ushering in a new republican Jerusalem; it remained a question of the degree of power the king should possess and how much he should be subject to parliamentary control.

Charles failed to press home his early advantage and to take London. In 1643 when the Parliamentary forces were thrown into disarray by the deaths of both Pym and Hampden, he failed to use his strength to come to terms with the moderates. By the end of 1644 the figure of Oliver Cromwell had emerged to press the Self-Denying Ordinances through Parliament which made a clean sweep of their inefficient, aristocratic army command. England's first disciplined professional army was raised and trained by Cromwell and Sir Thomas Fairfax, the New Model Army, on the basis of Cromwell's exhortation, 'Praise God and keep your powder dry!' In 1645 at the battle of Naseby in

Northamptonshire, it decisively beat the royalists.

After flirting with the Scots who first supported him and then reneged on him, by the beginning of 1647 Charles was in the power of the New Model Army. Cromwell, Fairfax and Henry Ireton presented him with the Heads of Proposals which would reinstate him as king but with a written constitution enshrining the rights of Parliament. Now Charles chose to do what he should have done earlier, to play off one faction against another, telling all, 'You cannot do without me.' But now he was dealing with the Cromwellians who controlled the most organized revolutionary body in England, the New Model Army, and who in their turn were being pressurized by the Levellers. The latter's Agreement of the People made the Heads of Proposals seem a pallid, old-fashioned document, with its demands for a total abolition of the monarchy and a Parliament truly representative of the people of England. Faced by Charles's obstinacy and resurgence of romantic arrogance, the Cromwellians broke off negotiations. The New Model Army then proved it could do without King or Parliament by marching on London and taking control of the capital.

In 1648 the second Civil War broke out, caused as much by severe economic difficulties as any great upsurge of royalist sentiment. Charles hoped to link with the Scots who yet again had turned their coats in his favour but Cromwell speedily doomed any such idea and within a few months all was quiet. The army was now demanding that 'Charles Stuart, that man of blood' be brought to account, and slowly Cromwell who had long favoured 'a settlement with somewhat of monarchical power in

it', came to his momentous decision. For the sake of English liberty Charles must not only die but the monarchy itself; or as Cromwell said, 'I tell you we shall cut off his head with the crown on it.' It was a staggering act to bring to public trial and execution an anointed king, the like of which was not again seen in Europe for nearly one hundred and fifty years.

At his trial Charles conducted himself with supreme dignity. He managed to say of Strafford (without stammering), 'An unjust sentence that I suffered to take effect, is punished now by an unjust sentence on me.' On a chill winter's morning, 30 January 1649, in a Whitehall packed with thousands of his subjects, he was executed. Charles died with even greater dignity, with the enthusiasm of the martyr he had determined to be and indeed soon became.

It is not difficult to sympathize with Charles's tragedy and admire his courage as a man; nor to have sympathy with him as a king who had to deal with the most politically advanced nation in Europe in militant, idealistic mood. But it is harder to swallow the persistent image of the wistfully handsome monarch who died so beautifully in Whitehall, murdered by a self-righteous fanatic called Oliver Cromwell. Charles's wistful, slightly effeminate features, though they may have appealed to future generations, held no attraction for his contemporaries, and he died because as a king he had been a disaster. He had neither the strength of purpose nor the bureaucracy to be an autocrat, nor

could he accept the necessity for balance and compromise. The Civil War into which Charles led his country was not inevitable.

Perhaps the worst aspect of Charles as a king was his total lack of scruples. As a man he was courteous if distant and kept his personal word, but as a king he lied, cheated and double-cheated from start to finish. Even *The History of the Rebellion and Civil Wars in England*, written by his loyal adherent and excellent historian, Edward Hyde, later Earl of Clarendon, underlines Charles's constant, inefficient treachery. It caused a parliamentary, though not unfriendly lady to comment, 'Men wondered that so good a man should be so bad a king.' What also doomed Charles was his failure to understand the spirit of England which Parliament did to an extent represent and which is so clearly shown in the calibre of his opponents, John Pym, John Hampden, Sir Thomas Fairfax, Henry Ireton, Oliver Cromwell, not forgetting that greatest of parliamentary and English poets, John Milton.

However, in recent years Charles has found some surprising bed-fellows in Marxist historians who view the Civil War as an early battle lost by the proletariat. According to Marxist theory Charles represented a doomed tradition but one which cared for the people, and the Parliamentarians were the bourgeoisie who denied the people their rights for another three hundred years. Without argument Shakespeare's words from *Macbeth* are applicable to Charles I, that 'nothing in his life became him like the leaving of it'.

Above Oliver Cromwell.

Left The execution of Charles I.

Charles II
r. 1660-85

'He never said a foolish thing. And never did a wise one.'

Until he was twelve years old Charles II matured in a warm, stable environment, even if he saw little of his parents. This solid base perhaps helped him to counter the slings and arrows that outrageous fortune showered on him in the next eighteen years. In the early hopeful stages of the Civil War Charles remained by his father's side and was present at the first inconclusive battle of Edgehill. After the Parliamentary victory at Marston Moor in 1644, his father's reaction was to send his fourteen-year-old son to Bristol as commander-in-chief of the loyal West Country. The boy was unable to impose any authority on the constantly bickering and wrangling royalists, or to use an adjective coined by one of their less quarrelsome members 'brangling'. After Naseby the Royalist cause was doomed and the young Charles fled further westward. For a period he sheltered in Henry VII's castle of Pendennis but by the time its starving garrison surrendered in August 1646 he was, on his father's orders, out of the country.

For the next three years Charles lived as a royal exile, first in France, then the Netherlands, but one not without hope. It was in The Hague that he learned of his father's execution when a fellow-exile addressed him as 'Your Majesty', a method which caused the young man to burst into tears and run from the room. All Europe greeted the news with horror and immediately recognized Charles II as the rightful King of England. Fortified by this reaction and their own outrage, Charles and his supporters decided to strike through one of England's vulnerable hostile flanks, Ireland or Scotland. Temperamentally Charles favoured Catholic Ireland but the news of Cromwell's brilliant, ruthless Irish campaigns put paid to any hopes of his landing there.

Charles therefore settled for Scotland. For six months austere, Calvinist but now pro-Stuart Scots and pleasure-loving, Catholic-inclined Charles played a grim game of compatability in pursuit of

the common end of defeating Oliver Cromwell's brand of Puritan republicanism. In the process Charles threw the one leading, always faithful Stuart supporter in Scotland, James Graham, Marquis of Montrose, to the Presbyterian hounds in much the same manner as his father had thrown Strafford to Parliament. But Charles was duly crowned King of Scotland in January 1651, and although Cromwell had heavily defeated the Scots at Dunbar on 3 September 1650, he nevertheless led an army into England. In his other realm he received little support and exactly a year later on 3 September 1651, he was decisively beaten at Worcester.

In the six weeks following the defeat at Worcester Charles's adventures were the stuff of legend, being hidden by loyal royalist subjects, many of them Catholics, disguising himself as a servant, spending the day in an oak tree while Cromwell's soldiers searched for 'The tall black man upwards of two yards high.' When Charles finally reached the safety of France he was a nine days wonder, but reality soon set in. The reality was that he had been defeated by his own subjects and Oliver Cromwell remained firmly in control. For the following nine years Charles led the aimless, wandering, dispiriting life of an uncrowned king, surrounded by even more 'brangling' supporters whose ranks dwindled as the European prestige of Cromwell's England rose. But Charles himself had changed. He had departed for Scotland a politically innocent, affable but moody young man. He returned a full-grown man who had learned that ambition made the strangest partners, that life itself could depend on stalwart friends, and how to mix with high and low. Probably Charles always had a cynical strain but after his harrowing education in Scotland and England in 1650–51 he became a complete cynic. Perhaps because he had no firm principles, partly from experience, partly from innate belief, he also emerged a tolerant man.

Opposite Charles at Edgehill, aged twelve.

Below Charles II.

In 1658, on his lucky date 3 September, Oliver Cromwell died. There was no immediate royalist revival, on the contrary thousands of people streamed past Cromwell's body as it lay in state and sang his praises. His son Richard became Lord Protector but Richard had none of his father's genius and at the beginning of January 1660 General Monck travelled towards London with his regiment of foot, already known as the Coldstream Guards. Monck was the ablest, most decisive of Cromwell's surviving generals and he correctly assessed the popular pulse. In February his Coldstream Guards enabled the excluded members of the Long Parliament – country gentlemen who had initially opposed Charles I but later Cromwell, too – to retake their seats. In March the longest of Parliaments dissolved itself and in April a new one assembled, with a House of Lords (which Cromwell had abolished). At the beginning of May the new Parliament considered the propositions General Monck had brought from Charles Stuart and on 8 May it proclaimed him king. On 29 May 1660 Charles himself entered London to a stupendous welcome from the crowds which twenty months earlier had mourned the dead Cromwell. It was Charles's thirtieth birthday and his restoration was almost as extraordinary as his father's execution had been.

From Holland, under the guidance of his father's old councillor Edward Hyde (soon created Earl of Clarendon), Charles had issued the Declaration of Breda. This promised pardon for his enemies, to uphold the Anglican Church but to grant toleration to other faiths, and that the monarch would submit all difficult matters to the will of Parliament. The shades of Pym, Hampden and the young Cromwell were already partly vindicated and that of his father should have risen from the grave. The exceptions to the general amnesty were those still alive who had signed Charles I's death warrant. On the anniversary of his father's execution, the bodies of Cromwell and Henry Ireton were exhumed from their resting places in Westminster Abbey and in their already decomposed state hung on Tyburn gallows. It was not a spectacle which Charles personally enjoyed but it satisfied the more rabid royalists.

The prestige of the country Charles re-inherited was high. Cromwell had a patriotism that was Elizabethan in its intensity and had proved no mean hand with a foreign policy more aggressive than Elizabeth's. He is never listed as one of the founders of the navy but the fleet was his particular pride (it was Cromwell who said that England should look to its moat, meaning the seas around.) Nor is Cromwell popularly regarded as a founder of the

British Empire but in his days colonial expansion was encouraged and the emphasis on trade grew, as England's routes to power and prosperity. Cromwell had also removed for his successor the most ardent republicans, the Levellers and the Diggers (and it is for these reasons that some Marxist historians regard him in such a poor light.) During the Civil War and with the growth of the self-reliant New Model Army, men of all types and classes had left their homes, moved around the country and grown more confident, and England had become a country without a peasantry as such. Charles did not till these seeds but eventually he paid attention to Cromwell's navy and earned his title as its royal founder. Charles also founded the Royal Society which did much to further scientific enquiry and knowledge, graced by such figures as Sir Isaac Newton, Edmond Halley (of Halley's comet fame) and Robert Boyle who formulated 'Boyle's Law' as a basis of chemistry. But the spirit which fostered the Society belonged to Cromwell's England, not to Charles's. It came from the Puritanism which believed in doing and that not to try was a greater sin than to fail.

Physically Charles was the dark man, six feet two inches tall, of the Cromwellian 'Wanted' posters. He was very swarthy – there was Moorish blood in his mother's ancestry – with the long nose, hooded eyes and sensual mouth shown in his portraits. Charles's boon companions were a group of hard-drinking, hard-swearing young men, including the Duke of Buckingham, Sir George Etherage and the Earl of Rochester. But if they lacked sensibility, they were not without a vigorous,

biting wit which showed itself in the Restoration drama of such playwrights as William Congreve and in Rochester's poetry. Charles himself loved the theatre – among those he licensed was Drury Lane – and also horse-racing which he established at Newmarket as 'the sport of kings'.

Above all he loved women, rarely with passion (few great womanizers do) but always with affection. He enjoyed his nicknames of Chanticleer, the cock of the walk, and Old Rowley, which derived from the leading stud in the royal stables. He embarked on his amorous path when he was in Jersey in 1646 and while he was in Holland he entered into his first serious liaison with Lucy Walter. She bore him his eldest son, the Duke of Monmouth, claimed that they had been secretly married and had the only royal relationship to end in acrimony. The reigning mistress in 1660 was Barbara Palmer, later Duchess of Cleveland, but she had a foul temper and tended to overplay her hand. There was Frances Stewart, 'La Belle Stewart', the most virtuous of Charles's conquests and one whose face is with us today because Charles used her as a model for Britannia on his coins, and it has never been changed. There was Moll Davis, quickly discarded for her more vivacious theatrical rival, Nell Gwynne. (If Charles licensed theatres, he nevertheless had to thank Cromwell for Moll and Nelly because it was during the supposedly austere Protectorate that actresses were first allowed on the English stage; previously of course boys had played female roles.) Nell Gwynne has deservedly acquired her permanent fame because she was a personally disinterested lass with a pungent honesty

and ready wit. At the height of the 'Exclusion Crisis' when religious passions were again seething, Nell's coach was attacked by a mob who thought it contained one of the foreign Catholic mistresses. Undaunted she stuck her head out of the window and shouted, 'Pray, good people, be civil. I am a *Protestant* whore!'

The mistresses who produced such charming enquiries as, 'Of foreign women why should we fetch the scum, When we can be so richly served at home?' were Louise de Querouaille and Hortense Mancini. In fact both were high-born ladies, Mancini being the niece of the all-powerful Cardinal Mazarin. Louise, later created Duchess of Portsmouth, was the one for whom Charles had the deepest affection and who therefore became the most influential. In 1667 Samuel Pepys reckoned that His Majesty was on his seventeenth mistress, and by mistress a reasonably serious affair of some duration was indicated, not casual indulgence. But Charles was good with and to his women; he rewarded them well and managed to keep swarms of them reasonably contented for years. The lady he actually married was Catherine of Braganza whom he treated with scrupulous courtesy, albeit amid the licentiousness of his court. But though the royal mistresses produced off-spring by the dozen, Queen Catherine was unfortunately unable to bear children.

Politically Charles found that the path of toleration was strewn with bigots, fanatics and straightforward opponents and that it required genius to follow it successfully in all but the most secure and economically prosperous periods. But he

Above Charles II's procession from the Tower to Westminster Abbey for his coronation on 23 April 1661.

Opposite Barbara Palmer, Duchess of Cleveland, the reigning royal mistress in 1660.

did his non-genius, unpassionate best in religious matters, and the focus of the early years was on foreign affairs. Charles had loyally retained his old councillors but, with the exception of the Earl of Clarendon, they were an untalented lot, and under their guidance England went to war with Holland. Since Elizabeth's day the Dutch had shown an amazing vitality, culturally, socially and economically, and could lay claim to being the most generally advanced nation in Europe. Protestant they might be but they were a particular threat to England in trade and colonial expansion. There was therefore some justification for the war but it was appallingly badly handled by the English, notably at sea.

In 1665, while the Dutch war effort flourished and the English languished, the last of the Great Plagues struck London. It was followed in 1666 by the Great Fire which, starting in Pudding Lane, raged for five days, destroying the old medieval and Tudor city. The fire was a blessing in disguise because it also destroyed the haunts of the plague, but at the time it seemed that one cataclysm had followed another. When in 1667 the Dutch actually sailed up the Thames and into the Medway, taking the flagship the *Royal Charles* back with them, England's chapter of disasters was complete. A peace treaty was hastily signed and Clarendon dismissed. (He then retired to the Continent to write his history of the Civil War.)

From 1667 to 1673 Charles ruled with an inner council of five whose main claim to fame was that they added a word to the English language, cabal – made up from the first letters of each councillor's name. During these years Sir George Downing tried to reorganize England's shattered finances and earned a minor immortality, not so much for what he achieved but for the houses he built in a quiet area off Whitehall, later named Downing Street. In 1670 Charles, partly urged on by his beloved sister 'Minette' who lived in France, partly from preference and fear of Dutch power, concluded a secret treaty with Louis XIII. But the problem which dogged his whole reign was his brother James. He was a good soldier, a loyal brother and a harder worker than Charles, but he had inherited most of the paternal weaknesses and was much influenced by his Catholic mother Henrietta Maria. Like his brother he was a womanizer, though not a cheerful one; Nell Gwynne called him 'Dismal Jimmy'. He had managed to seduce Lord Clarendon's daughter, Anne Hyde, which caused a considerable scandal, but Anne was a strong-willed Protestant and she bore her royal husband two daughters, Mary and Anne, and kept him under control. After her death in 1671 James, who

had already been secretly converted to Catholicism, married Mary of Modena, a pretty, quite intelligent princess, but a bigoted Catholic.

From 1674 the Earl of Danby became the strong man. He kept an anti-Catholic, anti-French Parliament quiet which enabled Charles to continue the delicate balancing act of allying himself alternately with the French and the Dutch. But Danby himself was basically anti-French and anti-Catholic and when he insisted on concluding a marriage alliance between James's elder daughter Mary and the young William of Orange, Charles's balance collapsed. Soon afterwards in 1678 the Dutch and French settled their differences in the Treaty of Nijmegen. England emerged with nothing but a mountain of debts and a furious, even more anti-Catholic, anti-French Parliament.

In such an atmosphere 'the Popish Plot' to kill the king was invented by Titus Oates. It was accepted seriously and took its hysterical toll of innocent Catholics. The Protestant Earl of Danby was impeached by Parliament and sent to the Tower when some of the secret negotations with Louis XIII, in which he had not been originally involved, were leaked. But the focus of the hatred became James, the known Catholic with the fanatical Catholic wife, who because Charles had no legitimate children was the heir-presumptive. Initially Charles, one of the few not to believe in the Popish Plot, acted sluggishly; he had inherited some of his father's passivity and was prepared to wait on events. But in what became known as the 'Exclusion Crisis', Charles was not faced by the calibre of opposition of his father's day and he himself had flexibility and in the end proved that he could act decisively.

From 1679 to 1681 the crisis raged, with two parliamentary factions, one supporting the unpopular legitimate Catholic James, the other clamouring for the popular (but infinitely stupid) Protestant illegitimate Duke of Monmouth. (Frantic efforts were made by Monmouth's supporters to find Lucy Walter's supposed marriage certificate which would make him legitimate.) In the process the opposition faction earned the name of petitioners (for Monmouth) and the court faction that of exhorters (for James); these terms were then derisively shortened to Whigs and Tories, the names given respectively to Scottish outlaws and Irish rebels. Thus was the embryo of a two-party political system conceived in England.

On the last lap Charles stood firm and made it clear that he was prepared to go to war in support of his brother's legitimate claim, though personally he much preferred his eldest son. In 1681 he showed a mastery of tactics by dissolving Parliament and

Below Charles's brother, James Duke of York, later James II.

Bottom Catherine of Braganza, Charles's wife.

calling the next assembly in Oxford, thus cutting off the Whigs led by Lord Shaftesbury from their most rabid supporters, the London mob. These wrangling Parliaments at least passed one imperishable Act, Habeas Corpus, by which no prisoner could be held indefinitely without trial.

The Whig bolt was finally shot by a group of extremists who planned to assassinate Charles and James and proclaim Monmouth king. The plot was easily foiled and by 1683 Charles was firmly in control of a Tory, Anglican England pledged to uphold the succession of his Catholic brother. This happened sooner than anybody expected when the apparently robust king was suddenly taken ill on 1 February 1685. As he apologized with sardonic humour for being 'such an unconscionable time a-dying', Charles was received into the Catholic Church which he had always personally favoured by Father Huddlestone, the priest who had helped save him after Worcester. On 6 February 1685,

aged fifty-four, surrounded by his mistresses and their children, he died. He begged James to look after them, adding, 'And let not poor Nelly starve.'

The most renowned verdict on Charles was written by the Earl of Rochester:

> We have a pretty witty king
> Whose word no man relies on:
> He never said a foolish thing;
> And never did a wise one.

It aptly caught Charles's lack of commitment and purpose but it was not entirely just, as he could be wise. But there was something missing and another less witty friend observed that he could 'more properly be said to have gifts than virtues.' But England had rejected the high principles and purpose of Cromwell and perhaps Charles was the right king to sail her back into monarchical waters. He undoubtedly had 'the common touch' and equally undoubtedly was the best of the Stuarts.

Below The Great Fire of London 1666.

George I

George II

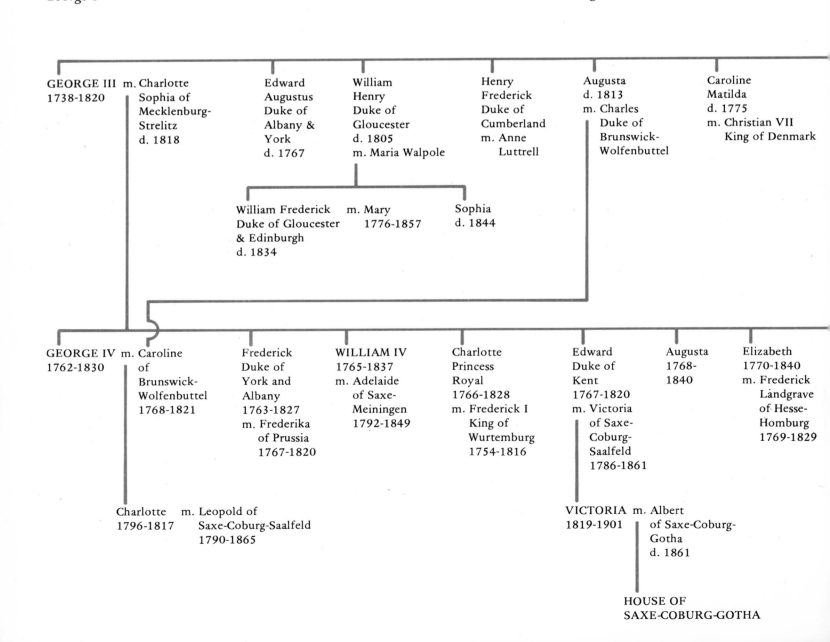

GEORGE III m. Charlotte
1738-1820　　Sophia of
　　　　　　Mecklenburg-
　　　　　　Strelitz
　　　　　　d. 1818

Edward
Augustus
Duke of
Albany &
York
d. 1767

William
Henry
Duke of
Gloucester
d. 1805
m. Maria Walpole

Henry
Frederick
Duke of
Cumberland
m. Anne
　　Luttrell

Augusta
d. 1813
m. Charles
　　Duke of
　　Brunswick-
　　Wolfenbuttel

Caroline
Matilda
d. 1775
m. Christian VII
　　King of Denmark

William Frederick　m. Mary
Duke of Gloucester　1776-1857
& Edinburgh
d. 1834

Sophia
d. 1844

GEORGE IV m. Caroline
1762-1830　　of
　　　　　　Brunswick-
　　　　　　Wolfenbuttel
　　　　　　1768-1821

Frederick
Duke of
York and
Albany
1763-1827
m. Frederika
　　of Prussia
　　1767-1820

WILLIAM IV
1765-1837
m. Adelaide
　　of Saxe-
　　Meiningen
　　1792-1849

Charlotte
Princess
Royal
1766-1828
m. Frederick I
　　King of
　　Wurtemburg
　　1754-1816

Edward
Duke of
Kent
1767-1820
m. Victoria
　　of Saxe-
　　Coburg-
　　Saalfeld
　　1786-1861

Augusta
1768-
1840

Elizabeth
1770-1840
m. Frederick
　　Landgrave
　　of Hesse-
　　Homburg
　　1769-1829

Charlotte　　m. Leopold of
1796-1817　　Saxe-Coburg-Saalfeld
　　　　　　1790-1865

VICTORIA m. Albert
1819-1901　　of Saxe-Coburg-
　　　　　　Gotha
　　　　　　d. 1861

HOUSE OF
SAXE-COBURG-GOTHA

The House of Hanover

GEORGE I m. Sophia Dorothea
1660-1727   of Celle
     1666-1726

GEORGE II m. Caroline   Sophia   m. Frederick William II
1683-1760   of Anspach   Dorothea   King of Prussia
     d. 1737   1688-1757

Frederick m. Augusta	William	Anne	Amelia	Caroline	Mary	Louisa
Lewes of Saxe-Gotha	Augustus	d. 1759	d. 1786	d. 1757	d. 1772	d. 1751
Prince of d. 1772	Duke of					
Wales	Cumberland	m. William IV			m. Frederick	m. Frederick V
d. 1751	d. 1765	Prince of			Landgrave	King of
		Orange			of Hesse-Cassel	Denmark

Frederick   Elizabeth   Louisa
William   Caroline   Anne
d. 1765   d. 1789   d. 1768

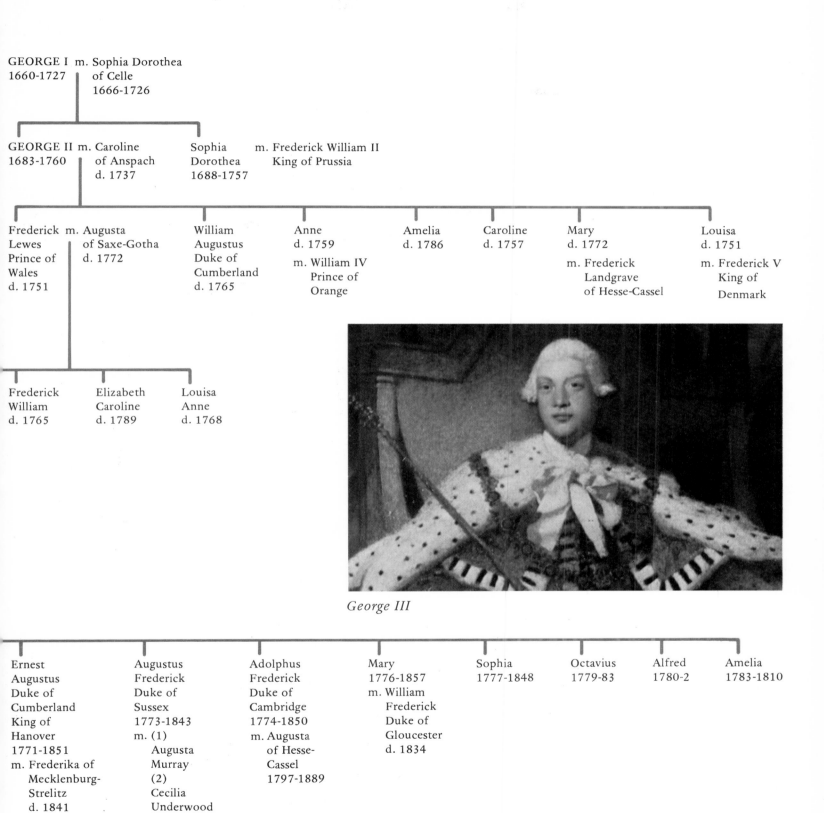

George III

Ernest	Augustus	Adolphus	Mary	Sophia	Octavius	Alfred	Amelia
Augustus	Frederick	Frederick	1776-1857	1777-1848	1779-83	1780-2	1783-1810
Duke of	Duke of	Duke of	m. William				
Cumberland	Sussex	Cambridge	Frederick				
King of	1773-1843	1774-1850	Duke of				
Hanover	m. (1)	m. Augusta	Gloucester				
1771-1851	Augusta	of Hesse-	d. 1834				
m. Frederika of	Murray	Cassel					
Mecklenburg-	(2)	1797-1889					
Strelitz	Cecilia						
d. 1841	Underwood						

George I
r. 1714-27

'The wee, wee German Lairdie.'

George I is one of the least known British monarchs and such reputation as he has is unfavourable – stupid, never learning to speak English properly, with a vindictive streak which led him to imprison his wife for thirty years, and two hideous mistresses known in England as 'the Maypole' and 'the Elephant'. In essence the unattractive portrait is true, but George was not entirely lacking in virtue and as the first king of a line which, though it has changed its name still sits on the English throne, he had a unique position in the development of his adopted country.

George Lewis, as he was called until he became King of England, was born in the German duchy of Brunswick–Luneberg (soon known as Hanover) on the day before Charles II re-entered London, 28 May 1660. His father was Ernest Augustus, a descendant of the ancient Guelph family, a man of limited intelligence and aims, unpassionately interested in food, horses and women. George's mother Sophia was a more interesting lady and it was through her that the claim to the English throne lay; her mother was James I's daughter Elizabeth and her brother was therefore Prince Rupert of Civil War fame. Sophia was intelligent, an excellent linguist, interested in the arts and sciences and would have made a good queen, but she had something of the passive Stuart strain and was able to accept her dull husband and his equally dull court at Herrenhausen.

George inherited nothing from his mother except the Stuart passivity, and was a carbon copy of his father, with an extra degree of shyness and more personal malice. Until the eighteenth century dawned his main claim to fame was scandalous. In 1682, in furtherance of his father's aim of enlarging the duchy, he dutifully married his cousin Sophia Dorothea of nearby Celle. It was a disastrous marriage because she was a vivacious, romantically-minded girl who unfortunately possessed neither her mother-in-law's intelligence nor fatalism. In 1689

she started to console herself with the handsome, unscrupulous Count Philip von Königsmark who had been appointed a Colonel of the Guards at Herrenhausen.

Despite friendly warnings to be more discreet because the family name was being dragged in the mud, Sophia Dorothea and Königsmark flaunted their relationship. In July 1694 Königsmark disappeared at Herrenhausen, in December George Lewis divorced his wife, forbade her to remarry or to see her children again. At the age of twenty-eight she was taken to Ahlden castle where she remained for the rest of her life. For years Europe had a first-class scandal to discuss, one with all the right ingredients: royalty, young lovers, secret murder, implacable husband and the sad prisoner of Ahlden. The scandal in no way affected George Lewis's position and when his father died in 1698 he ruled his reasonably prosperous, well-ordered, despotic little state efficiently. In his phlegmatic way he loved his obedient subjects and they him, but in 1700 an event occurred in England which completely altered George Lewis's prospects.

James II had duly followed his brother as king but had failed dismally to please his subjects. With a lunacy of which only he was capable the popular Duke of Monmouth had struck at the wrong moment and been executed. When the country could no longer stand Catholic James it turned to his daughter by his first Protestant marriage to Anne Hyde. In 'the Glorious Revolution' of 1688 – glorious because it was effected without bloodshed and Parliament got what it then wanted from the new monarchs – Mary and her husband William of Orange were installed on the throne. But Mary died childless and her younger sister Anne became the heir. In 1700 the last surviving child of Anne's innumerable pregnancies died and it became imperative to name an heir to succeed *her*, that was if the Protestant Succession and William III's mission were to be secured. The deposed James II was alive in France and by now had a son of his second Catholic marriage, James Francis Edward, whose claim was excellent. But William III's mission was to curtail the power of France so that his beloved Holland might thrive, and this was unlikely to be sustained by the two French-oriented James.

In 1701 William managed to get the Act of Settlement through Parliament whereby Sophia of Hanover and her heirs became next in succession to the crown after Anne. It was computed that there were fifty-seven descendants of James I who had as good a claim as Sophia, some of them Protestants too, but she had the vital qualification for William. For Hanover had been stalwart in its support of 'the common cause of Europe' against Louis XIV of France. William was not loved by his English subjects and had to pay dearly for his Hanoverian succession. Parliament insisted on further concessions, and the future Hanoverian successors were established not by the grace of God or even the king but by the will of Parliament. This was something George always accepted, even if he never understood it.

Sophia said her dearest wish was to have 'Sophia, Queen of Great Britain' inscribed on her tomb. Great Britain came into being in 1707, after it had become apparent that the dual monarchy of England and Scotland was not working. Either the two countries must again separate or become one. In 1707, after prolonged and bitter arguments and bargaining, the latter course was agreed upon and the Act of Union was signed in which Scotland lost its sovereignty and Parliament, though retaining its Church and Judiciary. Queen Anne was therefore the last monarch of an independent Scotland; henceforward the two countries were known as Great Britain and the term British came firmly into existence. James V's prophecy proved true, as the Scottish Stuart crown indeed passed with a lass, if one can so describe the corpulent, prematurely aged Anne.

George had no particular wish to have 'King of Great Britain' inscribed on *his* tomb but he appreciated that being such would enhance his European reputation and benefit Hanover. Throughout the waiting years Hanover supported England in the War of the Spanish Succession, William III's final effort to check France's power. Sophia and George kept a watchful eye on Hanoverian interests in London but they studiously refrained from becoming involved in the increasingly bitter political battles between Whigs and Tories which characterized Queen Anne's reign.

Sophia died in June 1714, aged eighty-four. She thus failed by less than two months to achieve her dearest wish because Queen Anne died on 1 August 1714. James II had died in 1701 and the two contenders for the crown were George Lewis as nominated by Parliament and James Francis Edward, already recognized by Louis XIV as the rightful James III and supported by many people in Britain because he was a legitimate Stuart and the Hanoverian claim was so weak. The dying Anne's ministers weighed the unsatisfactory alternatives; a Catholic Stuart who had spent all his life in enemy France? or a Protestant German who had supported the common cause of Europe? Having opted for the latter they acted with speed and decision and proclaimed 'Our only lawful and rightful liege Lord, George, by the Grace of God King of Great Britain, France and Ireland.' (France was a hang-

Overleaf opposite George I.

Overleaf Queen Anne.

Opposite George I's wife Sophia Dorothea with their two children.

over from medieval days, not finally discarded until the reign of George III.)

George failed to act with similar promptness and it was not until 18 September that he finally landed at Greenwich, in a thick fog which reflected his subjects' confused emotions. Lady Mary Wortley Montagu, the witty diarist, traveller and bluestocking, noted that he was surrounded 'by all his German ministers and playfellows male and female.' In fact one female playfellow was missing,

Above The Old Pretender with his son Bonnie Prince Charlie.

Mademoiselle Schulenberg, because she thought the English 'who were accustomed to use their kings barbarously, might chop off his head in the first fortnight.' Eventually Schulenberg appeared – she was the long thin mistress nicknamed the Maypole – became a naturalized British subject, was created Duchess of Kendal and lived to enjoy her ill-gotten gains until she was into her eighties. But George had the support of his other mistress Madame Kielman-segge – the enormous one nicknamed the Elephant – who rivalled Schulenberg in rapacity and eventually became the Countess of Darlington; also of his Turkish servants Mustapha and Mahomet whom he had captured in battle. (George was a courageous soldier.) An Englishman acidly observed, 'A flight of hungry Hanoverians, like so many famished vultures, fell with keen eyes and bended talons on the fruitful soil of England.' George, shy, suspicious and in unknown territory, naturally needed the support of his companions; however their greed (the pickings in England were rich) did nothing to further the new king's popularity.

In a blossoming pro-Stuart atmosphere the Jacobites finally raised the standard for James III in Scotland in September 1715. But the important towns of Edinburgh, Stirling and Glasgow stayed loyal to 'the wee, wee German Lairdie' (as George was contemptuously described by Scots Jacobites) and so did much of the Scottish nobility. Had the Jacobite leaders acted decisively they could have tipped the uncertain scales against George but they did not do so. They allowed a Jacobite force to straggle into England where it was defeated at Preston on 13 November 1715. On the same day, over the border, the inconclusive battle of Sheriffmuir was fought and the Highlanders followed their normal routine after a fight, particularly an inglorious one, and went home. In effect the Jacobite rebellion was broken but its star had yet to arrive and it was not until the end of December that James Francis Edward put in an appearance. Once landed he showed a typical Stuart mixture of stubbornness and weakness, and at the beginning of February 1716 returned to France. The Hanoverian succession was solidified, without England's loyalty being put to the real test.

Thirty years later in 1745 much the same pattern was repeated. The Young Pretender, Bonnie Prince Charlie, had far more charm than his father, attracted romantic legends like barnacles and caused greater panic in England. But he too lacked decision and failed either to lead successfully himself or to delegate authority properly. Yet again more Scots fought on the Hanoverian than the Stuart side, and this was the last throw of the Stuart dice.

In 1715 George and his ministers behaved with moderation towards the rebels (a pattern not, alas, repeated after Culloden in 1746 when hounded Jacobites rightly quoted Tacitus, 'Where they make a desert they call it peace'). But in 1715 only a few noblemen were convicted of treason and lesser lights sent to the American colonies as convicts. Among those few sentenced to death was the Earl of Nithsdale who earned a minor immortality by being one of a handful of prisoners ever to escape from the Tower of London. The escape was due to his wife Winifred's courage and initiative, for it was she who smuggled him out disguised as her maid. Throughout George's reign the Whigs, who had been the most enthusiastic supporters of the Hanoverian succession, remained dominant. Among those who swam quickly to the top were the Earls of Stanhope and Sunderland, the second-generation gentleman Charles Townshend, supported by his less exalted cousin Robert Walpole. Until 1720 the Whigs concentrated their attention on keeping in with the powerful Hanoverians, then trying to curtail their influence over the king; blocking George's attempts to put Hanover's interest before England's, and fighting between themselves for supreme power.

George was not as stupid, nor was his English as bad, as his reputation suggests. In the early days he proved that he could be firm and attended Cabinet meetings regularly. But he had never been interested

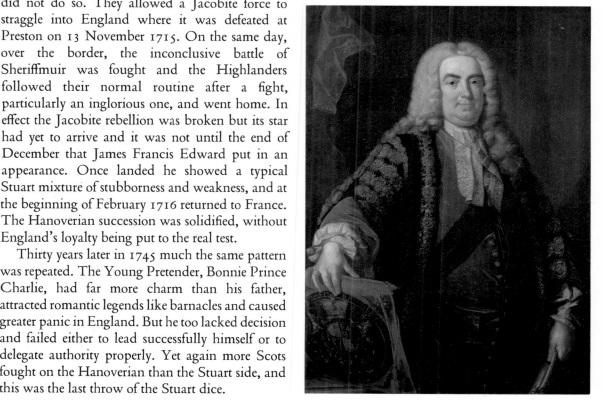

Right Robert Walpole.

in England as such and what he had learned since his arrival had not enchanted him, a nobility lacking in due deference, an obstreperous Parliament and a noisy populace. It only required some impetus to lessen his interest in its government and this was supplied in 1717 when a row erupted between George and the Prince of Wales. The two Georges had never got on well and after a stupid quarrel about the christening of the Prince of Wales's latest child, the heir and his wife were banished from court and separated from their children. Thereafter bad blood between father and sons became a Hanoverian tradition.

The Prince of Wales was slightly more intelligent than his father and had an infinitely more intelligent wife, Caroline of Anspach, and their banished court at Leicester House became the focus for all discontented, ambitious politicians. This grew into another Hanoverian tradition. The most important result of the royal quarrel was that the Prince of Wales was banned from Cabinet meetings. Previously he had interpreted for his father as his English was more fluent and slowly George ceased to attend. The seeds of parliamentary monarchy were thus further watered, with the shift of emphasis away from the king to the king's ministers.

The man who eventually tilted the balance by taking full advantage of George's absences to establish his own power was Robert Walpole. Usually acknowledged as the first Prime Minister in any modern understanding of the word, Walpole's route to power was not strewn with roses. He came from the Norfolk squirearchy, but society remained mobile, and he always had a bluff self-confidence. Despite the prevalence of bribery and corruption, which Walpole himself was expert at manipulating, he managed to inspire an aura of personal reliability which was not altogether misplaced. In 1717 Walpole's star was in the descendent but it rose when he became an habitué of Leicester House, formed a deep friendship with Caroline of Anspach, slowly won the trust of the Prince of Wales and in 1720 managed to effect a reconciliation between the king and his son.

Walpole's position was therefore improved when the South Sea Bubble burst. This had little to do with the South Seas and was the extraordinary speculative mania into which virtually everybody in Britain who had any money plunged, putting their cash into hundreds of daft, get-rich-quick schemes from trading in human hair to making oil from sunflower seeds. When the schemes collapsed the ruined disillusioned citizens shouted both for the culprits' blood and for a saviour. With a touch of genius later emulated by Charles de Gaulle,

Walpole retired to Norfolk before the crisis reached bursting point. Slowly the clamour grew for the return of a Whig minister who had not been in office when the government itself had started the speculative craze, who had not been personally involved (in fact Walpole had speculated but only minimally) and was free from the stench of corruption which hung over the court and other leading Whigs. George had the sense to accede to the clamour, even though he personally detested the upstart Walpole.

From 1721 until George's death Walpole increased his grip; aided by the fortuitous deaths of Earls Sunderland and Stanhope, he persuaded George to trust and rely upon him until he was indeed the first minister in the land. Walpole reorganized England's finances – he was the greatest finance minister since Thomas Cromwell – and set her firmly on the path of economic stability and growth, at home and overseas, for which the later Cromwellian revolution had prepared her. The unloved William III's curtailment of French power also played its part because it was not an exhausted Holland that benefitted but a thriving, thrusting England. Walpole's greatest strengths were his understanding of his countrymen – he became the personification of John Bull – and of Parliament.

George's general lack of interest and interference encouraged the arts as much as the political sphere. A brilliant crop of writers continued to flourish during his reign, Daniel Defoe (*Robinson Crusoe* was published in 1719), Jonathan Swift (*Gulliver's Travels* in 1720), Alexander Pope, Joseph Steele and Richard Addison. They all sharpened their satirical knives on the rapacity and corruption which the Hanoverians had introduced, albeit not unassisted by true-born Englishmen. George himself once said in his bad English, 'I hate all boets and bainters', but he had a love of music and the Anglo-German genius of Frederick Handel bloomed under his patronage. Handel's *Water Music* was composed for a royal fête on the Thames in 1717, though his masterpiece *The Messiah* did not appear until the reign of George II when the King established a tradition by rising for the 'Hallelujah Chorus'.

George died in June 1727, aged sixty-seven, appropriately on a visit to his beloved Hanover where he was duly buried. If his gifts to England were negative, they were most usefully so. George never tried to overplay his hand, he had a passive solidity and the good sense to back Robert Walpole. The citizens of Great Britain assuredly made the right decision, when from the two unsatisfactory alternatives, they chose the House of Hanover rather than the House of Stuart.

George III

r. 1760-1820

'Farmer George.'

In recent years George III's reputation has swung violently from the mad king who lost America to a paragon of virtue and sagacity who was the most cultured monarch ever to sit on the English throne. His apparent failures were due to bad luck and his being the victim of a physical illness whose symptoms seemed like insanity.

George was born in London on 4 June 1738. Perhaps fortunately he was a premature baby, because had he arrived a month later it would have been the date on which the American colonies issued their Declaration of Independence. He was the eldest son of Frederick who was in turn George II's eldest son, and Augusta of Saxe-Gotha. She was the dominant influence and his father, known as 'poor Fred', died before his son's thirteenth birthday whereupon George became the heir-apparent. The new Prince of Wales, or his mother and her close friend Lord Bute, followed the family tradition and opposed George II. During these years of being taught how to rule by Lord Bute, George was supposed to have fallen in love with a low-born Quakeress Hannah Lightfoot whom some gossips said he secretly married. The Lightfoot affair is wrapped in mystery but it seems unlikely that George married her because Lord Bute had instilled far too strong a sense of his royal responsibilities. In one of his youthful essays George wrote, 'The interest of my country shall ever be my first care, my own inclinations shall ever submit to it.'

In 1759 he became deeply enamoured of a more socially acceptable girl, Lady Sarah Lennox, a descendant of Charles II and Louise de Quer-ouaille. Lord Bute and particularly his mother opposed the match and George dutifully, if reluctantly acceded to their wishes. His grandfather George II died suddenly on 25 October 1760 and the next day twenty-two-year-old George was proclaimed king. Just under a year later he married the girl his mother had selected for him, Charlotte of Mecklenburg-Strelitz. Until the final distressing years it was a happy marriage and George could have done worse. Charlotte was plain, not over-bright and puritanical but George was seldom drawn towards intelligent women (the novelist and diarist Fanny Burney was an exception) and himself had strong moral convictions.

When George ascended the throne he was pleasant rather than good looking, with his heavy features, bulbous eyes and thick mouth. But he had a clear complexion, excellent teeth and a melodious voice and was the first King of England for nearly fifty years to speak English like a native. One matter in which his possessive mother had firmly instructed him was to 'convince this nation that you are not only an Englishman born and bred, but that you are also by inclination.' In his first speech to Parliament George duly echoed his mother, 'Born and bred in this country, I glory in the name of Britain.' The shy uncertain young man remained heavily under the influence of his mother and Lord Bute, both of whom saw themselves as powers behind the throne. (Frequent references were made to Queen Isabella, Roger Mortimer and the young Edward III, publicly and privately.)

Later accusations that Lord Bute taught his charge to be an autocratic monarch have been proved untrue. George was thoroughly versed in the English triumvirate of King, Church and Parliament and was horrified by the theory of 'the Divine Right of Kings', but his own words provide some clues to his limitations. He wrote, 'Thus have we created the noblest constitution the human mind is capable of framing'; 'This people will never refuse anything to a sovereign who they know will be the defender of their liberties'; and that all he wanted to do was 'to put an end to those unhappy distinctions of party called Whigs and Tories.'

George tried not so much to put the clock back as to keep it exactly where it was and how he thought it should be. The world's noblest constitution must not be altered but the right balance between a

Opposite George III.

unified strong Parliament and a strong king must be re-achieved because the king was the guardian of his people's liberty. George was the first person, but by no means the last, to try to banish party divisions. If only there could be a coalition of all the best talents from all sides! has been a frequent cry since his day. But man is a quarrelsome, argumentative animal and the English innovation of a party political system had developed into an effort to recognize and discipline this fact. In the latter half of the eighteenth century the parties (or factions) were in a particularly messy state and one sympathizes with

George's desire to be rid of them, but trying to do so was like Canute stopping the tide coming in.

To put his ideas into practice George had to break the Whig supremacy which had existed since 1714 but his early attempts to restore the unified authority of the king were not successful. Between 1760 and 1770 there were six ministries – the Duke of Newcastle's, the Earl of Bute's, George Grenville's, the Marquis of Rockingham's, William Pitt the Elder's and the Duke of Grafton's – several near misses and nearly five hundred changes of office. Apart from the constant ministerial crises, these years were disturbed at home by the activities of John Wilkes. Ex-member of the notorious Hellfire Club and personal libertine, Wilkes was an unlikely upholder of 'the English Liberty Tree' but for a period uphold it he did. Wilkes edited the *North Briton*, one of the many broadsheets which mixed serious grievance with scurrilous attacks on leading figures. On 23 April 1763 – an auspicious date, St George's Day – Wilkes launched a particularly swingeing attack. Instead of ignoring it, the Prime Minister George Grenville, urged on by George, had Wilkes arrested on a general warrant which specified no particular charge. After a furore in which Wilkes was released on a writ of Habeas Corpus and stirred up the London mob, he fled to France (he was hopelessly in debt.)

But by 1768 Wilkes was back. In the meantime Lord Rockingham's ministry had declared that general warrants were indeed dangerous and illegal, so Wilkes changed tactics and stood for Parliament as a champion of the people in one of the least bribeable of constituencies, Middlesex. After he had been elected George demanded his arrest and expulsion from Parliament, there were more scenes with Wilkes being released by the London mob, re-elected and re-expelled. Wilkes's radicalism was suspect; later he became a respectable citizen and was actually received at court. What he reflected was the growing frustration and resentment of the lower classes whose only official means of redress was their right to petition Parliament. At their worst they were a terrifying mob but they were also 'the people' and their determination to be heard was mounting.

It was Lord North who, when he became Prime Minister in 1770, tamed Wilkes by refusing to prosecute him. North seemed the answer to George's prayer, an odd-looking but personally pleasant man who led a blameless private life, an excellent manager of Parliament, yet prepared to listen to his king and carry back his wishes. In smoother waters North might have gone down as one of Britain's better prime ministers but he hit the stormy waves of the first colonial rebellion and has been bracketed with his king as 'the man who lost

Below Augusta, Princess of Wales, George III's mother.

Opposite Lord Bute.

America'. The American colonists were already growling when Lord North took office and their basic grievance was the English Parliament's right to impose taxes on them. The American War of Independence now seems inevitable; the very idea that the vast, twentieth century super-power should have remained under British jurisdiction for another hundred and fifty or more years seems ridiculous. But the vast countries of Canada and Australia did, and it was not until long after independence that the immigrants who made the United States flooded in. But Canada was always bitterly divided by its British and French colonization; Australia was only colonized after the loss of America and initially by convict labour; while America was mainly hardy British stock reared on the traditions of Cromwell and the Whigs but minus the landed aristocracy and caste system which the home-grown Whigs had introduced. The American colonists certainly wanted a semi-autonomous state freed from the English Parliament's apron strings, and as there was only a handful of men in England in the 1770s capable of accepting this idea, let alone implementing it, the inevitability is probably accurate. As George Washington said, 'It has been a kind of destiny.'

Nevertheless, if either George III or Lord North had been capable of understanding the mood of the colonists, Washington and America's destiny could certainly have been delayed. The colonists did not set out with the idea of complete independence and it was only when their petitions were rejected and their envoy Benjamin Franklin humiliated in London that the militancy spread. Even then there was no certain line from the first shots fired at Lexington and Bunker Hill in 1775 and the Declaration of Independence in 1776, to General Cornwallis's final surrender at Yorktown in 1782. But England was ill-equipped to fight a long war against determined adversaries fired with English-bred ideals. Since Cromwell's day the country had possessed no standing army and there was a horror of allowing anybody to control a large military force. Economically the war was crippling and when the merchants joined those few who had advocated early concessions, American independence became merely a matter of time.

George's reactions were typical. He told Lord North 'firmness is the characteristic of the Englishman', and 'the parent's heart is still affectionate to the penitent child.' That firmness on shifting sands was not a good idea and that the American child's heart was unpenitent did not occur to him. He kept poor North in office long after he had recognized that the war was unlikely to be won and certainly not by him. But George never

Gent.   No Gent.   & Re gent!!

lost his own courage and in the end he accepted his shattering defeat with dignity. When North finally resigned in 1782 George was faced with the resurgent Whigs. He had to accept three allegedly Whig ministries, Lord Rockingham's, Lord Shelburne's and an extraordinary coalition of Lord North and Charles James Fox; and he grew so depressed that he contemplated retiring to Hanover (which he had never visited.)

In December 1783 George showed what he had learned in his twenty-three years as king, namely a command of political tactics. In an astonishing coup he ousted the Whigs and installed a prime minister of his choice, twenty-four year old William Pitt the Younger. Pitt's ministry was defeated sixteen times in its first year of office and was kept there solely by the king. However Pitt's confidence grew and with one short break he remained as prime minister until his death in 1806. By one side Pitt is regarded as the saviour of his country and proof of the king's excellent political judgement; and by the other as the man who, supported by his king, enacted the most repressive legislation England has ever known: the 'Gagging Acts'. Pitt was particularly hated by contemporary radicals because he had originally fought for parliamentary and other reforms. In his first decade, until war broke out with revolutionary France, England undoubtedly surged forward. She picked herself up from the American trauma, sought new trade and colonies and changed into the full gear of the 'Industrial Revolution'.

Radicalism and discontent also grew, fuelled first by the vast industrial changes, then by the French Revolution. Most members of the ruling class from the king downwards, Whig and Tory, grew equally terrified that the England they knew would collapse and their terror was reflected in Pitt's 'Gagging Acts'. But England did not follow the French path. This can be attributed partly to the fact that she had been along it with Oliver Cromwell, partly to the English gentry's greater interest in the welfare of their country and in a curious way to their conservatism which had left the disorganized structure of English society unchanged for years. Nobody had a clear picture what was happening – the industrial activity was occurring outside London and it was Manchester which became the world's first industrial city. The reformers never threw up a great leader, and the structure was just sound enough to stand the strain.

George's personal popularity also helped, and when Lord Nelson died defeating the French fleet at Trafalgar in 1805 and Napoleon threatened England with invasion, it was clear whom the majority of Englishmen supported – their king and

his ministers. George had become the first monarch with whom the people identified as 'one of us' or at least what we might be. He was 'Farmer George', not over-clever but not stupid either, interested in sensible things like botany and agriculture, hard-working, personally kind, a devoted husband and father of a large family. In fact George did not manage his family well (he and Charlotte had fifteen children.) His relationship with his eldest son, later the Prince Regent and then George IV, was as disastrous as those between the unloving George I and George II and their offspring. The rebellious 'Prinny' became the boon companion of that other disreputable but more talented John Wilkes figure, Charles James Fox, whose radical-

ism was as suspect as Wilkes's but who also from time to time upheld 'the Liberty Tree' in some brilliant speeches and occasionally actions.

In 1788 George suffered his first major break-down, though he had been seriously ill in 1765 and his symptoms then were later linked to his 'madness'. For months he foamed at the mouth, talked incessantly for twenty-four hours at a time, frequently screamed sexual and other obscenities unknown to his normal, decorous conversation, and allegedly held a conversation with an oak-tree which he imagined to be Frederick of Prussia. By modern standards his treatment was horrendous, his mouth gagged, burning poultices applied to his body to drive out the evil humours, strapped in a

Opposite top Queen Charlotte, George III's wife, painted by Thomas Gainsborough.

Opposite bottom A contemporary cartoon provoked by the outrageous behaviour of the Prince Regent.

Above The Battle of Bunker Hill, 1775.

chair for hours (which in his lucid moments he ironically called his 'coronation chair'.) But George recovered and in the next twelve years suffered only a few minor attacks. Although his physical condition deteriorated and by 1805 he was nearly blind, it was not until 1810 that he lapsed into the condition which lasted until his death.

For years it was simply accepted that George III had suffered from periodic outbreaks of insanity which finally overwhelmed him in 1810. His unkindest critics implied that he had been mad all his life (hence the loss of America.) Then came the psychological explanations; George had suffered from repressed sexuality or an Oedipus complex or had succumbed to cumulative stress. In the 1930s porphyria was identified, a rare metabolic disease which can poison the nervous system and in extreme cases the brain and therefore seem like insanity. George III's symptoms were later analyzed from his doctors' reports and it was decided that he might have suffered from porphyria rather than mental unbalance. The defenders of George's reputation argue that the distinction is important because it redeems him not only from the slur of insanity but from the charges that he was mad all his life. The arguments also show how great a stigma we still attach to mental illness.

The one period when it would have been useful had the king been ill was in 1801 when the Act of Union between England and Ireland was effected. After the major Irish rebellion of 1798 which had been nurtured in Dublin's semi-autonomous Parliament, William Pitt decided that union was the only solution. But he also thought concessions to the Irish discontent were necessary and he promised that if the Irish Parliament would vote itself out of existence, he would implement Catholic Emancipation and thereby remove the restrictions on Irish Catholics holding public office. But George was in one of his lucid periods and considered that to emancipate Catholics would be to betray his Anglican coronation oath, and Pitt was forced into resignation. In any circumstances Pitt would have had a difficult task to get Catholic Emancipation passed; it was only twenty years since the vicious anti-Catholicism of the Gordon Riots had swept the country. With the king's backing Pitt had the strength to force through the measure; without it he was helpless and the Act of Union came into being in an atmosphere of betrayal which boded ill for the future relationship of England and Ireland.

George's reign effectively ended in 1810. The eruption of popular grievance known as the Luddite Riots, the assassination of the Prime Minister Spencer Perceval in 1812, the succession of Lord Liverpool who filled the post for fifteen years, the

Duke of Wellington's final defeat of Napoleon at Waterloo, the frenetic industrialization, the booming birthrate, the growing demands for reform, all passed him by. For ten long nightmare, Lear-like years George shambled round Windsor Castle, an

Above The Battle of Trafalgar, 1805.

unkempt, neglected figure for eventually his devoted wife became frightened and turned against him. Scant interest was shown by his large family whom a contemporary described without too much exaggeration, 'Good God, what a set they are . . .

rogues, laggards, fools and whores.' It was an infinitely sad and undeserved end for a man who had been devoted to his country and, in however reactionary a way, had provided sufficient stability to see it through sixty tumultuous years.

Victoria

r. 1837-1901

'I will be good.'

In 1818 there was a panic about the lack of legitimate children among George III's progeny which produced a rash of royal marriages. Among them was one between Edward Duke of Kent and Victoria of Saxe–Coburg and on 24 May 1819 a daughter was born of this dynastic union at Kensington Palace and christened Alexandrina Victoria. Eight month's later the Duke of Kent died and by 1830 it had become apparent that his daughter would be the successor to the crown after her uncle William, Duke of Clarence. When William IV himself died on 20 June 1837 and Victoria was summoned from her bedchamber to be informed that she was queen, she was just eighteen. As she said her childhood had been a sad, rather melancholy affair. Fatherless and bereft of companionship, she was alternatively bullied and wheedled by Sir John Conroy (another gentleman who saw himself as the power behind the throne) and over-protected by her ambitious, embittered mother.

It was a tribute to Victoria's strength of character that she emerged as well as she did. She had a quick, simple intelligence allied to a passionate nature; her dashing, inky writing with its frequent underlinings and exclamation marks emphasizes her positive mind. She was stubborn, courageous and honest. Mr Gladstone later described her as the most womanly of all women but she was also the most queenly of all queens, supremely conscious of the position in which destiny had placed her.

When Victoria ascended the throne Britain was changing at a faster rate than at any time in its history, and among the changes which could have occurred was the removal of the monarchy for the second time. There had been ten years of the 'mad' George III, followed by another ten of George IV who had squandered every talent except his artistic taste, with a further seven of William IV who if not quite as silly a Billy as anticipated had not polished the crown's lustre. But suddenly it was being worn by an enthusiastic, fresh, attractive girl and the country waited to see how she would handle affairs. Victoria started off extremely well, assisted by the current Prime Minister Lord Melbourne, her dear 'Lord M.'

Despite her strong will, the womanly side of Victoria needed a man whom she could trust and revere. Her uncle Leopold of Saxe–Coburg, king of the newly independent Belgians, was one such figure and Lord Melbourne was another. He was a charming, ageing cynic whose philosophy was, 'When in doubt what should be done, do nothing.' Officially a Whig, he believed reform to be the work of unrepresentative agitators. His influence on the young Victoria did not increase her awareness of the country's social problems or the need for change. Nor was Melbourne's indolent cynicism helpful in the 'Bedchamber Crisis' or the affair of Lady Flora Hastings. In the former he allowed Victoria's fondness for him and fear that her beloved Whig court ladies would be replaced by hated Tory ones, to keep the Tory Sir Robert Peel out of office, and himself in. When Lady Flora, who belonged to the queen's unhappy childhood, became ill and started to swell around the stomach, he let Victoria believe tittle-tattle about pregnancy and Sir John Conroy and then behave in a high-handed manner (though she was filled with contrition when Lady Flora died of a cancerous growth.) The result of both affairs was a decline in the young queen's popularity and two years after her accession it was not much higher than her uncles' had been. However, Lord Melbourne gave his charge some idea of the limitations of constitutional monarchy and certainly provided the close, friendly relationship she needed in the early days.

If the crown were to be secured and the queen's popularity restored, it seemed essential that she marry forthwith. Victoria had met her cousins Prince Albert and Ernest of Saxe–Coburg–Gotha in 1836 and since then had accepted her beloved

Opposite Queen Victoria in her coronation robes.

Above Princess Victoria aged eleven.

and privately. Over the years more Englishmen had become more convinced that they were God's chosen people, and Albert had to fight his way through this barrier. Much as his wife adored him she was the queen, and he had to cope with an emotionalism, a love of late nights and gossip which were alien to his disciplined, early rising, serious-minded temperament. But they both enjoyed music, riding and animals, particularly dogs.

If Victoria revelled in her role as doting wife, she was never able to produce a similar enthusiasm for that of mother. She positively disliked child-bearing and thought a much better method should have been arranged by the Almighty, but she did her duty. The Princess Royal (Vicky) was born in 1840, the Prince of Wales (Bertie) in 1841, Alice in 1843, Alfred in 1844, Helena in 1846, Louise in 1848, Arthur in 1850, Leopold in 1853 and Beatrice in 1857. The royal couple were extremely lucky in an era when medical knowledge had not kept pace with the general scientific progress because all their children survived to be adults. Their only serious worry was Leopold who inherited the dreaded disease, haemophilia. Prince Albert probably enjoyed his role as father more than that of husband, and it was he who popularized the Christmas tree in Britain as the focal point for the children. Both he and his wife took great pleasure in family life and in 1854 country-loving Albert finally persuaded his town-loving wife to buy Osborne House on the Isle of Wight; though it was a mutual love of Scotland which led to a new castle being built at Balmoral in 1853. Both residences were places where the family could relax in a compara-tively informal atmosphere.

Albert's only serious failure as a father, was his handling of his eldest son Bertie. It was the eldest daughter Vicky who had inherited her father's brain and Albert's attempts to turn Bertie into an intellectual were disastrous. Once freed from the paternal reins the Prince of Wales reacted by behaving in a toned-down 'Victorian' version of the Hanoverian libertine.

Slowly, tactfully Albert assumed more of the political burdens until his wife was claiming, 'We women are not *made* for governing.' In the latter part of the 1840s and in the 1850s, with the repeal of the Corn Laws splitting Sir Robert Peel's new Con-servative party down the middle and the general instability of political life, Albert's influence was considerable and on the whole beneficial. He increased his wife's interest in the problems that industrialization had brought to Britain, the appalling housing and factory conditions and the exploitation of labour, particularly women and children. But he also helped implant in his wife's

uncle Leopold's plan that she marry the younger Prince Albert, but when the moment came she showed a reluctance worthy of Elizabeth I. However, like Elizabeth she had an eye for male pulchritude and fifty-four years later in 1893 was able to recall her engagement day, 'Albert had been out hunting & looked so beautiful in a green coat with top boots, & that heavenly expression in his eyes.' On 10 May 1840 the young couple were married; unlike her illustrious predecessor Victoria was eminently suited to the role of adoring wife, and for her the marriage became the nearest approach to heaven on earth.

Albert had a harder furrow to plough, publicly

mind the idea that royalty, because of its intimate connections with the crowned heads of Europe, had a peculiar insight into foreign affairs. There were many battles with the jaunty, pragmatic Lord Palmerston who had no such belief and resorted to withholding decisions on foreign affairs from Her Majesty until after they had been implemented.

Albert's stock sank during the bungled Crimean War when he was believed to be pro the hated Russians, but Victoria increased her popularity when she instituted the Victoria Cross as the highest single award for valour, to be given to non-commissioned soldiers as well as officers. Victoria herself cared greatly for the citizens of her expanding Empire *en masse*, but had little understanding of their mass problems though she could always be touched by individual need.

The happiest, proudest day of Victoria's married life came in 1851 when she opened the Great Exhibition in the Crystal Palace in Hyde Park. She wrote, 'Albert's dearest name is immortalized with this *great* conception, *his* own, and my *own* dear country showed she was *worthy* of it.' Karl Marx, who had already issued *The Manifesto of the Communist Party* and was busy in the British Museum assembling the material which would in *Das Kapital* shake the foundations of the capitalist world, said, 'With this exhibition the world bourgeoisie erects its pantheon in the new Rome, where it proudly places on show the deities it has fabricated.' It was an accurate if incomplete assessment. For Albert the exhibition was an affirmation of his belief that his adopted country had led the world in a remarkable scientific and industrial revolution which could and must benefit the whole of mankind. Without Albert's unre-

mitting effort, knowledge and tact the startling glass structure of the Crystal Palace would certainly never have been erected and filled with objects from the sublime to the ridiculous.

Albert, for whom his wife finally obtained the title of Prince Consort in 1857, lived to see his first grandchild, the future Kaiser Wilhelm II, but on 14 December 1861 in his forty-third year he died. Albert killed himself by his grinding sense of duty which drove him to spend hours, at a time when he was already ill, amending despatches to Abraham Lincoln, which unamended might have led to Britain's armed intervention in the American Civil War. Albert earned the title of 'the Good', insufferably so to some twentieth century minds, but he really was a good, if over-conscientious man and his distracted widow's lament was not too biased, '... her adored, precious, perfect & great husband, her dear Lord & Master, to whom this Nation owed more than it can ever truly know.'

Had Victoria followed her husband to the grave, as she would then have wished, her reputation would have been high. The young queen, wife and mother who had not only refurbished the monarchy's image but had given it a new glow to be emulated by every respectable citizen. In fact Victoria's position as the ideal wife and mother was part of the constant paradox of the age which now

bears her name. The Victorians tried to turn women into docile, submissive, spiritual creatures whose preserve was the home, with men as the dominating, aggressive figures who operated in the great big world. Yet the woman on whom they modelled their image was the strong-minded head of the largest empire the world had known, who reacted to any encroachment on her position or infringements of her rights with fierce pride and jealousy.

Had Victoria died ten years after Albert her reputation would have been dismal. For a period it was accepted that the poor queen had suffered a shattering loss and could not face the ordeal of appearing in public. Victoria's grief was genuine, her sense of loss irrevocable, but she threw herself into them with every ounce of her emotional, stubborn nature. For the best part of a decade she immured herself on the Isle of Wight or at Balmoral, keeping some grip on her ministers' actions, but generally growing stouter and more stubborn. Mr Gladstone told his wife that the Queen now weighed 11 stone 8 lbs which, as he commented, was 'rather much for her height!' Her devoted private secretary remarked on 'the long, unchecked habit of self-indulgence that now makes it impossible for her, without some degree of nervous agitation to give up, even for ten minutes, the gratification of a single inclination, or even *whim*.'

Among the queen's more successful whims was *Leaves from the Journal of Our Life in the Highlands* published in 1868, which temporarily turned her into a best-seller and prompted Mr Disraeli's flattering remark, 'We authors' Ma'am!' But Her Majesty's deep friendship with her Scottish servant John Brown, created an immense scandal. In addition to the 'To Let' notices pinned to the railings of Buckingham Palace, scurrilous verses about 'Mrs Brown' circulated and by 1870, fired by the example of the Paris Commune, republicanism was on the upsurge again. Unfortunately for himself and the newish Liberal party of which he was now the leader, the man who had to deal with 'the royalty question' was Mr Gladstone.

William Ewart Gladstone and Benjamin Disraeli, the two giant figures of the nineteenth-century political arena, afford a further example of the contradictions of the Victorian age. Gladstone was a serious-minded, high-principled believer in the perfectability of the human race and God's infinite mercy. He was also a passionate gentleman who sublimated some of his sexuality into his endeavours to rescue prostitutes from their lives of sin. He became 'the People's William', a demi-god accorded the sort of worship nowadays reserved for pop singers and football stars, an internationalist who thundered against Britain's grabbing of land.

Disraeli was the cynic with the biting wit, only too aware of mankind's frailties and imperfectability, the outsider who had come up the hard way. To an extent Disraeli had more understanding of 'the people' than his rival and in his novel *Sybil* had written of 'the two nations' of England, the privileged and the poor; but he did not become the people's hero. It was Disraeli who encouraged 'the jingo spirit', the romance of empire and Britain's grabbing as much land as she could.

Gladstone was unfitted to deal with Queen Victoria in the situation of the early 1870s. Her famous remark that Mr G. addressed her as if she were a public meeting had validity; in fact he was an excellent conversationalist but he had no small talk and disliked gossip. The queen received the full barrage of his many-layered intellect and complained bitterly that he took hours to reach any point. They were both stubborn people and while Victoria's mind had largely atrophied when Albert died – as she said, '*his* wishes, *his* plans ... his views about *every* thing are to be my laws!' – Gladstone's was constantly on the move. They therefore clashed on the need for reform, but Victoria also had a very fundamental jealousy of Gladstone as 'the People's William' poaching on her territory. As he battled to persuade the queen to re-enter public life and to give the Prince of Wales more responsibility, the

Opposite The opening of the Great Exhibition in Hyde Park in 1851.

Above Balmoral Castle.

Above A contemporary cartoon of Mr Gladstone.

time and their friendship matured into full, heady bloom. Disraeli was not in awe of Her Majesty (curiously Gladstone was) and knew exactly how to handle her. He flattered her vanity and wisdom (not always unjustifiably), kept his official reports to the minimum, was personal and gossipy and avoided the fatal head-on approach. In fact Victoria herself was now ready to return to the world and under Disraeli's encouraging eye she opened Parliament, attended functions (including the unveiling of the Albert Memorial in Kensington in 1876) and appeared at royal weddings and garden parties. Also in 1876 Disraeli secured the title Empress of India for his queen. It was not a popular move – objections ranged from its being ridiculous, unnecessary or unconstitutional – but it appealed to the romantic, imperialistic side of the queen and her prime minister.

The issue which overshadowed much of Disraeli's 1874–80 ministry, and brought Glad-stone back to the centre of the stage, was 'the Eastern Question.' This focused on the corruption and weakness of the Turkish Ottoman Empire, particularly in its Balkan domains, and the fear of despotic Russia's expansion into the area. When the Turks massacred thousands of their rebellious Balkan Christian subjects, two camps formed in Britain. One, headed by Mr Gladstone, derided the Russian menace, supported Balkan nationalism, demanded that Britain cease to prop up the rotten Ottoman Empire and regarded the issue as a moral one. The other, headed by Queen Victoria and Mr Disraeli, considered the morality lay in Britain's strength and interests and that it was essential to counter Russia's aggression by continuing support for the Turks.

The political atmosphere became extraordinarily bitter and the queen was soon expressing her strong private views about 'that madman Gladstone' and 'the so-called but not real Liberals' who always behaved in the most shameful way and had no wish to help their country or their widowed and lonely sovereign. What Victoria failed absolutely to understand was that the two-party political system had emerged from loosely allied Whigs and Tories into Liberals and Conservatives who owed their allegiance not to the crown but to the people via their parties because the passing of the 1832 Reform Act and the 1867 Franchise Act had given more people the vote; and under Disraeli and Gladstone the parties represented different beliefs and ways of governing the country. During the furore over the Eastern Question Victoria grew so excited that even Disraeli moaned, 'The Faery writes every day and telegraphs every hour.' In 1878 he attended the Congress of Berlin to sort out the eastern problems,

previously amiable, if never close relationship deteriorated into one which on the queen's side sometimes came close to hatred. The actual effects of Her Majesty's opposition to reforming Gladstonian Liberalism have been debated but it certainly wore him down personally.

In 1874 Gladstone's ministry suddenly resigned and early the next year he retired from the leadership of the Liberal party. Queen Victoria was not upset. Mr Disraeli became prime minister for the second

except by now he was no longer plain Mr Disraeli but the Earl of Beaconsfield. He returned the hero of the hour, bringing 'Peace with Honour', having incorporated many of the Liberal demands into the treaty. Victoria recorded her satisfaction, 'High and low are delighted, except Mr Gladstone who is frantic.'

By 1880 the Conservatives had run out of steam and a General Election was called. Queen Victoria departed happily to visit her relations in Germany, certain that Mr Gladstone's recent barn-storming Midlothian campaigns would have no effect. To her unbelieving horror they had and the Liberals were returned with a thumping majority. She

threatened abdication but faced with the crunch decided that Mr Gladstone was the lesser evil and he became prime minister for the second time. His second ministry was dominated by Irish affairs because Catholic, largely peasant Ireland had found a magnetic leader in the Protestant, aristocratic figure of Charles Stewart Parnell. Victoria's Irish sympathies and understanding were not high. The Dublin crowds had insulted her beloved Albert on their one joint visit to the country, and she was surrounded at court by people who insisted that the Irish discontent was merely the work of a few agitators (in the manner of Lord Melbourne.)

Queen Victoria was helpful to Mr Gladstone in

Below The Duke of Wellington presenting a first-birthday gift to the Duke of Connaught.

the crisis which erupted over his extended Franchise Act in 1884 and averted a head-on collision between Lord and Commons. But by 1885 the Liberals had run into further difficulties over their plan to evacuate the Sudan which culminated in General Gordon's death on the steps of the Khartoum residency. Her Majesty accurately reflected the country's horror when she sent Mr Gladstone her famous, open telegram, 'These news from Khartoum are frightful, and to think that all this might have been prevented and many precious lives saved by earlier action is frightful.' (Normally all sensitive or confidential material was sent in cypher.) Later in 1885 the Liberals resigned but by 1886 they were back in office and in six whirlwind months Gladstone tried to force through a Home Rule Bill for Ireland. Had it been successful it might have solved some of the still festering Anglo–Irish problems but it failed, and Gladstone resigned with the Liberal party split down the middle over the Home Rule issue.

Lord Beaconsfield had died in 1881, gouty, rheumatic but retaining his wit, for when Queen Victoria offered to visit him at home during his last illness he said, 'No it is better not. She would only ask me to take a message to Albert.' The queen was almost as grief-stricken as by Albert's death but with Gladstone's resignation she entered into calmer waters. Her relationship with the new Conservative Prime Minister Lord Salisbury was most amiable, if lacking the personal warmth and magic of the old one with Disraeli. Her children were by now all married and she concentrated her mixture of genuine concern and practical wisdom, interference and selfishness on the problems of her proliferating grandchildren. Since being created Empress of India she had developed a passion for all things Indian, and when John Brown died in 1883 an Indian known as 'the Munshi' became her personal servant, causing as much resentment at court as Brown had, though not publicly this time.

For the longer Victoria reigned, the more she became the embodiment of the greatness of Great Britain and the Empire on which the sun would never set, and the Golden Jubilee in 1887 was an occasion for sumptuous pageantry. In 1892 the queen had to accept 'that dangerous old fanatic' Mr Gladstone, as her prime minister for the fourth time, but he finally retired in 1894 and she then had the more acceptable Lord Rosebery (though his Liberalism soon displeased her), followed by the eminently acceptable Lord Salisbury. The last ripple of anti-royalist sentiment was caused by the detested Mr Gladstone because when he died in 1898 and continents mourned the man whom the *New York Tribune* called 'the world's greatest

citizen', Queen Victoria refused even to mention his death in the Court Circular. She said, 'I am sorry for Mrs G: as for him, I never liked him, & will say nothing about him.' Her stubborn honesty was deeply resented and only redeemed by the Prince of Wales who, in the teeth of maternal opposition, acted as a pall-bearer at the great commoner's funeral in Westminster Abbey.

The apotheosis of Victoria's reign, indeed of the concepts of empire and monarchical rule, occurred at the Diamond Jubilee in 1897. The sixtieth anniversary of her accession was Victoria's final, never-to-be forgotten day. But she was ageing, death had taken a heavy toll of old friends and younger relations, and though she struggled through the celebrations the old zest was gone. Until the end of 1900 she continued to attend to ministerial papers but on 13 January 1901 the last entry appeared in the Journal she had kept so faithfully from the age of thirteen. On 22 January 1901 she died peacefully at Osborne, surrounded by her children and

grandchildren, in her eighty-second year. The funeral procession from the Isle of Wight to London, then across the capital for the last journey to Albert's mausoleum at Frogmore where Victoria's body was buried by his side, was an occasion of sombre magnificence and mass mourning.

Victoria had established the monarchy as a British institution for the foreseeable future, by the personal example of her family life, her early and later devotion to duty, and a feeling for the pulse of the country which more often than not was accurate. Unconsciously in her later years she had weakened the crown's position and facilitated the final transfer of power to Parliament. The Gladstonian Cabinet's reaction to her opposition had been the same as Lord Palmerston's and they also withheld controversial information until it was too late. When her beloved Tories returned to power, she was too old fully to appreciate what had happened and the trend continued.

When Victoria died the clear-sighted already knew that Britain had lost her industrial lead and faced the challenge of Germany and the United States. The bitterness of the Boer War had further revealed the division between pro- and anti-imperialists and the growth of the Labour movement heralded a new approach to social problems. On the long road since 1066 a plethora of contradictory characteristics had fused to make the English nation: energy, curiosity, greed, selfishness, genius for compromise, addiction to pragmatic improvisation, political maturity, dissenting bloody-mindedness, love of tradition, apologetic self-confidence. In the eighteenth century they had blossomed and in the nineteenth burst into full bloom. Whether they would carry Britain successfully through the new century, or whether she would need to make drastic readjustments, were questions asked by some of the late queen's resolutely hopeful but nonetheless enquiring, doubting subjects.

Above The Queen arriving in an open carriage at St Paul's Cathedral on 22 June 1897 for her Diamond Jubilee thanksgiving service.

149

George V

r. 1910-36

'I had no idea I was so popular.'

The second son of the Prince and Princess of Wales was born in London on 3 June 1865 and christened George Frederick Ernest Albert. His childhood was a happy one, particularly in comparison with most of his forebears', spent mainly at Sandringham, in the company of his elder brother Albert Victor (known to the family as Eddy), and three sisters, Louise born in 1867, Victoria in 1868 and Maud in 1869. (The youngest child, Alexander John, died twenty-four hours after birth in 1871). The Prince of Wales was determined that the mistakes of his own upbringing should not be repeated and had the right temperament to deal with most children: boisterous, extrovert and direct. The Princess of Wales, the beautiful Danish-born Alexandra – 'darling Princess Alix' of so many upper-class Victorian memoirs – was a disorganized, uncomplicated, warm-hearted lady. With the handicap of deafness and the knowledge of her husband's repeated, if discreet infidelity, she had a particular need of the family circle and lavished affection on her children, which was reciprocated. Until her death in 1925, for George she was always 'darling Motherdear'.

The princes' education was entrusted to the Reverend John Dalton (father of a leading minister in the first majority Labour Government of 1945, Hugh Dalton). He was a better choice than many royal tutors because in addition to a scholarly brain, he also believed in some extra-mural activity and in establishing a good relationship with his pupils. If Dalton did not succeed in turning Prince George into a scholar, he imparted his sense of order and detail and a devotion to duty. Queen Victoria further encouraged her grandson to be a model of Victorian virtue, 'I hope you will be a good, truthful boy, kind to all, humble-minded, dutiful and always trying to be of use to others!'

In 1877 the two princes were sent to naval college, not without opposition from Queen Victoria who considered the rough and tumble of naval life an unsuitable training for the heir-presumptive and his brother. In fact the life suited George admirably and he emerged from fifteen years' service in the Royal Navy with his devotion to duty and passion for detail enhanced, and a life-long love of the sea. He also learned something about his fellow men and of the world itself, his service including tours of duty in Australia, the Cape of Good Hope, the West Indies and the Mediterranean. Until 1892 it seemed that Prince George would pursue a successful naval career, as much on merit as on his royal birth.

But in 1892 Prince Eddy died suddenly from influenza which developed into pneumonia, and George became next in line to the throne after his father. His brother's death was a double blow because he and Eddy had been close and George had never seriously considered bearing the burden of kingship. However, from the angle of the British monarchy, Prince Eddy's death was almost certainly advantageous because he appeared to have inherited most of the Hanoverian vices and none of its or the House of Saxe–Coburg–Gotha's virtues. George, soon created Duke of York in honour of his new status, also acquired his brother's fiancée, Princess May of Teck, an intelligent, morally and physically upright young lady who probably also had long-term reason to be grateful for Prince Eddy's sudden demise.

Prince George and Princess May were married on a scorchingly hot day, 6 July 1893. Neither of their temperaments contained similarly scorching traits but their marriage developed into one of deep-rooted, rewarding, mutual devotion. Indeed George was soon able to write, 'I adore you sweet May', an unusually direct statement from a young man who was emotionally reserved except with his mother or sister Victoria.

His wife was even more reserved and had a permanent inability to express her feelings. This blockage went hand-in-hand with a dislike of the

Opposite George V on his horse Kildare.

processes of child-bearing and rearing even greater than Queen Victoria's but, as the old queen had before her, May did her duty. Edward (the future Edward VIII) was born in 1894 but always known to the family as David, Albert (the future George VI) in 1895, Mary in 1897, Henry in 1900, George in 1902 and the last born John in 1905. (John was, alas, epileptic and led an isolated life, dying in 1919). The serious-minded sense of duty led Princess May to subordinate her wider-ranging, livelier, more liberal mind to her husband's firm, common-sense but conservative one. Thus, while she admirably upheld Queen Victoria's conviction that she would be 'a good, devoted and useful wife', she was less than the ideal mother.

The first, and always best-beloved home was York Lodge in the grounds of the Sandringham estate. For the royal residence of a growing family it was remarkably cramped – George once wondered whether the servants lived in the tree-tops – and it was also singularly gloomy, hedged in by trees and shrubs. But it suited the unaesthetic, unsocializing, country-loving George, even if his wife had reservations. With the death of Queen Victoria and his father's accession to the throne in 1901, Prince George's horizons were perforce widened. He and his wife undertook an overseas tour to South Africa, Australasia and Canada – from which they

returned towards the end of 1901 to be created Prince and Princess of Wales – in the comparatively new roles of royal ambassadors to the Empire. In the process George shook hands 24,855 times (as he meticulously noted), and acquired a new confidence and sense of identity.

Edward VII encouraged his son to see state papers – as Queen Victoria had *not* done – and also gave him the old queen's private secretary, Sir Arthur Bigge (later Lord Stamfordham). Of Bigge, George V later said, 'He taught me how to be a King.' Soon after his return home Prince George delivered a 'Wake up England!' speech, whose frame of reference was the complacency of British manufacturers in the face of mounting competition. In other directions Englishmen, and women, had already obeyed his exhortations, and throughout his father's reign the signs that the old order was splitting at the seams became increasingly apparent.

In 1906 the Liberals reaped the harvest of awakening political and social consciousness when they were returned to power with a large majority. In 1909 Lloyd George introduced his 'People's Budget' which proposed old age pensions, to be paid for by increased duties and taxation. In their fury at this minor socialistic, soak-the-rich measure, the Conservative-dominated House of Lords threw out the Budget, thereby violating the old, hard-won

Left The royal family at Buckingham Palace in 1913.

Right The coronation of George V.

tradition that the Lords did not interfere with financial measures. In the General Election fought on the issue early in 1910, the Liberals lost their overall majority, showing how evenly divided the country was (though neither women, nor all men, yet had the vote). But the Liberals remained in power, supported by Labour and Irish MPs, and the prime minister, Herbert Asquith, announced his intention to introduce a Parliament Bill whereby the Lords' veto would be finally curtailed. As Lords and Commons donned their armour, with each side looking to the monarch for support, on 6 May 1910 Edward VII died. The country mourned 'good old Teddy' who had introduced a breath of fresh air into the reverential hush of the latter-day Victorian court. He had possessed something of the 'common touch', but had also left a mound of problems for his successor.

George V ascended the throne in a political atmosphere more bitter than for many a year, with social, labour, female and Irish unrest rumbling ominously. He noted in his diary, 'I have lost the best of friends and the best of fathers', but added, 'darling May will be my comfort as she always has been.' However, it was as Queen Mary, that his wife earned her redoubtable reputation. The stately towering figure and her shorter husband were later sometimes referred to as 'George and the dragon'; though the queen was only half an inch taller and it was the soon-famous headgear of toques that gave her height while, as already indicated, it was he, not she, who ruled the family roost. From the start the new monarch and his consort, if obviously reserved and considered dull in some quarters, transmitted an aura of devotion to duty, stability and reliability that augured well in troubled times.

In gentlemanly manner the political combatants called a truce on the Parliament Bill until the new king had found his feet. George V took seriously the monarch's rights to be consulted, to encourage and to warn his ministers. However, inexperienced as he was, and caught in the crossfire between politicians interpreting for themselves the other rights and prerogatives retained by the monarch, he spent a miserable, baffled, sometimes enraged first year as king. The Parliament Bill was passed by the Lords in August 1911, mainly because the king had finally, reluctantly, acceded to Mr Asquith's request that if necessary he exercise the monarch's prerogative of creating peers. Faced by the prospect of hundreds of Liberal peers swamping them, the Lords retreated; henceforward they could not veto any financial measure and their veto on other bills was restricted to three sessions (parliaments were also reduced from seven to five year terms).

The passing of the Parliament Act did not relieve

Above Money-raising stamps issued during World War I.

the tensions. When a fairly exhausted king and queen returned early in 1912 from the Coronation Durbar in India, they were met by massive discontent. The suffragettes led by the formidable Pankhursts had become more militant; although the king had no sympathy with 'Votes for Women', he protested forcibly to his Liberal Ministers about the women's treatment in prison, particularly forcible feeding which he considered 'something shocking, if not almost cruel'. Thousands of trade unionists had been and continued to be on strike (those who believe in the halcyon, pre-First World War days should study the history of strife- and strike-torn Britain between 1910 and 1914). But the most pressing matter was Ireland, whose nationalist MPs had given the Liberals support in order to carry Irish Home Rule.

In 1912 Asquith's Home Rule Bill passed through the Commons, to be immediately thrown out by the Lords. But by the terms of the Parliament Act it could only be rejected for three sessions, which meant it would become law in the summer of 1914. On one side were ranged the Liberals and Irish, convinced that failure this time would lead to disaster. On the other side were the Conservatives and Unionists equally convinced that Home Rule would be the disaster, focusing their opposition on loyal, Protestant Ulster forced against its will to accept southern Irish Catholic 'Rome Rule'. As the tension mounted, George V was caught in even more venomous crossfire and more ingenious political interpretations of his royal prerogatives. At times he was shaken by the fury of the battle but he emerged creditably, having tried (vainly) to solve the Ulster problem by means of an all-party conference at Buckingham Palace. By the king's refusal to act too precipitately or partially, the monarchy – which at one stage had been described as a football, being kicked by all parties – survived with its shape intact.

George V had experienced as gruelling a royal introduction as any monarch. He faced August 1914 with the gloomy expectation that Home Rule would mean the horror of civil war in Ireland, and the personal anguish of the monarch's constitutional position and involvement again to the fore. The horror that arrived in August 1914 was the First World War. As the young men of Europe and the European empires, and latterly the United States, died by their millions in the Flanders and Russian mud, the Dardanelles and Mesopotamian heat, drowned on the high seas, or fell from the skies in the new aerial warfare, King George and Queen Mary became the focus of patriotism for most of the citizens of Great Britain and its Empire.

George himself was intensely insular and

Above George V on his yacht Britannia.

Battenberg change his family name (which he did in the literal English translation of Mountbatten), and then he himself do likewise. In July 1917 George v, who had ascended the throne as the second ruler of the House of Saxe–Coburg–Gotha (even royal children took their father's name), became the first of the House of Windsor.

When a shattered, exhausted Europe ceased its blood-letting on 11 November 1918, George v had visited his armies in Flanders five times, held 450 inspections, personally decorated 50,000 of his servicemen, visited 300 military hospitals and made innumerable tours to munitions factories and bombed areas. He had also suffered an inglorious but nonetheless serious injury in Flanders in 1915, when his horse was frightened by the cheering troops, threw him violently, pinned him to the ground and fractured his pelvis. The majority of his subjects felt that the king had done his duty and more than fulfilled his royal purpose, and while the mighty Hohenzollern, Hapsburg and Romanov dynasties failed to survive the war, the new-old House of Windsor seemed more secure than ever. There were criticisms and cries for Britain to follow the European examples and rid itself of this archaic, elitist form of government. H. G. Wells launched a republican attack on the uninspiring, alien court to which George v countered, 'I may be uninspiring, but I'll be damned if I'm alien.'

Sir Edward Grey's elegaic remark on the eve of the war – 'The lights are going out all over Europe. We shall not see them lit again in our lifetime' – had not proved entirely true. The lights he cared for were dimming before 1914, and much of Europe's cultural, historical and in some areas reactionary glow had survived. Britain herself had emerged from the war, partially fought to defend the sovereignty of 'little Belgium' and the rights of small nations, with a considerably larger Empire, in the form of protectorates over defeated Turkish and German imperial territories (as had the French). But one part of the Empire wanted to depart, Ireland, and what then seemed the last act of the Anglo–Irish tragedy was played, with George v performing an effectively beneficial role. In January 1922 the Irish Free State came into being, with independent Dominion status, while six Ulster counties obtained a form of Home Rule within the United Kingdom. On the civil war which followed this betrayal, as some nationalist republican Irishmen saw it, England thankfully turned her back.

When Lloyd George's boast of 'a land fit for heroes' proved even less true than Sir Edward Grey's prophecy, it was the Labour party that benefited to the discomfort of the Liberals. In 1923 King George used his monarchical judgement and

patriotic, and had little love for Germany or his cousin, Kaiser Wilhelm II. (In earlier, happier days he had considered German a 'rotten' language and Heidelberg a 'beastly dull town'). Commendably, he was not infected by the hysterical xenophobia which led normally sane, decent English people to smash shop windows with, and attacks owners of, German names, and even to kill Dachshunds because they were German dogs. But the king was forced to accede to various anti-German demands, including one that his cousin Prince Louis of

For Your Splendid Work I Thank You

MAY 31ST 1916.

Above A souvenir of the Victory of Jutland, 31 May 1916.

Bolshevik miners, he said tartly, 'Try living on their wages before you judge them.'

As the years passed the king found himself less and less in tune with the strident, impatient new era of women with the vote, jazz, disrespectful flappers, socialists, communists, everybody demanding everything now, or in the idiom of the country whose power and prestige were notably increasing, the United States of America, 'like yesterday'. In his more irate moods he had Queen Mary to remind him that one must move with the times. After his serious illness in 1928–29, the king mellowed but when his temper did burst, the eruptions were often violent and the language extremely salty. During his long convalescence he had the comfort of his little granddaughter 'Lilibet', on whom he doted.

The ageing, ailing monarch had to face one final traumatic year. In 1931 the Statute of Westminster was promulgated, a curious, essentially English document which tried to define the twentieth-century relationship between the King-Emperor and the conglomeration of disparate countries over which he ruled. Several of the imperial countries were already independent dominions (Canada, South Africa, New Zealand and Australia, and the Irish Free State), others aspired to this status (notably India), while some were still fairly backward colonies. The linking factor in a free association of Commonwealth countries became

sent for Ramsay Macdonald to form a Government. The un-socialistic king behaved with scrupulous courtesy and impartiality to the somewhat bewildered newcomers, but noted in his diary, 'Today twenty-three years ago dear Grandmama died. I wonder what she would have thought of a Labour Government'. One can only echo, what indeed?

However, a minority Labour Government trying to govern through a hostile House of Commons, could not last long. At the General Election the Socialists were defeated and Stanley Baldwin and the Conservatives returned to power, and it was they who faced the General Strike of 1926. But the British Trade Union movement, like the British Labour party, was not a revolutionary body (a factor which their more militant, idealistic or wilder fringes failed to grasp), and the General Strike was a nine day wonder. The king's verdict on the orderly denouement of an admittedly potentially revolutionary situation was, 'Our old country can well be proud of itself . . . it shows what a wonderful people we are.' If George v had little understanding of the underlying issues and problems, he had equally little sympathy with arrogant coal-owners. When Lord Durham, a particularly wealthy coal-magnate, lambasted the

allegiance to the Crown although inherent in the Stat-ute was the situation whereby the English monarch could be the head of a Commonwealth of republics. While George V did not fully grasp the implications (few did), he understood the freedom of association and the pivotal position of the Crown.

The crisis of 1931 was the general world slump and Ramsay Macdonald's inability to continue governing with a second minority Labour adminis-tration. The king was severely criticized when he used his right to encourage, by urging Macdonald to head a National coalition government. Some said George V had overstepped his right, others that he had wanted to dish the Socialists by splitting their ranks. The Labour party was indeed split by Macdonald's action, but whether it was to their long-term disadvantage is a moot point. As a party they were left untainted by the failures of the next few years, and in the wilderness were given time for reappraisal and reorganization. George himself had no intention of overstepping constitutional boun-daries or breaking the Socialists. He was too little devious and too much of a stickler for duty for such methods, and he was following the old cry in times of stress for a coalition in the best interests of the country. The argument was more whether a National Government *was* in the best interests of the country, and whether he was the person to judge.

After the storms of 1931 George himself, if not his country, entered calmer waters. He marched with the times in agreeing to broadcast to his people in 1932, and the success of his subsequent Christmas messages gave him much satisfaction. But the warmth of the reaction during the 1935 Silver Jubilee took him completely by surprise. To the Australian Prime Minister Robert Menzies he confided, 'I had no idea I was so popular'.

By January 1936 George's strength was ebbing and via the medium of radio millions heard the words, 'the king's life is moving peacefully to its close.' On 20 January he died at Sandringham aged seventy and Queen Mary wrote, 'Am heartbroken. . . .' Many of their subjects were almost as heart-broken, and even those who opposed the monarchy had to admit the astonishing emotional grip.

In his youth Queen Victoria had told her grandson, 'It is in your power to do immense good by setting an example & keeping your dear Grandpa's name before you.' Whether the boy, or the man, had kept Albert's image before him is doubtful, but he had certainly set an example which, as a surprised George had noted, people actually liked. He had also created a new role for the monarchy, one which led a trenchant republican, Professor Harold Laski, to abandon hope of a sec-ond English republic in his lifetime because, as he wrote, the king had become 'an emollient, rather than an active umpire, between conflicting interests.'

Below The royal family entering St Paul's for the Silver Jubilee service of thanksgiving in 1935.

The royal arms of Queen Victoria and her successors

Elizabeth II

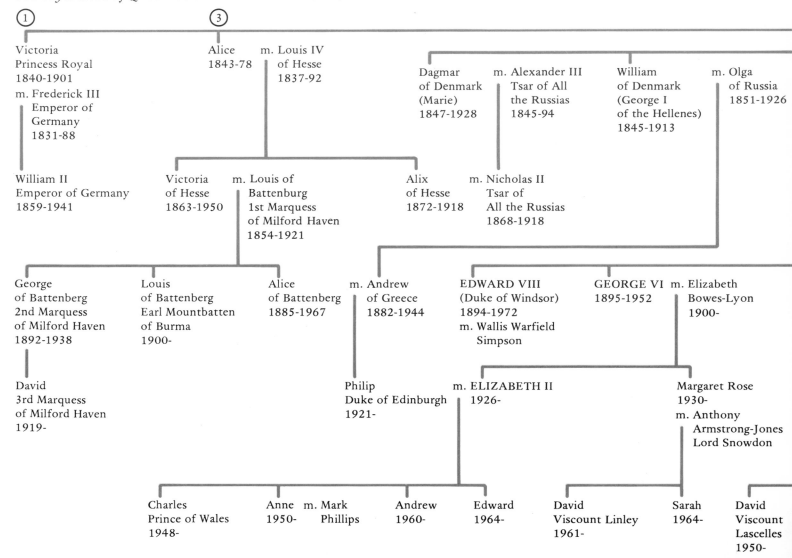

① ③

Victoria
Princess Royal
1840-1901
m. Frederick III
Emperor of
Germany
1831-88

Alice
1843-78   m. Louis IV
           of Hesse
           1837-92

Dagmar   m. Alexander III   William   m. Olga
of Denmark   Tsar of All   of Denmark   of Russia
(Marie)   the Russias   (George I   1851-1926
1847-1928   1845-94   of the Hellenes)
                                  1845-1913

William II
Emperor of Germany
1859-1941

Victoria   m. Louis of
of Hesse   Battenburg
1863-1950   1st Marquess
                  of Milford Haven
                  1854-1921

Alix   m. Nicholas II
of Hesse   Tsar of
1872-1918   All the Russias
                  1868-1918

George   Louis   Alice   m. Andrew   EDWARD VIII   GEORGE VI m. Elizabeth
of Battenberg   of Battenberg   of Battenberg   of Greece   (Duke of Windsor)   1895-1952   Bowes-Lyon
2nd Marquess   Earl Mountbatten   1885-1967   1882-1944   1894-1972   1900-
of Milford Haven   of Burma   m. Wallis Warfield
1892-1938   1900-   Simpson

David   Philip   m. ELIZABETH II   Margaret Rose
3rd Marquess   Duke of Edinburgh 1926-   1930-
of Milford Haven   1921-   m. Anthony
1919-   Armstrong-Jones
                                                                                                              Lord Snowdon

                    Charles   Anne m. Mark   Andrew   Edward   David   Sarah   David
                    Prince of Wales   1950-   Phillips   1960-   1964-   Viscount Linley   1964-   Viscount
                    1948-   1961-   Lascelles
                                                                                                                        1950-

The Houses of Saxe-Coburg-Gotha and Windsor

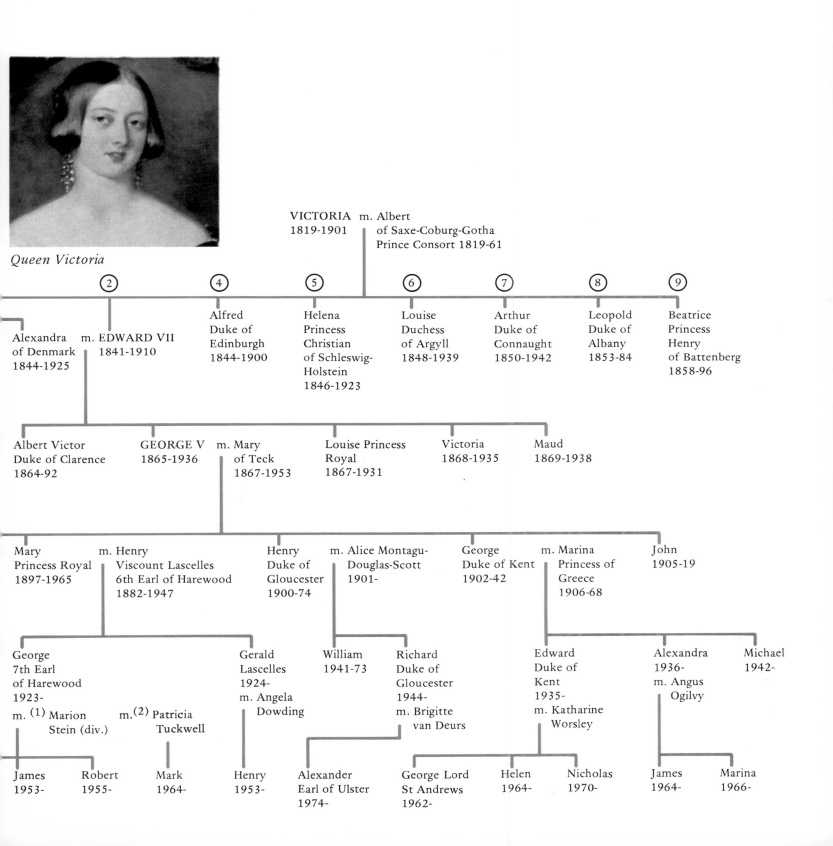

Queen Victoria

VICTORIA 1819-1901 m. Albert of Saxe-Coburg-Gotha Prince Consort 1819-61

② ④ ⑤ ⑥ ⑦ ⑧ ⑨

Alexandra of Denmark 1844-1925 m. EDWARD VII 1841-1910

Alfred Duke of Edinburgh 1844-1900

Helena Princess Christian of Schleswig-Holstein 1846-1923

Louise Duchess of Argyll 1848-1939

Arthur Duke of Connaught 1850-1942

Leopold Duke of Albany 1853-84

Beatrice Princess Henry of Battenberg 1858-96

Albert Victor Duke of Clarence 1864-92

GEORGE V 1865-1936 m. Mary of Teck 1867-1953

Louise Princess Royal 1867-1931

Victoria 1868-1935

Maud 1869-1938

Mary Princess Royal 1897-1965 m. Henry Viscount Lascelles 6th Earl of Harewood 1882-1947

Henry Duke of Gloucester 1900-74 m. Alice Montagu-Douglas-Scott 1901-

George Duke of Kent 1902-42 m. Marina Princess of Greece 1906-68

John 1905-19

George 7th Earl of Harewood 1923- m. (1) Marion Stein (div.) m.(2) Patricia Tuckwell

Gerald Lascelles 1924- m. Angela Dowding

William 1941-73

Richard Duke of Gloucester 1944- m. Brigitte van Deurs

Edward Duke of Kent 1935- m. Katharine Worsley

Alexandra 1936- m. Angus Ogilvy

Michael 1942-

James 1953-

Robert 1955-

Mark 1964-

Henry 1953-

Alexander Earl of Ulster 1974-

George Lord St Andrews 1962-

Helen 1964-

Nicholas 1970-

James 1964-

Marina 1966-

George VI

r. 1936-52

'I'm only a naval officer, it's the only thing I know about.'

Prince Albert Frederick Arthur George was yet another second son destined to become king. He was born at York Lodge, Sandringham, and committed the venial sin of arriving in the world on 14 December 1895. There was nothing wrong with the year but the date was the forty-fourth anniversary of the Prince Consort's death, an anniversary which Queen Victoria kept sacred. To placate the ageing queen, the Duke and Duchess of York offered to call the baby Albert – though he was always known by the diminutive, Bertie – and the peace-offering was graciously accepted.

From the moment of his inappropriate arrival, Bertie lay in the shadow of his brother David, a beautiful, golden-haired, charming, if moody boy, and was soon in the shadow of his sister Mary, the girl for whom his parents had longed. All the York children suffered from their parents' emotional inhibitions. George V imagined he was emulating *his* father but he lacked the easy-going gregarious-ness, and in his mouth Edward VII's chaffing (which was not loved by everybody, anyway) often emerged as a frightening, bullying sea-dog roar. Temperamentally, George V was more of a disciplinarian than his father, and his children were always being called to talk in the best naval tradition.

Of the five children (the youngest epileptic John was in a special category), the innately shy Bertie in particular suffered from the overt lack of affection and understanding. An unbalanced nanny fed him when and where she wanted, and he consequently developed gastric troubles which plagued him for much of his life; he was knock-kneed and made to wear corrective splints all night and much of the day; and he was naturally left-handed but forced to write with his 'proper' right hand. Unsurprisingly, by the age of six he had developed a stutter which grew into an agonizing stammer. Just occasionally, the boy released his misery in violent, incoherent temper tantrums but generally he was the with-drawn, backward child. As one of his naval tutors

put it, comparing Prince Albert with Prince David was like comparing an ugly duckling with a cock pheasant.

After a fairly dismal education in the hands of a considerably less able tutor than the Reverend Dalton, Bertie was sent to naval college in the footsteps of his father and older brother. The years at Osborne and Dartmouth were a fairly traumatic experience for the desperately shy, stammering young prince; bewildered, bullied and stuck with pins to see if his blood really was blue. His examination record hovered between 68th out of 68 or 61st out of 67 but there was a core of determination in Bertie, and fortunately he had several excellent and sympathetic naval tutors. By the age of sixteen, although still gauche in company, he had managed to make a few friends and had proved himself good at games, particularly tennis (at which he had been encouraged to use his despised left hand).

From 1913, when he officially entered the navy as a midshipman, until nearly the end of the war, Prince Albert was a serving officer, seeing action (though not much of it) in the confused, indecisive battle of Jutland in 1916. He always suffered from sea-sickness and never really loved the sea but he earned a reputation as a conscientious, capable, humane officer. However, it was his brother David, by-now the Prince of Wales, who attracted popular attention. Bertie accepted this as the natural order of things, and was only upset when persistent ill-health forced him to retire from the navy.

The end of the war found Prince Albert in much the same situation as many of his father's subjects, jobless and rudderless, if without their financial hardship. For a period in 1919 he joined the Air Ministry staff and determinedly learned to fly (he had been in the Royal Naval Air Service towards the end of the war). But flying had no more genuine appeal than the sea, and when poor health again intervened he went up to Cambridge for a year. At

the university he had the only training in the duties of a constitutional monarch that he was to receive before suddenly becoming king. In 1920 he was created Duke of York, which pleased him, but it did not solve his many problems.

Salvation was to hand. Prince Albert had first met Lady Elizabeth Bowes-Lyon, the ninth child of the Earl and Countess of Strathmore, at a children's party when she had kindly given him the glacé cherry from her cake. In 1920 they re-met at a dance, and she was to give him a great deal more than glacé cherries. Although he fell deeply in love, she did not immediately reciprocate, nor relish the prospect of exchanging a free, comparatively anonymous life for the restrictions and public glare enveloping royalty. However, Bertie had perseverance and in April 1923 Lady Elizabeth Bowes-Lyon and the Duke of York were married in Westminster Abbey.

The marriage was exceptionally popular with the press and public, and a good deal was made of a royal prince espousing a commoner. In fact, Elizabeth Bowes-Lyon was hardly the girl-next-door, being able to trace her ancestry to early medieval Scottish kings and to the Houses of Tudor and York; while the Strathmore family home, Glamis, was one of the most romantic, oldest inhabited castles in the British Isles, soaked in Scottish history. The young woman who captured the popular fancy by her sparkling, graceful informality also provided her husband with everything he had previously lacked and desperately needed: the warmth and serene confidence of her own happy family background; the patient understanding to cope with his always prevalent moods and eruptions of anger, arising from inherited short-temper and the long years of frustration; and a belief in him which helped her husband to believe in himself. An observer commented, 'She was his will power, his all.' She was not the actual instrument of her husband's greatest personal achievement, the conquest of the worst of his stammer, that being provided by a remarkable Australian therapist, Lionel Logue, but she gave unstinted support and encouragement.

With the birth of Princess Elizabeth in 1926, followed by that of Princess Margaret Rose in 1930, the Duke and Duchess of York acquired even greater popularity. In troubled, stressful times, they represented the stable, yet changing family unit in fairy-tale proportions; the charming, concerned wife and mother of two beautiful daughters who was also a successful royal career woman, and the prince who had conquered adversity (quite how much was not then fully known, though some of it was). But if the Duke of York had been something of an ugly duckling, he had never been a bad-

looking one, and with film and press photography growing apace, the continuing success of the British royal family owed a considerable amount to their photogenic qualities. Much of the world might still love royalty, but it preferred the twopence coloured to the penny plain variety (which remains true today).

The problem of finding a useful royal job was also solved. In 1919 the Duke of York was invited to be the patron of an incipient welfare service which had grown up during the First World War but was in danger of collapse. He agreed, 'providing there's no damned red carpet about it', and the organization became the Industrial Welfare Society. The duke, soon supported by the duchess, did his best to avoid the red carpet, insisting on talking to workers on the shop floor, asking and expecting answers about unsatisfactory management, and descending coal mines. If he did not, and could not, solve the problems of 'two nations', he at least tried to do more than cement the cracks.

In a further attempt to weld together the two Englands, he also inaugurated the Duke of York's Camps, at which admittedly carefully selected groups of boys from public schools and factories, joined under his auspices for a week of hiking, playing games and singing jolly songs round the camp fire. Today they would be largely viewed with derision – and they did not escape sniping at the time – but they were a minor break-through. Bertie was no revolutionary, but he sincerely believed that unless the royal family could prove its interest in and involvement with the people's needs and problems, then it was rightly doomed to extinction.

After his marriage, the relationship with George V improved considerably. Both the King and Queen Mary whole-heartedly approved of Bertie's wife (though George V, with his usual parental pessimism, had initially told his son that he would be damned lucky to win such a prize). The Duke and Duchess of York went on various Common-wealth goodwill tours, to East Africa, New Zealand and Australia, all of which they accom-plished with a high degree of success.

Their first married home was York Cottage in Richmond Park, but it was dominated by Queen Mary's tastes and hideously exposed to prying members of the public and press. Firmly but tactfully, they acquired their own more secluded house, 145 Piccadilly, but with the 1929 slump royalty was expected to draw in its horns, too, and the family moved into Royal Lodge in Windsor Park, a charming, if then delapidated folly designed for George IV. In the mid-1930s it seemed that the pattern of the Yorks' life was settled, a happy family

doing a good job in the royal second ranks.

When George v died in January 1936 and his eldest son was proclaimed Edward VIII, the latter's passion for Wallis Warfield Simpson was already well-known in restricted circles. Indeed it had caused a breach in the previously warm friendship between David and Bertie, as few members of the royal family considered Mrs Simpson a suitable close companion. While the Yorks had acquired their niche in the popular affection as the favourite royal family unit, the new king had earned a very

special popularity. He was the Prince Charming in tune with the age, anti-cant, anti-hypocrisy, determined to modernise the monarchy. But Edward VIII failed to distinguish between his own, very real popularity and the reverence still accorded to the crown. He also suffered from the common failing of impatient, woolly-minded reformers, in that it was easy to discover what he was *against* but more difficult to ascertain what he was *for*, or how he intended to implement change. Like the little girl with the curl in the middle of her forehead, when

Edward VIII was good he was very, very good but – as his advisers already knew – when his interest was not caught, he could be horrid: bored, selfish, unpunctual and petulant. Duty for him tended to be a personal affair.

When it became apparent that he was determined to marry the twice-divorced Mrs Simpson, the Abdication crisis ground into action. Although many people outside the royal circle also regarded her as an unsuitable consort, it was her divorced status, not her American nationality, which was the stumbling block in her marriage to a monarch who was also the supreme governor of the Church of England. For months the British press kept its pact of silence while newspapers throughout the world had a speculative field-day. Would the king marry the woman he loved? would he be KO'd by British stuffed shirts? and which was more important, one man's emotions or the monarchy itself? When the storm finally became public in Britain towards the end of 1936, although there were attempts to form a 'King's party' headed by Lord Beaverbrook and Winston Churchill, and there were demonstrations in Edward VIII's favour, the verdict of the majority of the country and the Commonwealth was against him.

Particularly surprising was the fervour with which the monarchy itself was supported. A king's desire to abdicate might have seemed, in the atmosphere of the 1930s, an excellent moment to decide that monarchy had had its day, even in Britain. But when Jimmy Maxton, the fiery Scottish Independent Labour MP, moved such an amendment to the Abdication Bill, it was defeated by an overwhelming majority of 403 to 5. It was estimated that if a definite republican motion had been put to the House of Commons, the maximum number in favour would have been fifty.

On 10 December 1936 Edward VIII signed the Instrument of Abdication, and in the evening of 11 December he made a farewell broadcast to his people, his resonant voice charged with emotion: 'I have found it impossible to carry the heavy burden of responsibility . . . without the help and support of the woman I love.' Had he remained in harness, the good side of his character might have risen to the challenge of majority Labour Governments, vast social change and the dissolution of the British Empire; as he lived until 1972 he would have had to cope with these matters. In the event, the bad side became more marked. As Duke of Windsor he flirted with Hitler's Germany; he refused to fly to Britain in the summer of 1940 when Churchill sent a desperately needed aircraft to collect him, unless he had the assurance that his wife would be greeted as *Her Royal Highness*; when Governor of the

Bahamas he banned any black man, of whatever status, from entering through the front door of Government House. After the war he led an increasingly selfish, useless life, though the passion for the woman he loved never dimmed.

The Duke of York had no constitutional need to accept the crown; it could have passed to one of his brothers. When the Instrument of Abdication was brought to him, as he wrote in his diary, 'I broke down and sobbed like a child', but he had inherited his father's stern sense of duty and there was no question of refusing the burden. The measure of his stunned, unbelieving emotion was further illustrated in remarks made to his cousin, Lord Louis Mountbatten, 'Dickie, this is absolutely terrible . . . I'm quite unprepared for it . . . I've never seen a state paper; I'm only a naval officer, it's the only thing I know about', because it was a long time since he had even been a naval officer. But he also said, '. . . you can be assured that I will do my best to clear up the inevitable mess, if the whole fabric does not crumble under the shock and strain of it all'.

The fabric did not crumble and on 12 May 1937 – the date originally set for Edward VIII's coronation – King George VI and Queen Elizabeth were crowned. He took the name George to emphasize the link with his father's reign, and with the little princesses in attendance at the ancient

Below Queen Elizabeth in 1941.

Above The royal family at Buckingham palace in 1942.

ceremony in Westminster Abbey, it was as a family that the Yorks ascended the throne. One alarming aspect of the Abdication crisis was the way in which it had overwhelmed the questions of Hitler's and Mussolini's ambitions and the Spanish Civil War. Winston Churchill said, 'Our Island might have been ten thousand miles away from Europe.' The first two years of George VI's reign, as he struggled to learn his job, were passed in the lengthening shadows of another war, with Britain's final abandonment of the policy of appeasement.

On 3 September 1939 the lugubrious voice of the prime minister, Neville Chamberlain, told his countrymen that for the second time in twenty-five years they were at war with Germany. It was a more openly divided, considerably more muted and unprepared Britain that went to war in 1939 than had done in 1914. But the Dominions followed Britain's example, though they had no need to, with the exception of the Irish Free State which preferred its own peculiar brand of neutrality. There followed eight months of the 'Phoney War', but when the

fighting started in May 1940 it was with a vengeance in which it seemed that nothing could stop the brilliantly disciplined, immaculately oiled, supremely confident Nazi war-machine. But as the mighty and lesser nations of Europe fell like the proverbial ninepins, Britain held out. Neville Chamberlain was told in Cromwell's words, 'You have sat in this place too long ... in the name of God go!', and Winston Churchill became the prime minister of a Coalition Government. The relationship between George VI and his new prime minister was initially strained, but by the middle of 1941 the king was writing, 'I could not have a better PM.'

Nor could the country, much as Churchill has been subjected to the microscopic inspection of historians and other critics in the post-war years. He provided the fire, vision and uplift, offering nothing but 'blood, toil, sweat and tears', while declaring, 'we shall fight on the beaches, we shall fight on the landing grounds, we shall fight in the fields and in the streets, we shall fight in the hills; we shall never surrender.' His Deputy Labour Prime Minister (a new wartime post), the unromantic, unemotional Clement Attlee, dealt with the nuts and bolts of wartime administration and the tensions of the coalition. Together they were a formidable partnership.

In this first war in which the entire civilian population of Britain was, to a lesser or greater degree involved, George VI became the patriot king in a manner which equalled, if it did not precisely resemble, Henry V. He and the queen visited the bombed areas, factories, Home Guard units and troops. They stayed in London throughout the Blitz and in their minds there was never any question of leaving for the safety of Canada, as was suggested. Queen Elizabeth said, 'The children cannot go without me, and I could not possibly leave the king.' (Though the princesses, like many other children, were evacuated, in their case to Windsor Castle). The queen echoed Churchill in saying she would fight to the last ditch, and assiduously attended rifle and revolver practice in the grounds of Buckingham Palace. The Palace itself was bombed nine times, once the king and queen came close to being killed, and she said she was glad: 'It makes me feel I can look the East End in the face.' The royal family also shared the pain of wartime death when the Duke of Kent was killed in a plane crash while on a mission to Iceland.

As the tide of war slowly turned in the Allies' favour, George VI visited his troops in North Africa and later in Normandy. (He and Churchill both wanted to sail with the first assault wave on D-Day itself but the possible deaths of the king and the prime minister was considered too great a risk). The occasion which the king said was one of the

Right King George and Queen Elizabeth on a tour of South Africa in 1947.

most moving of his entire life was when he sailed into battered, defiant Malta in 1943, standing at the salute on the prow of his boat, while what appeared to be the entire population lined Valetta grand harbour. Apart from discussing with Churchill all the major decisions, George played an extremely useful role as a royal emollient to the Allies' tensions and disagreements. He entertained countless visitors at Buckingham Palace, and in 1942 Mrs Roosevelt was both amused and impressed to find herself being served minute rations in a cold, draughty Palace, but off priceless gold and silver plates.

On 8 May 1945 the war in Europe ended, and an exhausted but proud nation swarmed to Buckingham Palace in a two-way salute between the royal family and its people. Apart from being exhausted, Britain also emerged from the war with much of her wealth mortgaged, bartered or spent during the five-year struggle. This was not immediately generally apparent, nor was the change that was occurring in what soon became known as 'the Third World', with its demand for independence from the old colonial empires and a larger share of the Western world's cake. It seemed that Britain's prestige, power and Empire stood as proudly as in the days of her 'finest hour' in 1940.

However, the social changes were heralded by the massive Labour victory when the longest Parliament since the country had become a United Kingdom was dissolved in 1945. George's relationship with Clement Attlee was initially less satisfactory than with Churchill; the latter had at least always talked, whereas Attlee's audiences were punctuated by long silences. But the king and the Socialist prime minister learned to respect each other. 1947 saw the Commonwealth strengthened with India's and Pakistan's entry as dominions, though Burma soon departed, followed by the new Republic of Eire.

After a long tour of South Africa in 1947 which

Above King George in naval uniform.

Above left Sir Winston Churchill.

it was hoped would soothe the remounting Boer emnity (temporarily it seemed to do so), the king and queen had the personal pleasure of their elder daughter's engagement and marriage. George VI lived to celebrate his own silver wedding, and the births of two grandchildren, Prince Charles and Princess Anne. But the war had taken a heavy toll of his always fragile health, and as Attlee commented, 'He was the worrying type, you know.' In 1948 only skilled medical attention saved the amputation of his right leg, in 1949 he had another serious operation, and by the autumn of 1951 his family knew he was suffering from cancer. But earlier in 1951 he had opened the Festival of Britain, the hopeful symbol of the country's resurgence. The king wryly commented that its centre-piece, the

Skylon, seemed an unfortunate choice, 'as it had no visible means of support.'

After a happy family Christmas spent at Sandringham, on 31 January 1952 George VI waved goodbye to his daughter Elizabeth and her husband, as they set off on a tour of East Africa. It was a bitterly cold day, and standing hatless on the tarmac the king looked worn and haggard. It was indeed his last public appearance, and, a few days later, on 5 February he died peacefully in his sleep at Sandringham. He bequeathed to his subjects his beloved daughter, Elizabeth, who had enjoyed the benefits of a close, warm family life and had, from the age of eleven, been trained in the curious, difficult role of a twentieth-century constitutional monarch.

Right George VI's lying-in-state in Westminster Hall, February 1951.

Elizabeth II

r. 1952-

'My whole life, whether it be long or short, shall be devoted to your service.'

Elizabeth of York was born in London on 21 April 1926 and twelve days later the General Strike started, which can be called a portent of things to come as industrial and social relations have dominated much of her reign. However, the likelihood of her becoming queen did not seem strong, as the Prince of Wales was then only thirty-one, would soon surely marry and have children. But the new baby had one unknowing distinction, being the last reigning monarch at whose birth the Home Secretary was present (at least in the house, not as previously in the bedchamber). A minister's attendance dated back to 1688 when supporters of a Protestant Succession claimed that the son unexpectedly born to James II's second Catholic wife (the future Old Pretender) was not hers at all. Thereafter, ministerial presence was deemed necessary to authenticate the birth of those closely in line to the throne. When Princess Elizabeth herself was confined with her first child, it was finally decided that this practice should be consigned to the curiosities of English history.

From birth the York children were the focus of popular attention and the process merely accelerated after George VI had so unexpectedly become king. But their parents tried to provide as free and as secluded a life as then appeared possible or seemly for royal children. It did not include going to school, mixing with other than a very select group or happily anonymous outings. When attempts were made to widen Princess Elizabeth's and Margaret Rose's circle, they were not oversuccessful, as those invited to be Brownies or Girl Guides at Buckingham Palace were on their unnaturally best behaviour. When the princesses were allowed such adventures as travelling on the London underground, they were quickly recognized and semi-mobbed.

If the normal horizons were limited, Elizabeth always had the companionship of her exuberant sister, and a well-balanced education in the hands of

a young, capable Scottish governess Miss Crawford (who achieved her own niche in the royal mythology as 'Crawfie'), and then later the Provost of Eton. Elizabeth was not intellectually brilliant, as her critics have frequently pointed out; but then nor is the majority of the human race. Personally she loved horses more than the arts or sciences, though fortunately for herself and her future role she was always interested in politics and history, appreciating that without knowledge of the past one is unlikely to have understanding of the present. And she had a good general intelligence, a receptive mind and a particularly retentive memory, together with her grandfather's and father's sense of order and attention to detail.

With the onset of adolescence, some of the natural charm and aplomb shown by the young princess evaporated, and the shyer, reserved, ungregarious side of her nature became more apparent. Apart from the physical and psychological changes affecting many teenagers, Elizabeth perhaps became more aware of her exposed, onerous position, while most of the war years had been spent in isolation at Windsor. On VE night 1945, the princesses descended from waving on the balcony at Buckingham Palace to mix with the crowds who had been cheering them (and for once were not recognized). While Margaret Rose wrote, 'It was absolutely wonderful. Everybody was knocking everybody else's hats off, so we knocked off a few, too', her father more sadly recorded, 'Poor darlings, they have never had any fun yet.'

Before the end of the war Elizabeth had begun to assume some official royal duties. In 1944, the Regency Act of 1937 was amended so that at the age of eighteen (rather than twenty-one) she could be one of the Counsellors of State, traditionally appointed to govern the realm in the monarch's absence. But it was not until the beginning of 1945 that she finally persuaded her father to let her be called up for National Service, as were other citizens

of the United Kingdom at the age of eighteen. Some of the stories connected with Second-Lieutenant Elizabeth Windsor of the ATS were myth, such as driving heavy lorries through the black-out and being treated exactly as if she were Miss Windsor from Wolverhampton. But for the first time in her life the princess mixed with 'ordinary' girls, proved herself a useful hand with a spanner and an above-average driver. When her grandmother Queen Mary came to inspect the unit and everybody dashed around in preparation she learned something else: 'Now I realize what must happen when Papa and Mummy go anywhere. It's something I'll never forget.'

Also before the end of the war Elizabeth had fallen in love, a situation which initially caused her parents some apprehension, not because they disapproved of the young man but because it seemed unlikely that her affections would remain fixed on the first, indeed sole, eligible bachelor she had

Opposite A family photograph to mark the engagement of Princess Elizabeth to Lieutenant Philip Mountbatten.

Below Princess Elizabeth and Princess Margaret in the gardens at Windsor in 1940.

known with any degree of intimacy. But Queen Mary, showing the shrewd liberalism which was not part of her popular image (particularly as she grew older and more stately in her out-dated toques), thought people could sustain youthful emotion, 'and Elizabeth seems to be that kind of girl. She would always know her own mind. There's something very steadfast and determined in her – like her father.' The old queen also thought the young man, Prince Philip of Greece, with his unorthodox schooling, forthright character and knowledge of the world, would prove a very useful member of the royal family.

Philip's connections with Greece were always minimal. His father Prince Andrew was of Danish blood (a Danish prince having been installed on the Greek throne by the European powers in 1863), while his mother was a daughter of Prince Louis of Battenberg who had become Mountbatten in the 1917 change of names. Philip was born in Corfu on 10 June 1921, but the whirlpool of Balkan politics led his family into exile in Paris, and apart from a year spent at Kurt Hahn's progressive school at its original home in Germany, he was wholly educated in Britain. (With Hitler's advent to power in 1933, Hahn and his educational ideas were considered a decadent corruption of German youth and after several traumas the school reopened in Scotland as Gordonstoun, with Prince Philip still among its pupils). When his parents separated in the 1930s, his mother's brother Lord Louis Mountbatten (later Earl Mountbatten of Burma) became his informal English guardian. In 1939 he entered Dartmouth naval college and subsequently had a distinguished operational war record.

By 1946 Philip himself had become more than interested in his third cousin Elizabeth whom he had met several times as a child, then on leave during the war. But their wish to become engaged ran into George VI's continuing belief that his daughter was too young and inexperienced. There was also the problem of Philip's Greek nationality, though he himself had long wished to be naturalized, particularly in order to continue his career in the Royal Navy. (As a wartime ally he had been able to serve as an officer but in peace-time only British nationals could do so). Early in 1947 Elizabeth duly accompanied her parents to South Africa but on their return, as it was obvious that the affection had not lessened on either side, the king and queen gladly consented to the match. In the meantime Philip had achieved his naturalization, if not without difficulty as the Foreign Office believed that the tense Greek political situation made it an unsuitable moment for a Greek prince to renounce his nationality. It was as Lieutenant Philip

Mountbatten RN that he became engaged to the heir to the British throne, though before the marriage George VI created his prospective son-in-law HRH The Duke of Edinburgh. (But it was not until his wife made him a Prince of the United Kingdom in 1957 that he could officially be called Prince Philip again).

The marriage took place, with most of the traditional royal trappings, in Westminster Abbey on 20 November 1947, in the dreariness of post-war austerity Britain, with its continuing rationing and shortages. But the groom was strikingly handsome in his naval uniform, the bride radiated happiness and a wintry sun managed to shine. Prince Charles and Princess Anne were born within three years of the marriage and many people decided that Princess Elizabeth and the Duke of Edinburgh had settled for young parenthood with the 'nuclear' family of two. But Queen Elizabeth and Prince Philip proved them wrong, by producing two more children after a ten-year gap, with the birth of Prince Andrew in 1960 and Prince Edward in 1964.

After the marriage, Philip continued to be a serving naval officer and for periods in 1950 and 1951 Elizabeth joined him in Malta, trying hard while pursued by photographers, to behave like any other naval wife (and eventually semi-succeeding). But with her father's declining health, she and her husband assumed more royal duties. Early in February 1952 they were enjoying a short respite on their East African tour – to be followed by one of Australasia – which included a visit to the old Treetops game observation post lying near the twin peaks of Mount Kenya. As a diarist wrote,' She became queen while perched in a tree in Africa.' Whether this was strictly accurate is a moot point but it had the right, irreverent 1950s touch. Her father's death was a sad blow but not an overwhelming, surprising shock, and the slight figure of the new queen was able to descend with composure from the aircraft which had immediately flown her back to London, wearing the mourning clothes packed for just such a contingency.

Elizabeth II was proclaimed in London on 8 February 1952, 'By the Grace of God, Queen of this Realm and of all Her other Realms and Territories, Head of the Commonwealth, Defender of the Faith.' The vague phrasing realistically and sensibly reflected the changed world and Britain's status in it, because her grandfather had been firmly proclaimed 'King of the United Kingdom of Great Britain and Ireland, of the British Dominions beyond the seas, and Emperor of India'. Unrealistically and unsensibly, many Britons believed that the queen's accession at the age of twenty-five, the same as her illustrious predecessor Elizabeth I, would somehow halt Britain's post-war slide, rejuvenate her weary citizens and send them buccaneering round the world to restore her economy, pride and prestige. But they would be buccaneers with a social conscience, aware of the imbalance between the affluent Western world and the emerging Third one, promoting *their* economies and well-being in the process. While those who stayed at home would perform similar miracles in transforming Britain into a vigorous, prosperous society in which Karl Marx's 'From each according to his abilities, to each according to his needs' would be implemented; but in a peculiarly British way, without the authoritarianism, totalitarianism, denials of liberty and new elitism which had overcome the existing Communist states. The dreams of a second Elizabethan age came as much from the Left as from the Right.

In 1956 the euphoria evaporated into the Suez crisis which split the country down the middle. How dare Britain join France and Israel in a naked act of aggression against Egypt, while proclaiming herself a champion of freedom? How dare she not secure the Suez Canal from the ambitions of a dictator? Apart from the passionate split in opinion, the debacle also revealed to all but the most short-sighted and jingoistic that Britain was no longer a front-rank power, that the Big Three of the war years had become the Big Two, America and Russia. The royal critical knives grew sharper.

Part of the criticism accepted that Britain had a monarch and that it was a good thing, but wanted the queen to behave differently and present a brighter image. There were moans about her dowdy, frumpish or alternatively over-fussy dress, and enquiries about the court circle – When will the Duke send the Old Gang packing? The most publicized attack came from Lord Altrincham in 1957, lambasting both the boring, conventional, horsey, upper class entourage and the queen herself as having the personality of a priggish schoolgirl, with a voice that was 'a pain in the neck'. It may be said that after this attack the priggish schoolgirl – or shy young woman – slowly grew more relaxed in public, while the voice that had given Lord Altrincham such a pain dropped several semitones in pitch and lost its more strangulated vowel sounds.

In more serious vein, when Sir Anthony Eden resigned after the Suez venture, the queen was criticized for sending for Harold Macmillan as prime minister, rather than the widely expected

Opposite A coronation portrait of Queen Elizabeth and Prince Philip.

Below The Queen returns from her coronation in the gold state coach.

candidate, 'Rab' Butler. It was said that she had overstepped her prerogative and interfered in party politics by forcing a leader on the Conservatives. In fact she had acted constitutionally, taking the advice of the party's two senior figures, Winston Churchill and Lord Salisbury, and the machinations within the Cabinet had nothing to do with her. Further criticism on the same lines occurred when Sir Alec Douglas-Home succeeded Macmillan in 1963. This problem was not resolved until 1970 when the Conservatives decided to elect their leader by a democratic vote, rather than the old 'emerging' process which had entailed the queen using her prerogative.

Implicit in these attacks was the question asked in 1957 – Does England really need a queen? The answer provided was basically no, with the argument that the British royal family had become the world's greatest soap opera, appealing to the lowest common denominator, generating nothing but snobbery and sycophancy. However, the monarchy might survive if it surrounded itself with up-to-date, intelligent men and women and could be viewed as a symbolic unifying element. Other critics focused on the monarchy as the symbol of the past impeding the future, and ruinously expensive. As long as it remained, the two nations would never disappear and there was no hope of a more just, egalitarian society.

Proponents of monarchy stoutly reposted that it was the continuous chain by which Britain had become a better society, whilst having remained the most stable in Europe. They also claimed that it was an essential check and balance in the British constitution, and while its wings had been clipped, it was *not* powerless. The queen remained head of state, to her the armed forces and legal luminaries swore loyalty, and she retained her prerogatives, if unused in normal circumstances. But in abnormal ones, with extremists of Left or Right threatening to take power, the monarch could effectively resume the role of protector of the people's interest. In the less extreme situation of evenly balanced political parties, the queen could use her accumulated political knowledge and judgement to avert a stalemate by inviting one party to form a Government.

The question of cost was arguable. The British royal family engendered an enormous amount of interest throughout the world which reflected well on the country and increased its 'invisible earnings'. In addition, royal pageantry and presence brought immeasurable pleasure into drab, unsatisfactory or downright miserable lives. While the ceremony of Trooping the Colour might now be archaic, it was more attractive to watch, and considerably less ominous, than displays of strutting troops, tanks and guns.

The uncertain '50s slipped into the briefly swinging '60s, with their more irreverent, satirical insistence that there were no longer sacred cows, only cows, and a debatable belief that if a thing was new it was good, if old bad. As for the monarchy, it was probably irrelevant but it was there, and not doing too much harm in an imperfect world. The Queen and Prince Philip were well aware that they were there, of the criticisms, and of the peculiar nature of their roles and functions in the second half of the twentieth century.

If the new Elizabethans had remained stuck in Britain's post-war social evolution and economic ills, Philip himself was always something of a buccaneering figure. He saw part of his task as ensuring that royalty moved with the times, come hell or high water (occasionally there was a bit of both). The royal household was reorganized, the Duke of Edinburgh Award scheme inaugurated, world wild-life supported, British industry encouraged. Debutante presentations at Buckingham Palace were out, more informal luncheons for men and women eminent in their fields were in. Later there were walk-abouts among the crowds and the royal family's appearance on a television film, which latter could be viewed as the soap opera to end soap operas or as a laudable attempt to humanize the monarchy.

Prince Philip also created a particular niche for himself as royal spokesman. Over the years it has become accepted that constitutional British monarchs have neither the right to express an opinion nor to reply to criticism, whatever their views might be, however wounding or inaccurate the attacks. While the idea that the monarch does not publicly disagree or interfere with any decisions or actions taken by ministers may now be fundamental, expressing opinions or replying to criticism seems a legitimate royal liberty. It is one that Prince Philip has taken, undoubtedly to some people's fury, though few of his remarks would cause such a stir if uttered by any other public figure.

Philip stated his views on the monarchy clearly, '. . . if at any stage people feel it has no further part to play, then for goodness sake, let's end the thing on amicable terms without having a row about it.' Neither he nor its central figure, his wife the queen, feel that stage has yet been reached. Harold Macmillan noted in his diary, 'She has great faith in the work she can do for the Commonwealth especially.' Elizabeth had in fact celebrated her twenty-first birthday and made the speech dedicating her life to her future subjects' service in South Africa (ironically, as South Africans ceased to be

Above A family group on the balcony at Buckingham Palace after the Trooping of the Colour in 1976.

her subjects in 1961). And increasing royal emphasis was placed on the increasingly amorphous Commonwealth, with the entertaining of its prime ministers or presidents and visits to their countries. Sometimes, as in the 1961 tour of Ghana or the 1964 one to Canada, these were in potentially dangerous or hostile circumstances. When over-protective male ministers urged that the visits be cancelled, the queen made it clear that her being a woman was irrelevant and that she was a public servant, not a film star.

The Commonwealth has been attacked as useless and expensive for ailing Britain to maintain, like the monarchy itself. But in a world bitterly divided by racial and economic differences, an amicable gathering of thirty-two countries, black, white, brown and yellow, such as occurred at the

Commonwealth Conference held in Canada in 1973, cannot be a bad thing. The critics say that all the Commonwealth countries have in common is a general use of English as an official language and the fact that for longer or shorter periods they were under British rule. By 1973 half the countries at the Conference were already republics, more will undoubtedly become so, and the situation inherent in the 1931 Statute of Westminster – the monarch as head of a Commonwealth of republics – could become a reality. If it does, the association would still seem worth preserving, with the a-political but highly informed and politically experienced British monarch providing the unifying symbol (a role often emphasized by the queen herself).

Back in 1960 Elizabeth made a Declaration in Council which gave her much personal pleasure.

Overleaf A family group at Balmoral in 1972.

Overleaf opposite A silver wedding picture of the Queen and the Duke of Edinburgh in November 1972.

On acceding to the throne, tradition had been reversed and the decision made that the queen and her heirs would continue to belong to the House of Windsor, rather than take her husband's name Mountbatten. In 1960 the queen declared that while she wished to retain the style of the House of Windsor, her descendants should be called Mountbatten-Windsor, honouring their father's name too. When Princess Anne married, her maiden name was duly entered on the certificate as Anne Mountbatten-Windsor.

The Queen and Prince Philip seem to have been remarkably successful in securing the balance between the public glare and a normal private life for their children, particularly for Prince Andrew and Edward. But the problem of balancing the human image of monarchy remains difficult. People consider they have a right to know about royal lives because they are glamorous public figures who, moreover, owe their position to an accident of birth.

But that accidental position has a mystique, a majesty, a nine-hundred year continuity that is part of its attraction. Thus while it is commendably human to hear Princess Anne saying, 'Oik, get off my dress' on her wedding day, or Prince Philip swearing (mildly) at intrusive journalists, in 1955 it was not considered right by large numbers of people for Princess Margaret (who dropped 'Rose' post-war) to marry the divorced Peter Townshend. British royalty has now to be of the people but remain different from them.

Whatever happens in the racially mixed and coloured society which is the tangible evidence of Britain's imperial past, as Elizabeth II celebrates the Silver Jubilee of her accession to the throne, few would deny that she has performed her difficult job with energy, professionalism, dedication and humanity; or that she has earned the respect and affection of millions of people who would echo the old cry, 'Vivat Regina'.

Bibliography

The Life and Times of the English monarchs series published by Weidenfeld & Nicolson (London), general editor Antonia Fraser, provides a useful next step. Lavishly illustrated, the series presents shortish biographies at a high level of popular history. For the English (later British) monarchs all but Henry II and the present Queen Elizabeth are covered:

William I Maurice Ashley (1973); *Richard I* John Gillingham (1973); *King John* Maurice Ashley (1972); *Edward III* Paul Johnson (1973); *Henry V* Peter Earle (1972); *Richard III* Anthony Cheetham (1973); *Henry VIII* Robert Lacey (1972); *Elizabeth I* Neville Williams (1972); *Charles I* D.R.Watson (1972); *Charles II* Christopher Falkus (1972); *George I* Joyce Marlow (1973); *George III* John Clarke (1972); *Victoria* Dorothy Marshall (1972); *George V* Dennis Judd (1973); *George VI* Keith Middlemas (1974).

Another useful series is the Collins/Fontana (London) paperback reprints of books originally published by Batsford. These cover each monarch from the late Saxon times and are written by experts in their period.

Saxon and Norman Kings Christopher Brooke (1967); *The Plantagenets* John Harvey (1966); *The Tudors* Christopher Morris (1966); *The Stuarts* J.P.Kenyon (1966); *The First Four Georges* J.H.Plumb (1966); *Hanover to Windsor* Roger Fulford (1966).

WILLIAM I
The Norman Conquest, D.J.A.Matthew (London 1966). A scholarly work.
William I and the Norman Conquest, Frank Barlow (English University Press reprint 1965). Scholarly but very readable and informative.
William the Conqueror, David C.Douglas (London 1964). A scholarly work.
The Normans and their World, Jack Lindsay (London 1973). Lengthy, informative book but aimed at the general reader.

HENRY II
The History of the Life of Henry II and the Age in which he Lived, George, Lord Lyttleton, (6 vols London 1769–73). The most massive biography but not easily obtainable and for those who like their history the old-fashioned way.
Henry Plantagenet, Richard Barber (London 1964). A good general biography.
The Devil's Brood: The Angevin Family, Alfred Duggan (London 1957). Highly readable account of Henry, Eleanor and their offspring.

RICHARD I
For one of the most popular medieval kings there are surprisingly few biographies.
Richard the Lionheart, Kate Norgate (London 1924). This remains the standard biography. Scholarly but readable it takes the popular view of the great Coeur de Lion.
The True History of Robin Hood, T. W. Walker, (West Yorkshire 1952). A devoted amateur historian's research among old records it establishes a strong case for 'the true story'.

JOHN
He has been re-assessed recently and there are several good biographies.
John, King of England, Edmund B.D'Auvergne (London 1934). One of the first books to query the black image.
The Reign of King John, Sidney Painter (Baltimore 1949). A distinguished American look at the whole reign.
King John, W.L.Warren (London 1961). Full length, scholarly, readable biography.
King John, Alan Lloyd (Newton Abbott 1973). Aimed at the general reader.

ROBERT BRUCE
Robert I has been the subject of several biographies including G.W.S.Barrow's excellent study *Robert Bruce and the Community of the Realm of Scotland* (London 1965). W.Croft Dickinson's *Scotland from the earliest times to 1603* (London 1961) and John Prebble's *The Lion of the North* (London 1971) provide less detailed information.

EDWARD III
There is a dearth of biographies of the longest reigning medieval king.
Edward III, James Mackinnon (London 1900). This is the only full-length biography but it has not worn well.
John Wycliffe and the Beginnings of English Nonconformity, K.B.McFarlane (London 1932). Scholarly but lucid short book to be recommended.

JAMES I OF SCOTLAND
King James I has been somewhat neglected by biographers. However, *James I, King of Scots* by E. W. M. Balfour-Melville (London 1936) tells his story and there is interesting information about his life and reign to be found in Caroline Bingham's *The Stewart Kingdom of Scotland 1371–1603* (London 1973) and her *The Kings and Queens of Scotland* (London 1976) as well as in John Prebble's *The Lion in the North* (London 1971). James I's poem *The King's Quair* edited by Mackay Mackenzie was published in 1939.

HENRY V
Henry V, Harold F.Hutchinson (London 1969). Now the standard full-length biography.
Henry V: The Cautious Conqueror, Margaret Wade Labarge (London 1975). A sympathetic transatlantic assessment.

RICHARD III
Richard III, Paul Murray Kendall (London 1955). An excellent biography.
The Yorkist Age: Daily Life During the Wars of the Roses, Paul Murray Kendall (London 1961). Again an excellent social history of the period.
Richard III: The Great Debate, edited and introduced by Paul Kendall (London 1965). Interesting reprint of Sir Thomas More's 'History of Richard III' which started the Machiavellian legend and Horace Walpole's 'Historic Doubts on the Life and Reign of King Richard III'. Written in the 18th century this was the first book to query the legend. Mr Kendall provides an authoritative modern commentary.

HENRY VIII
Henry is one of the more heavily written about English monarchs and my list is selective.
Henry VIII, J.J.Scarisbrick (London 1968). Now regarded as the definitive biography but not an easy read for the beginner.
Henry VIII, A.F.Pollard (London 1905). Written by an earlier authority on the period; still well worth reading.
Henry VIII: The Mask of Royalty, Lacey Baldwin Smith (London 1971). Complicated, stylish attempt to get behind the royal mask.
Henry VIII and his Wives, Walter Jerrold (London 1933). Remains a good popular short account of Henry's matrimonial ventures.

JAMES V OF SCOTLAND
A good recent biography of James V is Caroline Bingham's *James V, King of Scots* (London 1971). Interesting accounts of his reign are also to be found in Eric Linklater's study *The Royal House of Scotland* (London 1970) and Gordon Donaldson's *Scotland: James V–James VII*. (London 1965). Hester Chapman's *The Sisters of Henry VIII* (London 1969) also throws much light on the life and character of James V.

MARY, QUEEN OF SCOTS
A great deal has been written about Mary Stuart. Lady Antonia Fraser's *Mary, Queen of Scots* (London 1969) has become the standard work. Stefan Zweig's *The Queen of Scots* (London 1935) is another full scale biography. For a briefer account of Mary's life,

written from the Stuart viewpoint, there is Gordon Donaldson's *Mary, Queen of Scots* (London 1974). *The Crime of Mary Stuart* by George Malcolm Thompson (London 1967) concentrates on the Darnley murder while *Mary, Queen of Scots* (London 1972) by Roy Strong and Julia Trevelyan Oman is a beautiful little volume of words and pictures describing the personal details of Mary's daily life. For a study of the many writings about Mary Stuart from her own times onward Ian B.Cowan's *The Enigma of Mary Stuart* (London 1971) is highly recommended.

ELIZABETH I
There are again an enormous number of books.
Queen Elizabeth I, J.E.Neale (London 1934). Sir John Neale's most readable biography has stood the test of time and is probably still the best one overall.
Elizabeth the Great, Elizabeth Jenkins (London 1958). Another very good biography.
Elizabeth: A Study in Power and Intellect, Paul Johnson (London 1974). Highly readable, it concentrates on Elizabeth as a woman and an intellectual.

JAMES VI AND I
The life of James VI and I has been well covered by biographers. A good recent study is Lady Antonia Fraser's *King James* (London 1974). Another interesting biography is *The Wisest Fool in Christendom* by William McElwee (London 1958). His early years are described by Caroline Bingham in *The Making of a King* (London 1968) and Charles Williams in *James I* (London 1934) also chiefly concentrates on the Scottish part of the king's life. David Mathew's *James I* (London 1967) throws interesting light on the seventeenth century background.

CHARLES I
Another much written about monarch.
Charles King of England, Esmé Wingfield-Stratford (London 1949). Perhaps the best general biography. The author has written several other books on various aspects of the reign.
Charles I, Christopher Hibberd (London 1968). Lavishly illustrated, short lucid biography.
The King's Peace 1637–41; The King's War 1641–47; The Trial of Charles I, by C. V. Wedgewood (London 1966; 1966; 1967). Dame Veronica Wedgewood's illustrious histories of the reign from the King's viewpoint. For the other side two books may be noted:
God's Englishman: Oliver Cromwell and the English Revolution Christopher Hill, (London 1970). A brilliant lucid assessment.
Cromwell: Our Chief of Men, Antonia Fraser (London 1973). A massive biography.

CHARLES II
The most written about of all English monarchs; there must be literally tons of print.
Charles II, Arthur Bryant (London 1931). Rather suspect, pro-Charles biography but very readable.
The Private Life of Charles II, Arthur Irwin Dasent (London 1927). One of the more interesting, informative accounts of Charles's active private life but no longer in print.
The Tragedy of Charles II 1630–60, Hester W.Chapman (London 1964). Well researched, readable account of the early years.
Charles II: His Life and Likeness, Hesketh Pearson (London 1960). Readable biography of the man.
Charles II: The Man and Statesman, Maurice Ashley (London 1971). Currently the latest in the long line of full-scale biographies; by an expert on the period.

GEORGE I
One of the most underwritten British monarchs.

The First George, Lewis Melville (2 vols London 1908). The last full-scale biography but not a masterpiece.
England under George I, Wolfgang Michael (London 1939). A translation of a scholarly work in German.
The Four Georges, William Makepeace Thackeray (London 1861). A scathing look at the Hanoverians but the work of a novelist rather than a historian of genius.
Sophia Dorothea, Ruth Jordan (London 1971). Readable account of the divorce scandal and the subsequent sad life of George's wife.

GEORGE III
He has become fashionable in recent years. The trend was started by Sir Lewis Namier but his books are political and for the more advanced student.
King George III, John Brooke (London 1972). Much praised biography from which George emerges as a paragon of virtue.
George III, Stanley Ayling (London 1972). Sympathetic towards George but in my view more balanced.
George III and the Mad Business, I. Macalpine and R. Hunter (London 1960). The book that first advanced the porphyria theory.
George III, J.C.Long (London 1962). Interesting readable biography from the American viewpoint.
The Wickedest Age: The Life & Times of George III, Alan Lloyd (Newton Abbot 1971). Very much for the general reader.

VICTORIA
Not as over-burdened with biographies as might be imagined.
Victoria R.I., Elizabeth Longford (London 1964). Excellently researched, most readable biography; sympathetic but balanced.
Queen Victoria: Her Life & Times, Cecil Woodham-Smith (London 1972). The first volume of a projected full-scale life, again well-researched and readable.
Selections from Queen Victoria's massive correspondence have been published in three series but are of interest more to the specialist. The letters to her daughter Vicky, the Princess Royal, later the Crown Princess of Prussia, have a wider appeal. Edited by Roger Fulford they are: *Dearest Child, Dearest Child 1858–61; Dearest Mama 1861–64; Your Dear Letter 1865–71* (London 1964, 1968 & 1971).

GEORGE V
King George V: His Life & Reign, Harold Nicolson (London 1962). The official authorized biography; a particularly good one.
Queen Mary, James Pope-Hennessy (London 1964). The official biography.

GEORGE VI
King George VI, Hesketh Pearson (London 1937). Readable account of the early years.
King George VI: His Life & Reign, John Wheeler-Bennett (London 1958). The official authorized biography.

ELIZABETH II
The Work of the Queen, Dermot Morrah (London 1958). Authoritative account of the Queen's job.
Philip, Basil Boothroyd (London 1971). Chatty, informal biography.
Prince Philip: A Family Portrait, HM Queen Alexandra of Yugoslavia (London 1960). Useful for the early years.
Majesty, Robert Lacey (London 1977). This had not been published during my research period but has been immensely successful and will probably remain the standard biography for several years.
The House of Windsor, Elizabeth Longford (London 1974). Readable account of the whole family from George V to Elizabeth II. Many of the books listed are also published in paperback.

Acknowledgements

Photographs and illustrations were supplied or are reproduced by kind permission of the following:

The pictures on pages 4–5, 56 left and right, 80–1, 83 centre, 85, 88, 96, 113 above and below, 136 above, 141, 142, 143 below, 145, 147, 153, 161, 162 are reproduced by gracious permission of HM the Queen.

Associated Press: 167;
Barber Surgeons' Company: 84;
Bibliothèque Centrale, Ghent: 71;
Bibliothèque Nationale, Paris: 25, 39, 40, 44;
Trustees of Blairs College, Aberdeen: 91 (Robert Harding Associates), 128;
Bodleian Library, Oxford: 48–9 below, 50, 98, 110;
Bomann-Museum, Celle: 127;
British Federation of Master Printers: 122 left;
British Museum: 1, 2–3, 11, 14 above and below, 15, 17, 18, 20, 24, 26, 32, 33 (Picturepoint), 38, 42, 48–9 above, 52, 60, 61 above, 64 (Picturepoint), 66, 70 (Picturepoint), 136 below;
Duke of Buccleuch and Queensberry: 72;
Burgerbibliothek, Bern: 27;
Camera Press: 168, 174, 178;
Cooper-Bridgeman Library: 51;
Coram Foundation: 122 right (Cooper-Bridgeman Library);
Department of the Environment: 131;
Fishmongers Company: 159;
Major Gerald Flint-Shipman: 150;
Fox Photos: 158, 166, 168–9, 171, 173, 175, 177, 179;
Guildhall Art Gallery: 156–7;
Guildhall Library: 143 above, 148–9, 155;
Robert Harding Associates: 37;
Hatfield House: 57 (Angelo Hornak);
Michael Holford Library: 8, 9 above and below, 10, 13, 22–3, 29, 46–7, 97;
Angelo Hornak: 38 centre 65;
Imperial War Museum: 154, 156;
A.F.Kersting: 72–3;
Lambeth Palace Library: 63;

Edwin Leigh: 115;
London Museum: 121 (Cooper-Bridgeman Library);
Magdalen College, Oxford: 78;
Musée Calvet: 75;
National Maritime Museum: 103, 120 above (Picturepoint);
National Portrait Gallery: 58, 69, 76, 79, 82, 99 above, 109 right, 112, 114, 120 below, 124, 125, 132, 134, 135, 152, 164;
National Trust (Hardwick Hall): 89;
Sir David Ogilvie: 41, 92 below (and National Library of Scotland);
Picturepoint: 21, 35, 38 above, 46, 54, 61 below, 83 below, 116, 118, 137;
Popperfoto: 169;
Portsmouth Royal Naval Museum: 138–9;
Public Records Office: 12;
Radio Times Hulton Picture Library: 165, 172;
Royal Academy of Art: 123;
Duke of St Albans: 118–19;
Marquess of Salisbury: 102;
Scottish National Portrait Gallery: 53 (Tom Scott), 86 (Tom Scott), 87, 90 above, 90 below (Tom Scott), 92 above (Robert Harding Associates), 104 top right, 106 (Tom Scott), 108 above and below, 114–15 (Tom Scott), 117 (Tom Scott);
Ronald Sheridan: 6, 19;
Society of Antiquaries: 109 left;
P.Tweedie: 93;
University of London: 74 (Picturepoint);
Victoria and Albert Museum: 83 above (Marshall Cavendish), 99 below, 104 top left (Chris Barker), 129, 144 (Cooper-Bridgeman Library), 146 (Eileen Tweedy);
Weidenfeld and Nicolson Archives: 94;
Simon Wingfield Digby: 100–1;
Woodmansterne Ltd: 55;
Dean and Chapter of Worcester Cathedral: 30–1.

Royal coats of arms painted by Robert John Parsons BA, ATC, Herald Painter, College of Arms.

Index